The Mess Inside

Peter Goldie explores the ways in which we think about our lives—our past, present, and future—in narrative terms. The notion of narrative is highly topical, and highly contentious, in a wide range of fields including philosophy, psychology and psychoanalysis, historical studies, and literature. *The Mess Inside* engages with all of these areas of discourse, and steers a path between the sceptics who are dismissive of the idea of narrative as having any worthwhile use at all, and those who argue that our very selfhood is somehow constituted by a narrative.

After introducing the notion of narrative, Goldie discusses the way we engage with the past in narrative terms. This involves an exploration of the essentially perspectival nature of narrative thinking, which gains support from much recent empirical work on memory. Drawing on literary examples and on work in psychoanalysis, Goldie considers grief as a case study of this kind of narrative thinking, extending to a discussion of the crucial notion of 'closure'. Turning to narrative thinking about our future, Goldie discusses the many structural parallels between our imaginings of the future and our memories of the past, and the role of our emotions in response to what we imagine in thinking about our future in the light of our past. This is followed by a second case study—an exploration of self-forgiveness.

In this ground-breaking book, Goldie supports scepticism about the idea that there is such a thing as a *narrative self*, but argues that having a narrative *sense of* self, quite distinct from any metaphysical notion of selfhood, is at the heart of what it is to think of ourselves, and others, as having a narratable past, present, and future.

Peter Goldie was the Samuel Hall Chair in Philosophy at the University of Manchester.

The Mess Inside

Narrative, Emotion, and the Mind

Peter Goldie

OXFORD
UNIVERSITY PRESS

OXFORD

UNIVERSITY PRESS

Great Clarendon Street, Oxford, OX2 6DP,
United Kingdom

Oxford University Press is a department of the University of Oxford.
It furthers the University's objective of excellence in research, scholarship,
and education by publishing worldwide. Oxford is a registered trade mark of
Oxford University Press in the UK and in certain other countries

Published in the United States of America by Oxford University Press
198 Madison Avenue, New York, NY 10016, United States of America

British Library Cataloguing in Publication Data
Data available

Library of Congress Cataloging in Publication Data
Data available

ISBN 978–0–19–923073–0 (Hbk)
ISBN 978–0–19–870766–0 (Pbk)

To Sophie

As a rule is it with great difficulty that men abandon their physio-logical memories and the mould in which they are cast by heredity; to do so a man must be either particularly unpassioned and featureless or absorbed in abstract pursuits. The impersonality of mathematics and the unhuman objectivity of nature do not call forth those sides of the soul and do not awaken them; but as soon as we touch upon questions of life, of art, of morals, in which a man is not only an observer and investigator but at the same time himself a participant, then we find a physiological limit—which it is very hard to cross with one's old blood and brains unless one can erase from them all traces of the songs of the cradle, of the fields and the hills of home, of the customs and whole setting of the past.

(Alexander Herzen, *My Past and Thoughts*)

He would reason about people's conduct as though a man were as simple a figure as, say, two sticks laid across each other; whereas a man is much more like the sea whose movements are too compli-cated to explain, and whose depths may bring up God only knows what at any moment.

(Joseph Conrad, *The Warrior's Soul*)

Contents

Preface and Acknowledgements

This book is about the ways in which we think about our lives—our present, our past, and our future—in narrative terms.

Chapter 1 introduces the contentious notion of narrative. I argue, contrary to many views, that narratives need not be publicly narrated, but can be just thought through in acts of narrative thinking. In Chapter 1, I also introduce the notion of perspective, grasp of which is essential to a proper grasp of narratives. A perspective can be internal to a narrative, being the perspective of a 'character' in the narrative, or the perspective can be external to the narrative, being the perspective of for example, the narrator, or the audience. These perspectives can, of course, diverge.

Chapter 2 develops the notion of perspective in autobiographical narrative thinking, where the narrator, with his or her external perspective, is the very same person as the 'character' in the narrative. These potentially diverging perspectives are at the heart of narrative thinking about our past, and I show this through the idea of dramatic irony in autobiographical narrative thinking, where you now know things about your past that you then, in the past, did not know. And this in turn allows me to introduce a notion familiar in literary theory and narratology, but little discussed in philosophy: the notion of free indirect style, which is a literary device that is very common in modern literature. Very roughly, with free indirect style it becomes unclear whether the perspective being expressed in the narrative is that of a character internal to the narrative or that of the narrator. Drawing on some of the fascinating recent empirical work on personal memories, I then show how our memories of our past can be infused with the irony of what we now know, and what we now feel about what we now know, through the psychological equivalent of free indirect style.

In Chapter 3, as a kind of case study, I apply these ideas to narratives of grief, and, more widely, of narratives of past traumatic experiences. Against the vast majority of contemporary philosophical views about emotion, I argue that grief (and I believe other emotions too) is a kind of process, not a kind of mental state or event. Furthermore, I argue, a narrative is the ideal kind of account of the process of grief. I then discuss how our capacity to narrate our past breaks down after some kinds of traumatic experience, tragic loss being one such, and consider this in relation to what I call the desire for emotional closure. In both fiction and in real life narratives, emotional closure, like narrative closure in this respect, is something of an ideal: closure, however much aspired to, is never really reached, and remains illusory.

Chapter 4 turns to narrative thinking about our future, and its role in planning, forming policies, and making resolutions. Here I discuss the many structural parallels between imagination and memory, and the role of our emotions in response to what we imagine in making our plans. I then discuss how we can learn from our mistakes, and generally how narrative thinking about our past in emotional terms can inform our narrative thinking about our future.

In Chapter 5, in my second case study, I apply the ways in which we engage in narrative thinking about our future to self-forgiveness—a notion that many consider to be deeply suspect, as if by a simply *fiat* one can forgive oneself for some past wrongdoing. I show that self-forgiveness is not only coherent, but also that it is something that we often need for good ethical reasons (not just for reasons of self-interest), and that, when properly understood, it is by no means as easily won as its critics would suppose; the elusiveness of closure again plays a part here. Finally I contrast the possibility of self-forgiveness with the impossibility of self-pardon.

Chapter 6 is about the narrative sense of self: the sense that we have of ourselves as having a narratable past and future. I argue that the narrative sense of self is not at all the same thing as a sense of a narrative self. In fact, I think that there is no interesting notion of a narrative self: a self that is in some way constituted by the narratives that we tell about our lives. I also dissociate the narrative sense of self from questions of personal identity—one's narrative sense of self as I conceive it really has no direct connection with the metaphysical question of one's numerical identity over time, although I believe the narrative sense of self presupposes it. Generally, I argue that we can have a clear and distinct idea of what a narrative sense of self is without committing ourselves to any particular account of personal identity over time; and this, I believe, is a merit of my account.

Chapter 7 addresses a concern about narratives that is often voiced: whether narratives about our lives are capable of truth and objectivity. We need to be especially careful what we mean by these terms here: truth is not simply a matter of the constituent propositions in the narrative satisfying some minimal truth schema; and achieving objectivity is not simply a matter of providing or thinking through a narrative whose content expresses a perspective which can be shared by all reasonable people. But still, I argue, narratives are capable of truth and objectivity properly understood, and this in spite of the fact that, as a matter of human psychology, we tend to bestow our lives with a degree of narrativity which is often more appropriate to traditional fiction than it is to real life.

I have more people to thank than I could possibly mention here, including all those who have heard and commented insightfully on the ideas expressed in this book, and in journal papers and edited books. Special thanks for their help are owed to H. Porter Abbott, Simon Beck, Monika Bezler, Michael Bratman, Cindy Chung, Gregory Currie, Dorothea Debus, Ronald de Sousa, Russell Downham, Eric Eich, John Gibson, Charles Griswold, Tilmann Habermas, Paul Harris, Kathleen Higgins, Peter Hobson, Katharine Jenkins, Matthew Kieran, Peter Lamarque, Anthony Marcel, Alba Montes, Adam Morton, Kevin Mulligan, Robin le Poidevin, Anna Reboul, Robert Roberts, Jenefer Robinson, Louise Roska-Hardy, Marya Schechtman, David Shoemaker, Joel Smith, Helen Steward, Galen Strawson, John Sutton, Thomas Uebel, Samanatha Vice, and Gary Watson, many of whom took the trouble to read through and comment on all or large parts of earlier drafts. I also would like to thank Peter Momtchiloff and his colleagues at Oxford University Press for their support, as well as the anonymous readers for OUP, whose comments have been invaluable, and, finally and uniquely, Derek Matravers.

P.G.

October 2011
London

1

Narrative Thinking

Introduction: Finding the Right Place
for Narrative in Our Lives

Positions can get polarized. At one pole, there are the narrativists, as we might call them, who hold one or more of a cluster of strong views about the place of narratives in our lives. Our lives are, in some sense, lived narratives of which we are the authors. Our lives are somehow only comprehensible through a narrative explanatory structure. Our lives bear close similarities to (or are even fundamentally the same as) the lives of characters in literature. Our having the right kind of narrative of our lives is, in some sense, integral to or constitutive of our being the persons that we are. Our very survival depends on our having such a narrative.

At the other pole, reacting against these excesses of narrativity, there are the sceptics about the place of narratives in our lives. Narratives are not an especially interesting kind of thing. Narratives, whatever they might be, do not play any significant part in our understanding of our lives, or in living a life. Nor should they. Narratives of our lives are fundamentally perspectival, and can be deeply distorting of reality, of truth, of objectivity, and of what it is to be a person. Narratives have their proper home in literature, but no place in real life.

Between these two polarized clusters of views, however, much is possible. In this book, I will be arguing, in disagreement with the anti-narrativists, that narrative has a very important role in our lives: in our thinking about our own past and about our plans for the future; in our thinking about how things might have been; in our sense of ourselves as having a past and a future; and in other ways too. In doing this, however, I will not be arguing in favour of any of the above narrativist views. So the central task I have set myself is to find the *right* place for narrative in our lives, without any of the narrativist excesses that one sometimes finds these days, and without a recoil to an unwarranted anti-narrativist scepticism.

The first task, though, one for this chapter, is to give an outline of what a narrative is. I say 'an outline' because the details will emerge as I progress; to begin with, I just want to fix a rough idea.

What a Narrative Is

Roughly, then:

> A narrative or story is something that can be told or narrated, or just thought through in narrative thinking. It is more than just a bare annal or chronicle or list of a sequence of events, but a representation of those events which is shaped, organized, and coloured, presenting those events, and the people involved in them, from a certain perspective or perspectives, and thereby giving narrative structure—coherence, meaningfulness, and evaluative and emotional import—to what is related.

This is quite a dense statement, so I will try to unpack it, and to make some pointers towards more detailed unpacking in later chapters.

A narrative or story is something that can be told or narrated

There is a familiar distinction between a narrative as a product, and a narrative as a process. The product is the content of what is narrated—the story that is told. So when we say that someone's chosen narrative was the incestuous love of Phaedra for Hippolytus, it is the product that we have in mind—the content of the story that he or she chose to tell, the story *about* this incestuous love.

The process sense of narrative is the process, the activity, of producing a particular narrative, whether for the first time or not. It is this sense we have in mind when we say, for example, that the narrative at the dinner party of the incestuous love of Phaedra for Hippolytus took much too long, or that the narrative of Phaedra and Hippolytus unfortunately took place against the sound of a brass band playing in an upstairs room.

Sometimes we also speak of a narrative in a third sense, as a particular text, as we might say that the narrative of Euripides in the original Greek was in front of the person whilst he or she was narrating the story of

Phaedra and Hippolytus. In what follows, the meaning will usually be clear from the context, but where it is not I will disambiguate.[1]

The notion of a narrative as a product can be taken widely, to include anything that has what I will call *narrative structure*. Or it can be taken narrowly, to include only those things that have narrative structure and that *also* imply the existence of a narrator. In general, I want to take the notion widely, so that a narrative or story can include dramas, such as films, plays, or operas that have narrative structure, even though these media do not imply the existence of a narrator.[2]

A narrative can be just thought through in narrative thinking

Whether or not the notion of narrative is taken in this wide sense to include drama, most theorists of narrative, with a few exceptions, take the notion narrowly in another sense. They take the notion of narrative as product to be a notion of something that is necessarily public, involving written, or spoken, or signed, language, or some other product that in some way or other is necessarily already in the public domain.[3]

But this is too narrow. The notion of narrative as product can readily, and in an intuitively satisfying way, be widened to include the product of *narrative thinking*. Narrative thinking involves not text or discourse, but another kind of representation: thoughts. So, on this second wider notion of narrative as product, a narrative can be thought through, but there need be no public product as a result of a communicative event; there need be

---

[1] For discussion of these distinctions, see Lamarque (2004) and Wilson (2003). The Russian formalists made a distinction that should not be confused with the ones I have just made. This is between *fabula* and *syuzhet*, where (very roughly) the term 'fabula' picks out the events that are related, whilst the term 'syuzhet' refers to the order of events as they are presented in the narrative text. So the *syuzhet* of Almodovar's film *Broken Embraces* (2009) begins in the present day with the protagonist blind, and then flashes back to the 1990s, whereas the *fabula* of the film begins with the events that took place in the 1990s and that are being looked back on at the beginning of the *syuzhet*. French structural analysts have used *histoire* or *récit* for *fabula*, and *discours* for *syuzhet*. All these terms can be confusing for native English speakers, partly because the terms 'plot' and 'story' cut across the distinctions that are being made (Brooks 2002: 130–1). So I will from now on avoid use of these terms.

[2] Not surprisingly, it is controversial whether film, for example, necessarily involves a narrator, but it is a dispute I wish to avoid.

[3] See e.g. Peter Lamarque, who says that 'Narratives must be related: that is how they come into being' (2007: 396, cf. 394, 402, 404). And Robert Scholes, James Phelan, and Robert Kellogg begin their book *The Nature of Narrative* thus: 'By narrative we mean all those literary works which are distinguished by two characteristics: the presence of a story and a story-teller' (Scholes, Phelan, and Kellogg 1966: 4).

no public act of narration. A narrative that is thought through in this sense will involve certain sequences of thought, feeling, and imagination—sequences that have, as I will argue, narrative structure. On this doubly wide notion of narrative, then, a narrative is something that can be, *but need not be*, told or narrated to others in a variety of different ways: it could be spoken, written down, drawn, acted, sung, mimed, danced, filmed, or communicated through some combination of these. Narrative thinking is *narratable, communicable*, but need not be publicly narrated or communicated to another person.

This wider notion of narrative, as publicly narratable but not necessarily actually publicly narrated, is by no means arbitrary or ad hoc: it is part of our everyday, commonsense idea of what narrative is. To show this, imagine that Italo Calvino conjured up in his mind one of his inimitable short stories, and, before he was able to write it down or communicate it to anyone in any other way, he died. Surely we would say that the world had lost something—we had lost a wonderful story of Calvino's. Or, to make the same point with a different example, imagine that something surprising happened to me whilst I was walking the dog this morning, alone on the beach; when I return home, after a bit of rehearsal to myself about how best to relate what happened, I might say to my partner, 'I've got an amazing story to tell you about my walk this morning.' The story, the narrative, is already there, in my mind, waiting to be told to another for the first time.

I can think through a narrative in a variety of ways, each of which will be relevant in different ways in subsequent chapters: remembering, perhaps episodically or experientially, some events that happened to me or that I observed; hypothesizing what might happen in the future; thinking through a narrative propositionally; mentally rehearsing it, as one might mentally rehearse a speech; using perceptual imagination to, for example, visualize what might happen; thinking through an episode of events coolly with little or no emotional engagement; thinking through the episode vividly and highly emotionally; thinking of 'that terrible quarter of an hour when I thought that all was lost'; thinking through how things might have turned out differently if I hadn't made that terrible mistake; and in lots of other ways, many of which cross-cut with each other.

Generally, I will use the term 'thinking through' to encompass all kinds of narrative thinking by which an episode comes to be mentally represented in narrative form. So thinking through is very much like *conceiving*, understood in the relatively loose sense used by the *Oxford English Dictionary* of take into or form in the mind, where in narrative thinking what is taken into or formed in the mind is a narrative.[4] This sense of conceiving is meant to be neutral as to where, on any particular occasion, conceiving falls within the spectrum of ways in which an episode can be represented in narrative thinking. It is also meant to be neutral as to whether the thinking through takes place as a process carried out deliberately and with conscious intent, perhaps with methodical care; or whether the narrative is thought through or conceived more or less 'all at once', in a single spontaneous moment of thought, without any conscious intention on the thinker's part.[5] More specific terms, such as 'imagine' or 'remember' or 'plan' or 'reconstruct' or 'think over', are often more natural ones to use than 'think through' or 'conceive', but what I need here are terms that are as neutral as possible both as to the kind of content of the narrative that is thought through and as to the manner of thinking through of the narrative.

It might be objected here that this notion of narrative thinking fails to maintain the distinction between narrative as process and narrative as product. But this is not so, as can be seen by considering the narrative of that *mauvais quart d'heure*. Without ever having related it to anyone else, I can readily refer to that narrative as product, without, in so referring to it, actually going through the process of thinking it through; I might, for example, think to myself , 'Don't think about that *mauvais quart d'heure.*' We can also see that the distinction remains in place by considering how one tries to work through a narrative in one's mind. The two-timing spouse might be trying to craft a mendacious story to tell her husband about what she was doing earlier that evening—she doesn't yet have a persuasive narrative, and that narrative, as a product, is precisely what she is trying to work through in the process of narrative thinking.

Of course, there is an important difference between narratives that are just thought through, and narratives that are publicly narrated. The former are much more indeterminate. They are more indeterminate as to activity in the sense that our activity of thinking through a narrative will characteristically not have a precise beginning and end: a problem at work pops

---

[4] For discussion, see Gendler and Hawthorne (2003). For those who believe that there is such a thing as non-conceptual content, conceiving in this sense could be non-conceptual.
[5] This will be especially relevant in relation to traumatic memories, which I will be discussing in Ch. 3.

into your mind whilst you are queuing to buy a lunchtime sandwich; this thought prompts you to begin to think through a way out of the problem; and then you hear a voice 'Cashier number seven, please', and the thread is lost, perhaps to be picked up later, perhaps not. (The same kind of thing can happen in conversation between friends.) And they are more indeterminate as to content simply because the thoughts that make up a thought-through narrative might not be fully formed, so that they can readily be made explicit in speech. For example, your thoughts about the way out of your problem at work might only be partially formed in your mind. E. M. Forster's famous 'How can I tell what I think till I see what I say?' is instructive here, except that it might give the impression that the issue is simply an epistemic one, as if there is something determinate that you are thinking but you cannot know what it is until you utter the words. The mind is messier than that.

A narrative is more than just a bare annal or chronicle or list of a sequence of events

A narrative is distinct from what it is a narrative *of*. To fail to maintain this distinction is to lose the distinction between, on the one side, language and thought, and, on the other side, the world, between representation and what is represented. An effect of the mistake is also to lose the distinction between those narratives (such as historical narratives) that aspire to be true, and those narratives (such as novels) that do not aspire to be true in this sense. All narratives share certain properties in their structural dimension; in other words they all have narrative structure. But not all narratives are alike in their referential dimension: some aspire to reference and to truth and some do not.[6]

Of course, the simple fact that our lives, or episodes in our lives, are not narratives (that is, they are not *identical* to narratives) does not imply that narratives and narrative thinking cannot play a central part in how we lead our lives. We think, talk, and write *about* our lives by narrating or thinking through narratives, and how we do this can profoundly affect our lives as such. What emerges, then, is that our narratives of our lives, or of segments of our lives, can be embedded in the lives that we lead, which themselves are not narratives. A simple example can illustrate the point. One evening you are in a restaurant with a friend about to order dinner. It is very stormy

---

[6] I will come back to this in Ch. 7 when I discuss the question of truth in narrative, comparing real-life narratives with fictional narratives.

outside. There is a sudden flash of lightning, and the lights suddenly fuse. You then say to your friend, 'This reminds me of something that happened to me in Bali in 1987,' and you then proceed to tell her all about it. Your thoughts about those events in Bali in 1987, and what you tell your friend about what happened, are narrative in form. And when your friend listens to what you say, she is engaging with a narrative. This perhaps might make her feel jealous, thinking of your life before she knew you. But those events that took place in Bali in 1987 and that make your friend jealous are themselves no more a narrative than are the events that took place in the restaurant that very evening. There are thus two things to be kept apart: a sequence of events; and a narrative or story of the events, where this is taken as a product in the doubly wide sense that I have been discussing.

It is helpful to compare narratives with annals and chronicles. Annals and chronicles are like narratives in one sense: annals and chronicles are distinct from the events that they are a record of, and in this sense they have a referential dimension just as a narrative has when it is concerned with real-life events. But a mere annal or chronicle of events lacks narrative structure—it does not have the same structural dimension as a narrative. Let us consider some examples. Hayden White gives a nice example of an annal from the *Annals of Saint Gall*, covering events in Gaul in the eighth to the tenth century AD, part of which is as follows:[7]

709. Hard Winter. Duke Gottfried died.

710. Hard year and deficient in crops.

711.

712. Flood everywhere.

713.

714. Pippin, Mayor of the Palace, died.

715. 716. 717.

718. Charles devastated the Saxon with great destruction.

719.

720. Charles fought against the Saxons.

721. Theudo drove the Saracens out of Aquitaine.

---

[7] From the *Annales Sangallanses Majores, dicti Hepidanni*, ed. Idlefonsus ab Arx, in *Monumenta Germaniae Historica*, series *Scriptores*, ed. George Heinrich Pertz, 32 vols. (Hanover 1826), i. 73–85, trans. H. White, and cited in White (1980: 7).

Somewhat closer to a narrative, perhaps, but still a long way short, is the chronicle. This is an example, cited by Bernard Williams ('here' in the text means 'in this year'):[8]

Here the sun grew dark. And Eorcenberht, king of the inhabitants of Kent, passed away. And Colman with his companions went to his native land. The same year there was a great plague among men . . .

Here Theodore was ordained archbishop.

Here King Egbert gave Reculver to Bass the mass-priest in which to build a minster . . .

Here there was a great mortality of birds.

Diaries too can have elements of narrativity but still fall short of a fully fledged narrative. The diaries of Samuel Pepys are an interesting case in point. With an eye on the above chronicle, contrast the first paragraph of Pepys's diary for 25 September 1662 with the first paragraph for the following day:

25. Up betimes and to my workmen: and then to the office, where we sat all morning. So home to dinner alone and then to my workmen till night; and so to my office till bedtime, and after supper to my lodgings and to bed.

26. Up betimes and among my workmen. By and by to Sir W. Batten, who with Sir J. Mennes are going to Chatham this morning. And I was in great pain till they were gone, that I might see whether Sir John doth speak anything of my chamber that I am afeard of losing or no. But he did not, and so my mind is a little more at ease. So all day long till night among my workmen; and in the afternoon did cause the particion between the entry and the boy's room to be pulled down, to lay it all into one—which I hope will please me and make my coming in more pleasant.

What do annals and chronicles lack when compared to narratives, and what does Pepys's diary entry for 26 September have that is missing from the entry for the day before? To answer these questions, I now need to say what narrative structure is.

A narrative is a representation of events which is shaped, organized, and coloured, presenting those events, and the people involved in them, from a certain perspective or perspectives, and thereby giving narrative structure—coherence, meaningfulness, and evaluative and emotional import—to what is narrated.

---

[8] The Anglo-Saxon Chronicles, the Winchester MS (A), AD 664–71, cited in Williams (2002: 238).

This process, which, following Paul Ricœur (1984), I will call *emplotment*, is one by which a bare description of events, such as one might find in an annal or chronicle, can be transformed into a narrative, giving coherence, meaningfulness, and evaluative and emotional import to what is narrated.[9] I will try to show what is involved in emplotment by breaking it down into four parts: the raw material for emplotment; the process of emplotment itself; the outcome of the process, which is the narrative or the story, which can be but need not be publicly related; and the possible effects of the narrative or story on a thinker, hearer, or reader who grasps its import.

The raw material for emplotment comprises descriptions and names of persons and actions, and of objects and events generally. These descriptions can be rich. That is to say, the raw material does not have to be restricted to, for example, impersonal descriptions using only concepts that are congenial to the physical sciences. To demand that the process of emplotment should begin at such an impoverished level is to demand too much of it. Emplotment is not alchemy, seeking to turn the base metal of impersonal physical concepts into the gold of a narrative. Accordingly, the raw material for emplotment can include, for example, rich descriptions of people's thoughts, feelings, moods, and emotions, rich descriptions of people, including their character traits and personality, rich descriptions of people's actions, and rich descriptions of other things, such as institutions, cultures, cultural practices, and customs. This is very much what the cultural anthropologist Clifford Geertz had in mind in his notion of a *thick description* as the essential starting-point for ethnography (Geertz 1973).[10]

This idea of a rich description is most familiar in relation to *actions*.[11] A particular action can be variously described, depending on how widely the intention behind the action is drawn. Elisabeth Anscombe has a famous example in her *Intention* (Anscombe 1957), of 'the man who (intentionally) moves his arm, operates the pump, replenishes the water supply, poisons the inhabitants'. Anscombe argues that the man is

---

[9] Ricœur bases his discussion of emplotment on Aristotle's *Poetics*, but diverges from him in a number of respects; similarly, I diverge from Ricœur in a number of respects, as anyone familiar with his work will see.

[10] Geertz nicely characterized ethnography as intermediary 'between author-saturated texts like *David Copperfield* and author-evacuated ones like "On the Electrodynamics of Moving Bodies"'. In Geertz, *Works and Lives: The Anthropologist as Author* (Stanford, Calif.: Stanford University Press, 1988), 141, cited in Inglis (2000: 109).

[11] See in particular MacIntyre (1981).

performing just one action and not four: one action which has four descriptions, 'each dependent on wider circumstances, and each related to the next as description of means to end'. So, as she says, 'it is not wrong' to say that the man is poisoning the inhabitants in reply to the question why he is moving his arm (1957: sect. 26). This would be a richer description than to say that the man is operating the pump, and such a less rich description, whilst true, can at the same time fail to be narratively appropriate. Richness comes in degrees.

Determining what is the narratively appropriate description as raw material of a person, of an event, or of an action, from amongst a variety of possible descriptions, ranging from richer to less rich, is part of what is involved in the process of emplotment. When it comes to actions, the raw material for emplotment will not include ultra-impoverished descriptions, often because such descriptions simply will not be available. Consider the fielder catching a ball at the crucial stage of a Test Match or a World Series. A rich description might be 'clinching the series', and a less rich one might be 'catching the ball', but we might not be able to characterize the action, qua action, any less richly than that, in a way that does not appeal in one way or another to *the ball* and to what the fielder was *trying* to do. Notably, even annals and chronicles contain rich descriptions, as we have seen from the examples just given ('Theudo drove the Saracens out of Aquitaine'; 'Theodore was ordained archbishop'), and there is no good reason to expect the raw material for a narrative to be less rich than these.

So much for raw material; now I turn to the process of emplotment, which mediates between the raw material and the narrative itself—the narrative as product. Essentially, emplotment brings together the raw material, organizing into a coherent whole what is a mere succession of events, actions, objects, individuals, and thoughts, feelings, moods, and emotions. The process involves agency; it is not like the process of the ripening of a tomato in the sun—something that can happen without human involvement. As we saw earlier, however, conscious intention is not a necessary feature of the process of emplotment. This point is especially relevant when we consider those narratives that are merely thought through. For example, someone can suddenly come to see certain things that happened to him as having a narrative structure, or as being of a form that can be narrated, and yet he did not consciously set out to see things in that way. Or the whole 'plot' of the way out of your current difficulty at work can come into your mind unbidden, perhaps whilst dozing in a half-awake state as you lie in bed in the morning.

The process of emplotment involves *shaping, organizing,* and *colouring* the raw material into a narrative structure. Shaping involves selecting raw material with the appropriate degree of richness, and shaping it in a way that is appropriate to the narrative. Organizing involves configuring the raw material into a narrative, with a beginning, middle, and end. And colouring (not a necessary ingredient of emplotment, perhaps, but a typical one) involves bestowing evaluative and emotional import to what might otherwise be a bare description of what happened. The process of emplotment is often a *tâtonnement,* a tentative, groping procedure: one might begin with an idea of how the narrative should be shaped, and, once one has developed it somewhat, one might be able to see saliences that one could not see before, and then find it appropriate to go back and reshape the narrative in this new light. More than that, the *tâtonnement* typically involves a groping search for the appropriate evaluative and emotional import of what is narrated. All these go together: it is not as though there is, first, a completed narrative, and then, second, an evaluation and emotional response to the narrative; rather, the evaluation and emotional response themselves infuse the narrative, shaping and colouring it. This point will be especially important in what follows.

The manner of this shaping, organizing, and colouring is informed by something that is at the heart of my account of narrative: the narrator's perspective or point of view from which the events are narrated. As we will see, it is important here to keep separate two kinds of perspective: the possible multiplicity of perspectives of those who are internal to the narrative; and the possible multiplicity of perspectives of those who are external to the narrative, including, of course, the narrator. But I need to ask for an interlude in my account of narrative to consider briefly the notion of perspective that is at work here. I will then be in a position to turn to the outcome of the process of emplotment: narrative as product.

What sorts of things have perspectives? First, there is a weak notion of perspective according to which all and only things that have sentience have perspectives. This is *sentience-perspective.* Not everything in the world has sentience-perspective; a volcano does not, nor does a stone or a lamppost. To have sentience-perspective is to be a subject of experience such that there is *something that it is like* to be that thing: something with sentience-perspective has an egocentric view on its environment, and it is able to find its way around in its world through its sense modalities.[12] Another way of capturing this weak notion of sentience-perspective is in terms of explanation of behaviour: the behaviour of a rat or a dog, for example, can best be explained in terms of how things seem to it. One might even want to go so far as to say that creatures with only sentience-perspective have minds, where to have a mind is to have the property of *intentionality*, which is the mind's capability of being directed onto things in the world.[13]

Whether or not one would want to allow mindedness to such creatures, we human beings have a perspective on the world that involves a much richer sense of mindedness. To begin with, unlike creatures with only sentience-perspective, we human beings are also able to think of ourselves *as* having a perspective, and as being capable of thoughts and feelings. Thus we humans can have a perspective on our own perspective and can conceptualize it as such.[14] Moreover, a number of other abilities come with the ability to think about, and respond to, our own thoughts and feelings, and one such is the ability to think of others—other humans—as having perspectives, as capable of thoughts and feelings just as one is oneself. This personal perspective, as I will call it, through which we can have perspectives on perspectives, can thus be first-, second-, or third-personal, singular or plural.

We humans not only have a personal perspective in the literal sense, as we might contrast our visual perspectives on an object (it is to my left and to your right), but also we have a personal perspective in the more metaphorical, evaluative sense, as we might contrast our evaluations of some action (that action of yours might seem a reasonable response from your perspective, but it strikes me as being thoroughly unreasonable).

---

[12] This is the notion captured by Thomas Nagel in his famous paper 'What Is It Like to Be a Bat?' (Nagel 1974; cf. Flanagan 1994: 193–4). There is a notion that is, perhaps, even weaker than sentience-perspective: Daniel Dennett discusses the idea of the biological self, which is a 'minimal proclivity to distinguish self from other', and is a distinction that 'even the lowliest amoeba must make, in its blind, unknowing way' (1992: 414).

[13] For an account of intentionality along these lines, see Crane (2001). As Lynn Rudder Baker (1998) reminds us, there is something like an intermediate stage between having a sentience-perspective and the personal perspective. This is the ability for self-recognition that is manifested by certain sorts of chimps; they seem to be able to recognize a face in the mirror as being their face; see Gordon Gallup (1977).

[14] The point is sometime put in terms of the capacity for 'meta-representation'; for discussion, see Currie and Ravenscroft (2002).

As we will see in Chapter 2 and beyond, the interplay between diverging perspectives in a narrative—between literal and evaluative, as well as within the evaluative domain—is one of the main sources of its power as a medium of thought in explaining and expressing what it is to lead a life as a person.

I will now turn to the outcome of the process of emplotment: narrative as product. Narratives have narrative structure to a greater or lesser degree: coherence, meaningfulness, and evaluative and emotional import.

Narrative Structure

It is no part of my intention to give a set of necessary and sufficient conditions for something to have narrative structure, even if such a thing were possible; I will just outline three characteristic features of a narrative— features that give narratives their special explanatory, revelatory, and expressive power, and that are not possessed by a mere list, or annal, or chronicle—in the words of Elbert Hubbard, just one damn thing after another. Instead of necessary and sufficient conditions, narrative structure is a property that can be possessed as a matter of degree: it can be present to a greater or a lesser extent. For example a chronicle that lacks significant narrative structure might nevertheless have elements of it that make it more narrative-like than an annal, but less than a diary.[15] And narratives can range from being what Bernard Williams calls mini-narratives, 'short and unambitious' (2002: 233), such as the narrative of my going to the gym this morning, to something saga-length such as Boris Pasternak's *Doctor Zhivago*.

The idea that narrativity and narrative structure are properties that admit of degree happily makes room for the claim that a narrative's being perspectival also admits of degree, down to a vanishing point at which the perspective, whether internal or external, is more or less completely effaced. Consider, for example, being presented with a text that begins with the race card for the 1959 King George VI and Queen Elizabeth Stakes at Ascot. Considered superficially and on its own, this race card seems to be completely lacking in narrative structure; indeed, if one imagined turning the pages of the text only to find further race cards for

---

[15] Greg Currie argues persuasively that what he calls narrativity is a matter of degree (Currie 2006, 2010).

further races that day in 1959, one would reasonably enough form the opinion that what one is presented with is, in fact, a *race card for Ascot for that day*; in which case it would be a text with properties more like those of a mere list than those of a narrative. But instead, let us imagine that the text continues with something that clearly has many of the properties of a plot, introducing internal characters whose lives, in one way or another, depend on the outcome of this particular race event. Then we can see the force of Noël Carroll's point, that having narrative structure (and being perspectival) is not something that is essential to narratives in the sense that all narratives must have narrative structure throughout, but rather that all narratives must, to some degree or other, have narrative structure (and be perspectival).[16]

To start with, I will follow the tradition of narrative theory, and speak of a narrative as something that is publicly narrated, and is thus accessible to an audience or to a reader; so, at this point, emplotment will be a process undertaken by the narrator as such. Then, once the three characteristic features of narrative are in place, I will extend the notion to narrative thinking, where, of course, there is no text, no discourse, no narrator as such, no reader, no audience.

Coherence

The first characteristic feature of a narrative is that it has *coherence*, in the sense that it reveals, through the process of emplotment, connections between the related events, and it does so in a way that a mere list, or annal, or chronicle, does not. Emplotment, as Paul Ricœur puts it, 'extracts a configuration from a succession' (Ricœur 1984: 66).

Narratives characteristically have much in common with ordinary causal accounts. Like these, they are idiographic (Collingwood 1946: 165–70); that is to say, they are concerned with particular facts, events, and individuals. Secondly, like a causal account, a narrative cannot be concerned with just a single simple event; it must be about one thing happening after another, and the notion of coherence is concerned with how these things happening one after another hold together in some way.[17] And, thirdly,

---

[16] Thanks to an OUP reader for pressing me on this point, and for referring me to Kendall Walton's discussion and his example of the 'effacement' of narrators in his 1990: 367.

[17] A narrative can, though, be concerned with a single *complex* event, such as the Second World War.

causal relations often play a central part in the coherence of a narrative. Let me illustrate this with an example.

I tell you a little story—short and unambitious—about what happened to me this morning, and in particular how my dawdling over my breakfast at home (C) caused me to miss my train to work (E). There are causal relations between events C and E in the narrative, but, as is typical in idiographic accounts, C is not causally sufficient for E, such that if C happens then E would be bound to happen. Nor is C necessary for E. My dawdling over breakfast (C) was what J. L. Mackie has called an *INUS* condition for my missing the train (E)—an Insufficient but Necessary part of an Unnecessary but Sufficient condition.[18] In other words, a whole cluster of elements, of which my dawdling was only one, was a sufficient causal condition for me to miss the train, the other elements of the cluster being unmentioned in the narrative—for example, the train being on time (as it usually is when one is late). But this cluster of elements, of which my dawdling is a part, was not a necessary condition for my missing the train, because another wholly different cluster of elements might have had the same effect—I might, for example, have sprained my ankle as I left the house, or my wife's lover might have burst in and started a fight, and either of these elements, suitably combined with others, would have been sufficient to have caused me to miss the train. Now, considering my dawdling as an element in this cluster, it on its own was insufficient to cause me to miss the train without the other elements; perhaps one such other element was my partner's being unwilling to give me a lift in the car (as usually happens when one is late). But my dawdling was nevertheless a necessary element, because, if all the other elements had been in place, I would not have missed the train: and this is the sense in my saying 'If only I hadn't dawdled, I wouldn't have missed the train.'

What is helpful about this idea for our understanding of narratives is that it provides a structural explanation of how both causal explanations and narrative explanations typically work. As David Lewis says in his discussion of causal explanations, 'Any particular event that we might wish to explain stands at the end of a long and complicated causal history' (Lewis 1986), and in our explanations we very seldom (if ever) appeal to all the elements

---

[18] The following points, made familiar by J. L. Mackie in his work on causation (1980), have been subtly brought to bear in recent philosophical debate on narrative by Noël Carroll (2001).

in that history. Rather, we appeal to the elements that are relevant to our interests, and to the interests of our audience. Lewis puts the point nicely in relation to the multiplicity of causes of a particular car crash:

> If someone says that the bald tyre was the cause of the crash, another says that the driver's drunkenness was the cause, and still another says that the cause was the bad upbringing which made him so reckless, I do not think any of them disagree with me when I say that the causal history includes all three. They disagree only about which part of the causal history is most salient for the purpose of some particular inquiry. They may be looking for the most remarkable part, the most remediable or blameworthy part, the least obvious of the discoverable parts. (Lewis 1986: 215)

Similarly, in narrative explanations, the elements that the narrative mentions will depend on our interests. I might say that I missed the train because my partner refused to give me a lift in the car (she was too busy, she said), whereas she might say that I missed the train because I dawdled so much that walking to the station would not get me there on time (and she really was too busy to give me a lift). All of this will be very relevant when we come to questions of perspective and truth in narrative, and when we come to counterfactual narrative thinking, and it is interesting here to see that narrative explanation has a partner in crime in causal explanation.

In spite of having much in common, the relation between a narrative account and a causal account is not a simple one, and it would be wrong to think that a narrative account is simply a causal account plus some other added element or elements. Nor do we need to insist that causal relations are necessary for narrative; coherence between represented events is not the same notion as a causal relationship between those events.

However, returning to Noel Carroll's notion of narrative structure, whilst it is certainly true that narratives need not involve causal relations between the events that are related in the narrative, for, as David Velleman (2003) and Gregory Currie (2006) have argued, notably against Carroll's (2001) account of narrative in relation to INUS conditions, we need room for coincidence, as exemplified in Aristotle's story in his *Poetics* of how the murderer of Mitys was killed by the falling statue of Mitys. Nevertheless, Carroll effectively makes the point that it would be a strange story indeed if it involved no representations of causal relations whatsoever; after all, it was the falling of the statue of Mitys that *caused* the death of Mitys' murderer. Arguably, all narratives, whether fictional or not, must be broadly subject to plausible causal constraints, and this will be so in spite of the undoubted possibility of counterexamples in particular cases, of which coincidence is one kind; and there are others that we will turn to in more detail in later chapters. And of course these constraints of a causal nexus apply a fortiori when we turn to history, to biography, and to autobiography.[19]

Meaningfulness

The second characteristic feature of a narrative, which has important connections to the first feature of coherence, is *meaningfulness*. A narrative can be meaningful in at least two ways. These two ways are distinct, but, as we will see, they are intimately related in interesting and complex respects. First, a narrative can be meaningful by revealing how the thoughts, feelings, and actions of those people who are internal to the narrative could have made sense of them from their perspective at the time—that is, from their internal perspective. And, secondly, a narrative can be meaningful by revealing the narrator's external perspective: his or her thoughts and feelings that throw light on why the narrative was related (or just thought through) in that particular way. Bound up with these two kinds of meaningfulness are the two ways in which a narrative can have evaluative and emotional import. Again, this can be internal or external to the narrative, revealing evaluative and emotional import from the perspective of those who are internal to the narrative, or revealing them as part of the thoughts and feelings involved in the external perspective of the narrator. In this chapter, I will focus on the first, internal, kind of meaningfulness and evaluative and emotional import, and, in Chapter 2, I will turn to the narrator's external perspective, and to the complexities of the relationship between internal and external perspective. But from the outset it is important to appreciate that the internal meaningfulness of a narrative emerges because the narrative is the product of the external narrator.

Internal meaningfulness

When I write of the perspective of those people who are 'internal' to the narrative, I mean simply the perspective of those people who are part of the content of the narrative. Thus, in a narrative of Mrs Jones's first

---

[19] I will return to these issues in Ch. 7, when we consider the possibility of truth and objectivity in narrative; thanks to an OUP reader, though, for suggesting I introduce this important point at this stage.

meeting with her Harley Street consultant, Mrs Jones and the consultant are internal to the narrative. In contrast, the narrator, whoever it might be, is external to the narrative. This distinction will be central to the discussion in Chapter 2. In narrative thinking about one's own past or future, the internal and external perspectives will both be one's own. For example, in Mrs Jones's story of her first meeting with her consultant, Mrs Jones will be both internal to the narrative, and, as narrator, external to it, and these perspectives will not be the same, even though they are both perspectives of Mrs Jones.

Finding meaningfulness in, or making sense of, the thoughts, feelings, and actions of people who are internal to the narrative will often appeal to the psychological states of the people concerned. For example, the brief mini-narrative of Mrs Jones's meeting might be:

> Mrs Jones went to her first meeting with her Harley Street consultant. She felt overawed because of his domineering manner. She decided that it was best to say nothing for fear of saying something stupid and ignorant.

Here the narrative invites the audience to 'pick up on' Mrs Jones's perspective (rather than that of the consultant). As audience, we might simply understand *that* Mrs Jones felt overawed and so on. Or we might go beyond merely representing Mrs Jones's thoughts, by coming to appreciate how awful it must have been for her to be in that situation, and the narrative might be coloured in a way that encourages us to do this. And beyond that, we might, perhaps, imagine what it would be like for her in this situation.

We can see that even such a minimal narrative is clearly asymmetric in the kind of engagement that it encourages the audience to enter into with the evaluative perspectives of those internal to the narrative: in the above narrative it is Mrs Jones whose thoughts and feelings we are encouraged to engage with, and not the consultant's. The asymmetry could easily be reversed:

> For no reason that the consultant could make out, Mrs Jones sat silently through her first meeting with him.

A narrative that tells us nothing about Mrs Jones's inner life or about the inner life of the consultant—'Mrs Jones said little in her first meeting with her consultant'—will be lacking in internal meaningfulness, although it is possible to use one's inventiveness and imagination to fill in the gaps.[20] But we can gain some kind of an insight into Mrs Jones's thoughts and feelings if the narrative *shows* her perspective, without actually *stating* what is in her mind. Consider for example this:

> Mrs Jones was silent in her first meeting with her consultant, who had a domineering manner.

The last clause yields internal meaningfulness: the narrative does not state that it was *because* of the consultant's domineering manner that Mrs Jones said little, although, because of the way the sentence is crafted, we are invited to fill in the gaps in this way. This asymmetry too could be reversed, showing but not stating the consultant's internal perspective:

> For no apparent reason, Mrs Jones was silent in her first meeting with her consultant.

Here we are asked to fill in the gaps by postulating that the consultant, perhaps like the external narrator, finds himself to be somewhat baffled by Mrs Jones's silence.[21]

There are many other ways of providing internal meaningfulness to a narrative beyond enabling the audience to gain a grasp of what is actually in the mind of one or more of the people internal to the narrative. In making sense of people's actions in narratives, we often go beyond appeal to their actual psychological states, and these kinds of explanation often interweave with each other in any particular narrative.

First, we sometimes provide a *desirability characterization* for an action, as Elisabeth Anscombe calls it. Returning to her example that we looked at earlier, of the man who was poisoning the inhabitants by operating the pump, the narrative might add that his motive was revenge, and this can be true without the notion of revenge as such entering into the man's mind; perhaps his thought was 'This is what those bastards deserve after all they did to us.' Once we appreciate that his motive was revenge, we are left to

---

[20] And of course the narrative of the eruption of a volcano will have no internal meaningfulness, simply because there is no internal perspective. Whilst I think that it is perfectly possible to have narratives of events that involve no people, they will not be my concern here.

[21] This discussion is in the interesting and fruitful territory of *free indirect style*, which I will introduce in Ch. 2, where we will see how internal and external perspectives in a narrative can relate in complex ways.

fill in the gaps in the *detailed* goings-on in the mind of the person doing the action, without those being either stated or shown in the narrative.

Secondly, we can find internal meaningfulness in a narrative through appeal to a character trait of which that action is an expression: 'He lent her the money because he is a generous person.' The character trait of generosity is, roughly, a disposition reliably to have certain kinds of motives in certain kinds of situation, and thus reliably to act in certain kinds of ways. Again, this kind of narrative explanation just points towards a general sort of motive—generosity, helpfulness, and so on—without being concerned with the precise details of what was going on in the person's mind at the time of the action. We fill in the gaps.

Thirdly, we can find internal meaningfulness when a narrative reveals influencing factors on the person's mind that are not themselves part of the content of his mind: states such as being drunk, being under the influence of drugs, having a bad cold, being depressed, and having had a sleepless night. 'He proposed marriage to her at the party because he was drunk' points towards this kind of explanation. His being drunk was a cause but not a reason for him to propose—it was not a consideration in its favour that entered into his mind. Yet the implication in the narrative is that he would not have made the proposal if he had not been drunk (it was an INUS condition), and his proposal cannot be made sense of without that piece of information.

The fourth way of finding internal meaningfulness pulls together the first three, and goes beyond them. Narratives often provide explanations of why someone had a particular motive, or why someone has a particular character or personality trait, or why someone was drunk, depressed, or angry. And the explanations that we get are narrative-historical explanations: they locate the motive, the trait, the undue influence on thinking, within a wider nexus, in a way that enables us to understand more deeply why someone did the thing that they did through appeal to aspects of their personal history or circumstances. For example, we explain that she acted inconsiderately because she was brought up in a family where considerateness in any form was always taken advantage of; or that he shouted at his child (in spite of being a loving father) because his job has been under threat and he cannot bear his boss; or that Mrs Jones was silent at her first meeting with her consultant because she was brought up by her father to treat men in authority with unquestioning respect. This should remind us of David Lewis's emphasis on the 'multiplicity of causes and the complexity of causal histories', and his example of the car crash where '[t]he roots in childhood of our driver's reckless disposition . . . are part of the causal chain via his drunkenness, and also are part of other chains via his bald tire' (Lewis 1986: 214, 215).

These observations about the variety of ways of finding internal meaningfulness reveal why narratives characteristically leave substantial explanatory gaps to be filled in, where we typically need to have some knowledge of the range of real-world possibilities (Currie 2007: 53–4), including possibilities about the psychology of the individuals who are internal to the narrative. As a result, narrative explanations often appear to be more explanatory than they really are. To show this, it is helpful to contrast explaining or making sense of an action with predicting action. Predicting how people will act is a perilous affair, for whilst each of a range of possible actions could readily be explained or made sense of in the circumstances, it is the job of prediction to determine which of that range of possible actions will in fact be done, when any of them could be explained. A fairly everyday example will illustrate the difficulty.

Jerry is Ben's non-paying guest in a restaurant, and the waiter brings Jerry a flavour of ice-cream that he did not order. The waiter explains to Jerry that they have run out of the chocolate flavour, which Jerry ordered, and that this is why the waiter has brought him the strawberry flavour instead. What will Jerry do? Will he tell the waiter to take it back; will he eat what he is given; will he leave the ice-cream uneaten; will he throw the ice-cream at the waiter and walk out of the restaurant; will he offer the ice-cream to Ben, his host; will he pour the ice-cream onto Ben's lap? Given this array of possible actions, if you are asked to predict what Jerry will do, the sensible reply is 'Well, it depends.' Of course it depends partly on *Jerry*, but even knowing what is in Jerry's mind is often not sufficient for prediction; for Jerry at the time might know perfectly well what is in his mind, and yet still not himself have decided what he is going to do.[22] Imagine, for example, that Jerry is intent on showing Ben how angry he is at being given the wrong flavour of ice-cream: it could still make sense for him to do any one of the things just canvassed (if he were to eat what he was given, he would need to eat it *angrily*—something easily done, as any teenager will readily demonstrate).

[22] This raises a whole range of issues concerning self-knowledge and the personal perspective that I will be considering in Ch. 6.

Let us now return to explanation, and let us assume that Jerry in fact asked the waiter to take the strawberry-flavoured ice-cream back. We can readily give a narrative explanation which makes sense of this action in terms of Jerry's psychological states, or in terms of one of the other ways of finding meaningfulness that I have been discussing. But the readiness of this explanation is belied by the simple fact that the explanation does not explain why Jerry did *that* action, and not one of the other actions that, as we have seen, would also have made sense for him to do, and that would have been equally explicable. This is a significant reason why narrative explanations, when properly delved into, leave substantial explanatory gaps to be filled in. The narrative of Mrs Jones's meeting with her consultant might explain that she said nothing because she felt overawed by her consultant's domineering manner. But her feeling overawed might equally explain her nervous volubility.

Finally, we should not forget how often narratives can simply fail to explain what happens and what people do. Not all narratives are narrative *explanations*. Life is full of surprises; people can do things that even they cannot make sense of. And the appropriate narrative should not seek to reveal internal meaningfulness when none can be given. One kind of case involves a crucial moment in a life. In Joseph Conrad's *Lord Jim*, when Jim, abandoning all his eight hundred passengers, makes his fateful leap off the *Patna* which he thought was about to sink, neither Conrad, nor his internal narrator the wise Marlow, sought to provide an explanation of that leap; as Marlow put it, it had 'happened somehow' (Conrad 2002: 81).[23] Another kind of case, related to the first, involves a breakdown in thinking—conflict and confusion in the mind—which characteristically happens at a time of radical change in one's life. I will discuss these cases in Chapter 6, where the possibility of finding internal meaningfulness eludes one; even one's agency seems threatened in such cases. Not all narratives explain, and not all narratives should seek to explain everything; sometimes the best that they can do is relate what happened—what 'happened somehow'.

Evaluative and emotional import

Bound up with internal meaningfulness in a narrative is the third characteristic feature of a narrative: *evaluative and emotional import*. In its internal manifestation, what we are concerned with are the evaluative and

---

[23] For a careful discussion of Jim's leap in the context of narrative explanation, see Abbott (2010). I will return to this in Ch. 6.

emotional responses of those who are internal to the narrative in the sense I been discussing. As with meaningfulness, I will turn in more detail to the external manifestation of this phenomenon in Chapter 2.

The idea here is really very simple. Things matter to people, and a narrative involving people can capture the way things matter to them. We already have this in the story of Mrs Jones: she felt overawed because of her consultant's domineering manner, and she thought it best to say nothing for fear of saying something stupid and ignorant. The internal meaningfulness of Mrs Jones's behaviour is thus bound up with the evaluative and emotional import that the situation had for her: her evaluation of her consultant as being domineering, and her fearful response.

Let us return to the events involving Jerry and Ben in the restaurant, and flesh out the following narrative:

> Jerry, Ben's guest at the restaurant, had ordered chocolate ice-cream. The waiter brought him a different flavour, saying they were out of the chocolate. Jerry was angry that there was no chocolate ice-cream available, given that it was on the menu, and given that the waiter had inconsiderately failed to advise him in advance of its unavailability. Thinking his anger to be justified, Jerry expressed his feelings by angrily eating what the waiter brought him. Ben resented both Jerry's anger and the rude way in which he chose to express it, thinking it unjustified by such a trivial incident, attributing Jerry's reaction to a deeper-seated anger towards him generally. Jerry, however, thought that Ben's unfeeling arrogance showed that he lacked the sensitivity to appreciate just how much these things mattered to him.

This narrative is unusually (and thus intentionally rather clunkingly) explicit in the way that it reveals the internal evaluative and emotional import of the situation for Jerry and Ben; a more subtle narrative will be much less explicit than this, leaving gaps to be filled in by interpretation:

> Avoiding Jerry's fierce stare, keeping his eyes fixed on his plate, Ben silently and resentfully ate what the waiter had put in front of him.

Narratives such as these are typical in communicating evaluative and emotional import through the use of *thick evaluative concepts*—a term first introduced by Bernard Williams (and not to be confused with Clifford Geertz's notion of thick description) (Williams 1985/2007: 128–30, 140–6; see also Williams 1965/1973). Thick concepts, such as *rude, inconsiderate, insensitive, arrogant,* are evaluative concepts that have more descriptive content than thinner evaluative concepts such as *good* and *right.* Thoughts involving these thick concepts, such as Jerry's thought about Ben's unfeeling arrogance, can be directly attributed to those who are internal to the narrative, helping to explain the emotions and actions that are involved, including perhaps Jerry's angry response. It is substantially because of its use of thick concepts that one can say, as Williams puts it, that a narrative 'seemingly runs together fact and value' (Williams 2002: 235).

It is an important feature of narrative that it can be unclear whether the values expressed in the narrative, whether through the use of thick evaluative concepts or in other ways, are the values of a person who is internal to the narrative or the values of the narrator, who is external to the narrative. Let us return once more to Mrs Jones:

> Mrs Jones was silent in her first meeting with her consultant, who had a domineering manner.

We have seen that, through the last clause, the narrative implies that it was because of the consultant's domineering manner that Mrs Jones was silent. But perhaps—it really is not clear—the narrative is also suggesting that the narrator, external to the narrative, not only considers that the consultant's manner was indeed dominating (so his perspective in that respect agrees with that of Mrs Jones), but also that the narrator thinks that this is not the kind of manner which Harley Street consultants ought to have (poor Mrs Jones, forced to be silent when she could have had so much to tell). Or perhaps the narrator does not know that this is what he thinks, but still his narrative reveals it. Or perhaps the narrator is subtly hinting to his audience that this might be what they should think whilst intentionally not being explicit; in the famous words of Francis Urquhart in Michael Dobbs' *House of Cards*: 'You might very well think that, but I couldn't possibly comment.'

One might think, even at this early stage, that narratives, including narrative thinking, are deeply problematic. For, according to me, not only do narratives express multiple perspectives, internal and external, but they also do so in ways that are inherently and perhaps ineluctably evaluative, and, even worse, they often do so in ways where it is unclear just whose evaluative perspective is being expressed. But I suggest that these features of narratives, which might seem like faults, are actually merits: the powers of narratives to express multiple perspectives, often in ways that are unclear, are powers of narrative that, in part, explain their pervasiveness in our lives, given the way our lives are, and given the way we think about our lives.

Conclusion

That completes my rough outline of what a narrative is, and how the notion can readily and naturally be extended to include narrative thinking. What needs to be filled in, though, is a more detailed account of the external perspective of the narrator and of the audience—and in particular of external meaningfulness, and external evaluative and emotional import. In Chapter 2 and beyond, I want to develop this in relation to the *ironic distance* that the external perspective allows and that is at the heart of narrative. I will then apply this to the role of narrative in thinking about our own present, past, and future. What I hope will emerge as I progress are the ways in which the special explanatory, revelatory, and expressive power of narratives can be put to work in places where all the subtleties and complexities of our lives are involved.

2

Narrative Thinking about One's Past

Introduction: Internal and External Perspectives in Narrative Thinking

So far, then, we have seen how internal meaningfulness in a narrative is bound up with internal evaluative and emotional import: the narrative reveals what the narrated events mean to those who are internal to the narrative, and what evaluative and emotional import they have from their internal perspective. This left outstanding a detailed examination of these things in relation to various kinds of external perspective. In other words, what we now need is an account of the external perspective in terms of meaningfulness and evaluative and emotional import.

Someone who is internal to a narrative, having a role as a 'character' in the narrative, can also be external to it, having also the role of external narrator. This is the case in autobiographical narratives. I will show that, first in autobiographical narrative, and secondly in autobiographical memory, these two kinds of perspective are intimately bound up with each other. To lead into this discussion, I will begin with drama and literature in order to introduce and explain two key notions that are essential to understanding how evaluative perspectives can differ and yet at the same time interweave. They are, first, dramatic irony, and secondly, free indirect style.

Dramatic Irony

What do I mean by dramatic irony? The term in its original use comes from drama, where the theatre audience knows something that one or more of the characters in the drama does not know. The idea is as old as drama itself: in Sophocles' *Oedipus Rex*, the audience knows that Oedipus killed his father at the crossroads, but Oedipus believes that he killed a stranger.

In Shakespeare's *King Lear*, there is a scene that involves a very powerful use of dramatic irony. Gloucester, who has recently been cruelly blinded, wants to die. He asks Edgar to take him to the 'very brim' of the cliffs of Dover, to 'a cliff whose high and bending head | Looks fearfully in the confined deep' (Act IV Scene i). Edgar misleads him into thinking that he has done just that:

> Come on sir; here's the place: stand still. How fearful
> And dizzy 'tis to cast one's eyes so low!
> The crows and choughs that wing the midway air
> Show scarce so gross as beetles; half way down
> Hangs one that gathers samphire, dreadful trade!
> Methinks he seems no bigger than his head.
> The fishermen that walk upon the beach
> Appear like mice, and yond tall anchoring bark
> Diminish'd to her cock, her cock a buoy
> Almost too small for sight. The murmuring surge,
> That on the unnumber'd idle pebbles chafes,
> Cannot be heard so high. I'll look no more,
> Lest my brain turn, and the deficient sight
> Topple down headlong.   (*King Lear* IV. vi)

The audience knows what Gloucester does not know: that, contrary to what he thinks, he is not on the edge of the cliffs of Dover, and thus not able with one step to cast himself over the edge to his certain death. This is dramatic irony. In order to appreciate it, the audience has to appreciate both what Gloucester believes to be the case, and to appreciate what in fact is the case. The term 'irony' might seem oddly out of place here, but there is this in common between dramatic irony and irony: to appreciate irony, one has to grasp what is literally said, and one has to grasp what the speaker means, and one has to grasp them independently and in contrast one to the other; and in dramatic irony there is a similar structure, requiring the audience to grasp independently how things in fact are and how another thinks they are, and also to grasp the contrast between the two. To appreciate the dramatic irony of this scene in *King Lear*, the audience has to be aware that Gloucester is not in fact at the top of the cliffs of Dover, and also to be aware that it seems to Gloucester as if he is. Edgar's subtly deceptive words spoken to Gloucester brilliantly capture the way things look when one is at the top of a cliff with the sea below, so the audience is in a good position to gain a clear imaginative grasp of how Gloucester, so recently blinded, believes things to be. On its own, the audience's grasping Gloucester's perspective in imagination cannot yield up any dramatic irony, nor on its own can the audience's own perspective on how things in fact are. The audience has to hold both in mind at the same time—their own perspective, and that of Gloucester—and it has to appreciate how they diverge or potentially diverge.[1]

Appreciation of dramatic irony is an ability that a child typically does not develop until after the age of 4. There is an experiment in developmental psychology, generally known as the false belief task, which demonstrates this. For those who are not familiar with it, I will give a very quick summary of what is involved in the original experiment, from which there have been innumerable variations since.[2] The child is asked to watch a puppet show, in which Maxi the puppet puts a chocolate in a box. Maxi then goes out to play. Then, whilst Maxi is out, the child watches Maxi's puppet mother move the chocolate to a cupboard. The child is then asked where Maxi will look for the chocolate when he returns. The 3-year-old reliably gets the answer wrong, saying that Maxi will look in the cupboard; after all, that is where the chocolate is. The 4-year-old child, unless he is autistic, reliably answers as an adult would: Maxi will look in the box because that is where Maxi, falsely, believes the chocolate to be—understandably enough, because Maxi was out of the room when it was moved.

This is, precisely, dramatic irony. The 4-year-old child who first passes the false belief task has shown the beginnings of a grasp of it—of being able to hold in his mind at the same time both how someone thinks things are (the other's perspective) and how they in fact are (his own perspective): the child realizes that Maxi believes something that is not the case, just as the audience realizes that Gloucester falsely believes that he is on the edge of the cliffs of Dover.[3] But even if the false belief task reveals a significant

---

[1] My discussion of dramatic irony does not depend on any particular theory of irony. For a helpful discussion of irony in narratives, and for a defence of the pretence theory of irony, see Currie (2010).

[2] The *locus classicus* is Wimmer and Perner (1983).

[3] Given the structural similarities that I mentioned just now, I take it that it is no coincidence that autistic children have difficulties appreciating not only dramatic irony, but also irony.

change in this respect in children of about this age, the evidence points towards a progressive developmental story in the grasping of diverging perspectives, rather than something that comes about, all at once, at this age. For example, children seem able to grasp diverging desires before they are able to grasp diverging beliefs. And after they are able to pass the false belief task, and thus demonstrate a grasp of diverging beliefs, there remains a delay before they are able to grasp what the implications are of having false beliefs for emotion, even though they might be able to grasp what the implications are of false beliefs for action. This is interesting and somewhat puzzling. Consider the story of *Little Red Riding Hood*—a wonderful example of dramatic irony. Little Red Riding Hood has the false belief that it is Grandma whose teeth she is admiring, and the four-year-old child, in engaging with the narrative, is able to appreciate this. Surprisingly, though, it is not until around five to six years old that the child is able to appreciate the emotional implications for Little Red Riding Hood of her false beliefs—that it is understandable that she should be unafraid as she knocks on Grandma's door, and as she discusses the size of 'Grandma's' teeth. The four-year-old child projects his own fear onto Little Red Riding Hood, whilst not projecting his own belief. Moreover, children manifest the same failure to appreciate emotional implications of false beliefs in their own case: for example if the child is, like Maxi, the unwitting victim of a chocolate switch, looking back on their past feelings, they would 'claim to have felt the emotion they now feel, having discovered the actual situation'.[4]

Thus it would seem that, as children grow up, they find their way slowly into a world of diverging perspectives, becoming increasingly able to appreciate the implications of these diverging perspectives in ways that, I would maintain, are required for anything like a fully fledged appreciation of narrative. Perhaps it is very early on that the young child is able to give a breathless, babbled narrative to her mother of what happened to her on the bus on the way back from playschool, and this is done from a perspective, but this in no way suggests that she is able to appreciate the narrative possibilities that emerge with dramatic irony and diverging perspectives.

---

[4] Many thanks to Paul Harris for discussion here; the citations are from personal correspondence. See also his (1989).

As We Grow Up: Diverging Perspectives in Literature and in Real Life

Our ability to appreciate diverging perspectives is a skill that we continue to foster and develop into maturity. Novels are the most wonderful source of the phenomenon: in novels there can be diverging perspectives between two or more characters internal to the narrative, between character and external narrator, between external narrator and internal narrator, between character and reader or audience, between external narrator and implied author, between implied author and author, between implied author and reader, between reader and reader, between actual reader and ideal reader, and many more besides. To understand these possible divergences is part of what it is to understand and appreciate a novel.[5]

Usually we take all this for granted, as it comes to us so easily. But at times it is something of a struggle to achieve and the effort makes evident to us what is also involved in the effortless cases. Let me illustrate this with Willa Cather's novel *My Ántonia*. It makes use of an interesting framing device: an Introduction that sets the scene for the first-personal narrative that is to follow, at the same time giving the rest of the novel a false and superficially misleading air of factuality or reality. The use of a framing device is found in Vladimir Nabokov's *Lolita*, and versions of it are very common in the novels of Joseph Conrad.[6]

In Willa Cather's wonderful novel, we have Jim Burden's first-personal childhood story, set in frontier Nebraska, of the incredible hardships in the life of his friend, Ántonia Shimerda, an immigrant from Bohemia with whom he grew up. But Willa Cather sets the scene with the Introduction, in which an unnamed character, writing in the first person, tells of meeting Jim Burden, a childhood friend, on a train. Burden, now old, a railroad lawyer, unhappily married, and full of disappointments, reflects on that Bohemian girl whom they had both known all those years ago, and tells

---

[5] Sometimes in literary theory the term 'external perspective' is used when we are speaking or thinking of the characters in novels as characters, and so in that sense 'externally'; see e.g. Lamarque and Olsen (1994) and Currie (2010). For example, in this sense we might say that Pierre in *War and Peace* is a better-drawn character than Levin is in *Anna Karenina*, whereas if we were to say that Pierre was a man of great sensitivity yet capable of terrifying and blind rage we would be taking an internal perspective on Pierre. Although useful in many ways, this is a different (although related) internal–external distinction from the one that I wish to draw.

[6] For discussion of framing devices, see Mullan (2006).

this person, the narrator of the Introduction, that he had been writing down what he remembered of Ántonia. The Introduction ends as follows:

When I told him [Jim] that I would like to read his account of her, he said I should certainly see it—if it were ever finished.

Months afterwards, Jim called at my apartment one stormy winter afternoon, carrying a legal portfolio. He brought it into the sitting-room with him, and said, as he stood warming his hands, 'Here is the thing about Ántonia. Do you still want to read it? I finished it last night. I didn't take time to arrange it; I simply wrote down pretty much all that her name recalls to me. I suppose it hasn't any form. It hasn't any title either.' He went into the next room, sat down at my desk and wrote across the face of the portfolio the word 'Ántonia'. He frowned at this a moment, then prefixed another word, making it 'My Ántonia'. That seemed to satisfy him.   (Cather 1918/1980)

And then we have Jim Burden's story, narrated by Jim. What this Introduction does, in a rather moving way, is to open up and make starker the diverging perspectives: we have Willa Cather the author; we have the first-personal narrator of the Introduction (and what is this character's relationship to Willa Cather?); we have Jim Burden as a young lad; we have Jim Burden as a disappointed railroad lawyer with a failed marriage looking back on his life, making dismissive remarks about the lack of form in the writing; and so on. As readers of the novel, we have to make a real effort to keep track of these diverging perspectives and the dramatic ironies that are involved. The difficulty is not like the difficulty that we found in grasping multiply embedded propositional attitudes (Mary believes that John hopes that Joseph wants that Peter . . .), where beyond a certain level of iteration it becomes psychologically impossible to keep track. Rather, the difficulty, as we read the novel, is of keeping in mind, and evaluating, this variety of perspectives that can diverge from each other and from our own. And we need to maintain an external perspective in order to do this. If we merely put ourselves in the shoes of one of these characters or people—Jim the narrator, say—we will lose the dramatic irony. That is to say we will lose sight of the divergence between Jim's perspective and our own, and of the divergence between the perspective of Jim as narrator, now an unhappy old man, and of Jim as a young boy, full of hopes.

But here you might object. Surely the ideal reader of a novel is expected to shift his or her perspective to that of one or other of the characters in the novel, to imagine 'from the inside' what it is like for him or her. Am I not flying in the face of millennia of great narrative works of fiction? I think not. The very fact of dramatic irony shows that imagining the perspectives of those who are internal to the narrative is not sufficient for narrative appreciation: one cannot appreciate the plight of Gloucester without appreciating how it is for him and at the same time appreciating that things are not as they seem to him.

Reading great literature, then, can remind us of the complexities of diverging perspectives—perspectives that sometimes come into view only with careful attention. The point applies not only to fictional narratives, but to works of history, to autobiographies, to diaries and contemporary historical documents, and to confessions. All kinds of narrative, when concerned with people, have this special explanatory, revelatory, and expressive power, which can remind us of, and throw light on, the subtle and complex ways in which perspectives can diverge, and it is for this reason that good literary works can be a kind of training ground for appreciating and dealing with dramatic irony and other kinds of diverging perspective in the so-called 'real world', and for evaluating and responding to those perspectives that diverge from our own: the therapist's perspective diverges from our own qua patient, the bank manager's from our own qua customer, the house-buyer's from our own qua house-seller, the child's from our own qua parent, the colleague's from our own qua colleague, the politician's from our own qua voter, and so on. It was surely with this in mind that Prime Minister Harold Macmillan, himself a great reader of Trollope, once impatiently told an ambitious young politician to go away and read a novel.

Free Indirect Style and the Narrator's External Perspective

One way in which a narrative can reveal the narrator's external perspective is by revealing the narrator's specific thoughts, feelings, and intentions. A narrative is in just this sense the product of an intentional activity of a thinking person, and, as with any action, it is possible, at least in principle, to grasp the reasons why the person chose to produce that particular narrative in that particular way and at that particular time. For example, I might decide to tell you how I was cruelly treated by my father in order to elicit your sympathy—that was my specific reason for telling you.

However, a narrative can be expressive of, and thus revelatory of, more than just the narrator's thoughts, feelings, and intentions that were his specific reasons for producing that narrative in that way and at that time. It can also express aspects of the narrator's character and personality, very much as, for example, someone's way of dressing or of driving can reveal the sort of person that they are. It is a familiar point that a literary style can be expressive in this way (Robinson 1985), and although the term 'style' is perhaps most appropriate to literary narratives, if it is understood in a fairly minimal sense of being a 'way of telling', then very much the same thing can be true of a more everyday narrative that we might tell about part of our own life.

It follows from this that what is expressed and revealed in a narrative can be more than the narrator intended. For example, just as a person's way of dressing or driving can reveal, in a way that he did not intend to reveal, his carelessness, so a way of telling a narrative can be careless, muddled, confused, or convoluted, and these too need not be things that the narrator intended to reveal. Indeed, sometimes a narrative can be expressive and revelatory of what the narrator firmly intends *not* to reveal, aiming rather to hide something from view—his impatience perhaps, or his mendaciousness—as well as things of which he is not consciously aware—his vanity, or his suppressed feelings of envy or guilt perhaps. This applies particularly to autobiographical narratives, simply because the subject concerned is what Kant called the 'dear old self'. For example, I might tell you how I was cruelly treated by my father, thinking that I am doing so in order to elicit your sympathy, but really I am doing it in an unconscious effort to expiate my guilt for having failed to pay him any attention as a person over all those years. When we read Jean-Jacques Rousseau's *Confessions*, these questions of interpretation arise in a way that they would not if the narrator and the protagonist were not one and the same person—if it were a biography and not an autobiography. What, for example, are we to make of this: 'I believe no individual of our kind ever possessed less natural vanity than myself' (Rousseau 1861: 10)?

So when a narrative is expressive and revelatory of the narrator's external perspective, this can be what the narrator intends, or it can be what the narrator does not intend, or it can be some combination of these. When I talk of the narrator's external perspective, I mean it in this inclusive sense. It can be communicated as part of the explicit content of the narrative, or it can expressed in other ways, in the framework of the narrative. (A framework is not the same as a framing device, which

I considered earlier.) As Gregory Currie explains, a framework is 'a preferred set of cognitive, evaluative, and emotional responses to the story', communicated, intentionally or unintentionally, 'not as something represented, but as something *expressed* in the process of representing the story' (2010: 86, his italics).

Appreciation of the perspectives of those who are internal to the narrative, and appreciation of the external perspective of the narrator, are bound up with each other in highly complicated ways. To develop this theme, which is central to my account of autobiographical narrative and autobiographical memory, I will now introduce the idea of free indirect style. To begin with, I will continue the discussion in terms of the narrator, understood as identical here to the author—although, as we will see, the same ideas will apply, *mutatis mutandis*, to the narrative thinker—to the person who thinks through the narrative without publicly narrating it.

Free indirect style is a particular expression of the ironic gap between perspectives. As we saw earlier, in drama, where dramatic irony has its home, the ironic gap is between the perspective of those characters who are internal to the narrative—Gloucester, for example—and the external perspective of the author or narrator and of the audience. Free indirect style expresses this ironic gap in a special way in the narrative. The idea is introduced thus by James Wood in his marvellously concise *How Fiction Works*:

[With] free indirect style, we see things through the character's eyes and language, but also through the author's eyes and language too. We inhabit omniscience and partiality at once. A gap opens between author and character, and the bridge— which is free indirect style itself—between them simultaneously closes that gap and draws attention to its distance. This is merely another definition of dramatic irony: to see through a character's eyes while being encouraged to see more than the character can see (an unreliability identical to the unreliable first-person narrator's).[7]

Consider this simple example from James Wood (2008: 10):

Ted watched the orchestra through stupid tears.

---

[7] Wood (2008: 11). For discussion of free indirect style, see also Banfield (1973); Cohn (1978); Genette (1980, 1988); Bal (1997); Rimmon-Kenan (2002; 111ff.); Mullan (2006: 76–8); Currie (2010: 140–4).

This illustrates a number of important properties of free indirect style. It shows that free indirect style can express more than just what the character is actually thinking, or what the character 'says to himself'—whatever precisely that means. Beyond that, it can express the character's 'behaviour' understood more widely, such as, in this case, the expressiveness of Ted's tears.[8] It can express the ironic gap between character and narrator with an economy of style that is part of its attraction, and that provides the material for one of its great strengths, which is that it captures an important indeterminacy or openness to interpretation as to whose perspective is being revealed. As Wood puts it: 'What is so useful about free indirect style is that in our example a word like "stupid" somehow belongs both to the author and the character; we are not entirely sure who "owns" the word.'[9] Whether or not Jane Austen was the first English novelist to deploy free indirect style in a significant way (see Gunn 2004; but see also Lodge 2002), her subtle use of it in capturing the thoughts, feelings, and behaviour of her heroines is a source of endless delight to her readers. Consider the second proposition in the following passage, in which Emma is wondering whether Mr Elton is suitable for Harriet. Understanding of how this works shows us that it would be a mistake to interpret this as revealing only Emma's sentiments. It reveals also the sentiments of the narrator and, indeed, possibly those of the reader as well. And it does so in such a way that there is, as there ought to be, no determinate answer to the question of whose sentiments are being reported. 'The longer she considered it, the greater was her sense of its expediency. Mr. Elton's situation was most suitable, quite the gentleman himself, and without low connections; at the same time not of any family that could fairly object to the doubtful birth of Harriet.'[10] As with Wood's example of the stupid tears, one simply must not ignore the narrator's presence; it is at the heart of appreciating the way dramatic irony can be captured through free indirect style. It is central to appreciation of the modern novel from Flaubert to Woolf.

[8] Matters are made even more complex because much of the discussion of free indirect style/speech is in French and German and the terms do not seem to have precisely the same meaning across the three languages (*style indirect libre* and *erlebte rede*). I hope that none of these complexities will impinge on what follows.

[9] Wood (2008: 11).

[10] Cited in Gunn (2004: 40). The cited passage is from *Emma* (1816/1983: 27). I am indebted to Gunn for his nuanced discussion and for this particular citation.

As a final example from literature, let us consider the famous opening paragraph of Kafka's *Metamorphosis*:

One morning, as Gregor Samsa was waking up from anxious dreams, he discovered that in bed he had been changed into a monstrous verminous bug. He lay on his armour-plated back and saw, as he lifted his head up a little, his brown, arched abdomen divided up into rigid bow-like sections. From this height the blanket, just about ready to slide off completely, could hardly stay in place. His numerous legs, pitifully thin in comparison to the rest of his circumference, flickered helplessly before his eyes.

What Kafka so brilliantly invites us to do is to see things through Gregor Samsa's eyes, and yet at the same time see through the author's eyes and through our own, from a perspective that is external to that of Samsa. In other words, we do not just engage with how it is for Samsa from the inside, we also engage with it from the external perspective, and these two ways are bridged by means of free indirect style. In the last sentence we are told what Samsa sees, but we are told in terms that are not, precisely, his: using Wood's helpful way of putting it, we can ask 'Who *owns* the words "pitifully" and "helplessly"—author or character?' They cannot be precisely Samsa's words for he surely would not see his own legs in this way; rather, his legs are described as we might see them, and yet the sentence (including 'before his eyes') seems to be telling us what Samsa saw and how he felt—how things were for him.

Free indirect style may be relatively new in the novel, but elsewhere it is surely as old as narrative discourse. We often use it to express another person's perspective whilst at the same time distancing ourselves from that perspective in a way that, as with our literary examples, involves indeterminacies in interpretation that must be seen as an interpretative gain and not a loss. Anne Reboul has a very nice example of how it arises in ordinary everyday discourse; the last sentence is clearly in free indirect style: 'I met Mrs. Smith last Sunday. As usual she was complaining. It was raining all the time, her children never came to visit her, and she'd missed *The Archers* three times in a row because she had to go to the doctor for her lumbago . . .'[11] Free indirect style in literary narratives expresses the ironic gap between character and author or narrator. Although structurally the same, in autobiographical narrative, in contrast, free indirect style expresses the ironic gap not between the perspectives of two different individuals, but between the two perspectives of one individual—between *you then*, as

---

[11]   Thanks to Anne Reboul for correspondence and for the lovely example.

someone—a 'character'—who is internal to the narrative, and *you now*—
the narrator—who is external to the narrative. It is because of this gap
between you then and you now that the ironic gap can open up:

> I watched the orchestra through stupid tears.

A couple of examples might help to make clear this essential distinction
between internal and external perspective in autobiographical narrative,
where the narrator is the very same person as the person who is internal to
the narrative. Later I will turn to autobiographical narrative thinking and
autobiographical memory, which are, as we will see, structurally parallel to
autobiographical narrative.

As a first, fairly straightforward example, let us consider a narrative that
I tell about an amusing incident that occurred when I was playing tennis
doubles:

> My partner and I were both chasing the same lob, and then we
> hilariously fell over each other in a tangle.

In relating this narrative, I tell how at the time I was highly amused. This
emotional response is internal to the narrative in just the sense that it is I *in
the narrative* who felt amused—I as the internal character at the time found
the incident to have this particular internal emotional import. Now, as
external narrator I still consider what happened to be amusing, and this is
expressed in my narrative.[12] So in this first example, internally and externally the evaluative and emotional import and response are of the same
kind, and there is no significant ironic gap. If I no longer think of
what happened as amusing, as meriting amusement, I would conceive a
different narrative of the episode, which would express a different external
evaluative and emotional import.[13]

---

[12] This emotion that I have as external narrator is what Dorothea Debus (2007) nicely calls
an autobiographically past-directed emotion (an APD emotion). She argues, in a way that
supports my claims here, that all such emotions are 'new' emotional responses to what is
remembered, and not simply a memory of the emotion experienced at the time.

[13] David Velleman (2003: 20) considers the external emotional response, which he calls a
'subjective understanding', to be a sort of projective error. He says, agreeing with Hayden
White on historical narratives: 'The understanding conveyed by the narrative form of
historical discourse is not an objective understanding of how historical events came about
but a subjective understanding of how to feel about them.' I would reply that if one's
evaluations and emotions about a narrative are, in fact, the appropriate ones, as they arguably
are in this example, then they are only 'subjective' in one sense of that slippery term, and they

Now let us complicate things a little by considering a second example of autobiographical narrative in which the two evaluative and emotional perspectives differ and where the ironic gap opens up. Let us imagine that I was at a meeting with a number of colleagues at the place where I work, and during the meeting I was humiliated in front of everyone by the most senior person there. This is how I relate what happened:

> I was humiliated in a meeting the other day, left feeling deeply embarrassed. But I now realize the way I was treated was inappropriate and unfair, and I am angry and resentful.

In this mini-narrative I reveal that I, internal to the narrative, felt embarrassment or shame at the time—that was how I then felt, because I then thought that the way I was treated was humiliating. But, with my external perspective on what happened, I also reveal that I now feel differently: I now feel anger and resentment at what I now realize was an injustice. These latter emotions are external to the narrative, as I did not feel them at the time, but my narrative reveals that I now think that what happened is such as to make these external evaluations and emotions appropriate.

So the ironic gap opens up in this second example of autobiographical narrative, where my evaluation and emotion that is internal to the narrative differs from my external evaluation and emotion as narrator. But what is notable about this second narrative is how the internal and external perspectives are kept apart; it is this that makes the narrative sound rather stilted and unnatural.

Let us at this point turn to my third example of autobiographical narrative, where internal and external perspectives fuse through free indirect style. I tell the story of how last night I went to the office party. Having had one or two drinks too many, during the dinner I stood up on the table and sang 'Love is like a butterfly' at the top of my voice. At the time I felt a kind of heady delight, seeing all my friends thoroughly enjoying the performance. But now, when I tell the story the following day, I tell it how I now see it, with a triply ironic gap. I now realize that they were all laughing *at* me, not *with* me as I thought at the time: this is an epistemic ironic gap—I now know what I did not know then. I now

---

are not a projective error. I return to this in Ch. 7 where I discuss questions concerning objectivity and truth in narrative.

consider my whole behaviour to have been ridiculous and shameful: this is an evaluative ironic gap—I now think differently of my behaviour than I did at the time. And I now feel ashamed at what I did: this is an emotional ironic gap—I now have a retrospective emotion that I did not have at the time. This triply ironic gap is, echoing the words of James Wood, opened up and simultaneously bridged in how I narrate what happened, through free indirect style: 'I shamefully made a ridiculous fool of myself last night, getting up on the table and gleefully singing some stupid song.' In relating the narrative in this way, I invite the audience to think of what happened as I now think of it, and yet, bound up with this, I also invite the audience to see it as I then saw it—blithely, gleefully thinking that everyone was enjoying my performance as much as I was at the time.

And here is a fourth example:

> Last Saturday I went to the football ground to watch the match, and stupidly bought a forged ticket from a conman. I ended up missing the game and trudging home fifty pounds worse off, wet, angry, and feeling pathetically sorry for myself.

In this example, we have me as a character in the narrative, trudging home, realizing, as part of the narrative, how stupid I had been earlier that day. So within the narrative there is an ironic gap that has opened up between two internal perspectives of mine. And then we have my external perspective as narrator, looking back on the day, and now evaluating my feeling sorry for myself as rather pathetic, as if the worst thing in the world had happened to me; now I have a rather amused emotional distance to my day's travails. Again, internal and external perspectives are bound up with each other; again the ironic gap is opened up and then bridged with the free indirect style of my autobiographical narrative, so that in this example we can ask rhetorically who *owns* the word 'pathetically'.

With these examples of autobiographical narrative to hand, I now want to bring narrative back inside the mind—to turn to narrative thinking about one's past, and then to autobiographical memory. We will see that free indirect style—or at least its psychological counterpart—is central to autobiographical memory just as it is to autobiographical narrative.

Autobiographical Narrative Thinking and the Problem of the Audience

But before I turn to autobiographical memory, there is a concern that I must address about the very idea of narrative thinking and the external perspective that is particularly plain in the case of autobiographical narratives. The concern is, roughly speaking, as follows. My claim is that a narrative, *whether or not narrated*, requires an external perspective. According to me, a narrative can be a sequence of thoughts with the three characteristic features of narrative: coherence, meaningfulness, and evaluative and emotional import. And the thinker is the person who occupies the external perspective of narrator—he is the external narrator just in the sense that it is he who thinks through the narrative. So it is the thinker who is able to grasp the coherence and meaningfulness of what is thought through, and the thinker who, from his external perspective, is able to evaluate and respond emotionally to the events related in the narrative. The narrator, the thinker in this case, will often use free indirect style to bridge the gap between the internal and external perspectives—albeit here the perspectives are those of one and the same person. Then, if the thinker chooses to relate the narrative, he will *thereby* reveal his perspective, and also invite the audience to take its own external perspective on what is narrated, and to evaluate and respond emotionally to the portrayed events in the way that the narrative encourages.

Now, the concern is this: how can this notion of narrative really make sense when the narrative remains unexpressed to another person—when there is no audience as such? To whom does the narrator address the narrative? Does there not have to be an audience? Do we not have an equivocation of the very idea of narrative when it is private in this way, just as there is an equivocation of the idea of talking when we 'talk to ourselves'. I will call this the *problem of the audience*.

The immediate and obvious answer to the problem of the audience is that the audience is the thinker—the narrator is addressing himself. But this answer, although true, needs embellishing in a number of respects—some of which I will turn to in later chapters, where I will be discussing such things as the role of narrative in thinking about one's future and in forming intentions and making plans (Ch. 4), and the role of narrative thinking in self-forgiveness (Ch. 5).

The first embellishment is that I might be thinking through a narrative in preparation for narrating it to someone else. For example, one morning I might be rushing on my way to an important meeting for which I am seriously late, and as I rush I think through the best way to tell to my colleagues the story of why I am late. In doing so, in thinking through the narrative, I imagine how my colleagues, as my intended audience, will respond to what I am planning to say. In other words, I imagine what *they* will consider to be the evaluative and emotional import of my narrative. And then we can see that part of my aim in thinking through the narrative in advance in this way is so that I can have an evaluative and emotional response that arises *in the light of* the imagined response of my audience. So, in this example, I might think through the story of why I am so late as if it were an amusing disaster, with just one thing going wrong after another; I then imagine my audience's response to the way I tell the story, and in turn I evaluate their imagined response—both what they might think of my story, and what I might think of being such an object of amusement as a result of the story that I tell. What this example reveals is that sometimes the narratives that we think through can be *nested*: I first think through the narrative of why I am late; and then in turn I think through my act of narration—the 'higher-order' narrative of myself narrating the narrative of why I am late. And this allows me to revise my narrative of why I am late in the light of the other higher-order narrative. It is a very familiar idea, that we *rehearse* what to tell, and this rehearsal is manifested in precisely the process of *tâtonnement* that I discussed in Chapter 1.

The second embellishment on the idea that it is the narrative thinker who is the audience is that one might have another person in mind as audience, and yet not plan to tell the story to that other person; indeed, it might be impossible to do so. For example, I might think through a narrative that aims to vindicate my rather unseemly behaviour towards my friend, and imagine telling the story to my dear dead uncle, imagining him looking over his half-moon spectacles in his characteristically sceptical manner. As a result of imagining my uncle's response, I might draw back from such a wholesale vindication. Again, we can have the same nested structure as part of the process of *tâtonnement*.

The third embellishment is that the audience—the ultimate audience—can be oneself in another guise. For example, I might think through a narrative explanation of my past behaviour where I myself—my 'better self' let us say—am the audience. Or in resolving to undertake a project that involves a lot of hard work before any benefits emerge, I might adopt a hortatory role, imagining my future self and approving of my success. Narrative thinking thus exploits our capacity for self-reflectiveness. One sees one's past or future self as another, and, in just this respect, one is at the same time both actor and spectator, both narrator and audience, and both agent and judge, judging both the events in which one's past or future self is implicated, and judging the narrative itself.[14] In thinking through a narrative about one's past or future, seeing oneself as another, we some-times in a sense address that past or future self: 'you fool!' we say, thinking back on that very silly practical joke that went wrong; 'brave, clever you!' we say, imagining ourselves succeeding in some future exploit.[15] But still, the audience of the thought-through narrative is *you now*, not *you then*, for it is you now who is evaluating what you did as foolish, or what you will do as brave and clever, and responding accordingly.

In these ways, then, there remains the possibility of an evaluative and emotional gap between oneself as narrator and oneself as audience: I think through the story and then ask myself what I think of it: Is it persuasive? Is it honest? Is it faithful to the past? Am I putting a self-serving gloss on what happened? So whilst my evaluation and emotional response as audience is ultimately that of me as narrator (the very same person), in responding to my narrative there remains the possibility—a life-long possibility—for me to rehearse, and if necessary revise, my narrative in the light of my own response to what I think through in narrative form. Our past thus remains permanently open for reassessment. Just as one's response as a reader or audience of a great novel or drama can change as one gets older, so one's response to one's narrative thinking about one's past can change over the years. Watching Verdi's *La Traviata* the young man might identify with the young and impetuous Alfredo, but in later years he might come to understand more deeply the honourable motivations of Alfredo's father. And the young man, thinking back on his own youthful indiscretions, might be less censorious than he is when he reflects on his past from his perspective of twenty years later. (To anticipate, though, what we will see shortly is that the way one remembers one's past can colour the memories themselves, through the psychological correlate of free indirect style.)

---

[14] Cavarero (1997: 40). See Ricœur (1992) for the importance of seeing oneself as another.
[15] For discussion, see Cohn (1978).

We will turn to self-addressed narratives in further detail in later chapters, when we consider planning and self-forgiveness, but it is important to see here that this notion of the narrator, you now, as audience does not simply remove the possibility of deceiving or disappointing yourself in the story that you tell yourself. One can be honest or sincere with oneself in the way one thinks through one's past or one's future, and also one can be dishonest or insincere. And one can quite often readily observe that in thinking about one's own narrative: 'Come on, you *know* that wasn't how it really happened!' But for now, the solution to the problem of the audience is that the narrator is indeed also the audience, but this leaves plenty of room for an ironic gap in perspective between narrator and audience.

Autobiographical Memory and General Events

The essential idea that I now want to exploit in relation to autobiographical narrative memory follows on from my earlier discussion in this chapter: the idea that there is, in autobiographical memory, an ineluctable ironic gap (epistemic, evaluative, and emotional) between internal and external perspective, and that our memories are themselves infused with this irony through the memory equivalent—the psychological correlate—of free indirect style. I could put it like this: I want to emphasize the *biography* in autobiographical memory.

I intend autobiographical memory to be not simply memory in which the rememberer features as internal to what is remembered. In addition, the memory must be narrative in form, with narrative structure of the kind I outlined in Chapter 1. It will, in other words, be a variety of narrative thinking, involving the external perspective which is essential for narrative, and thus for narrative thinking, and thus for narrative thinking about one's own past.

The raw material for autobiographical memory will include memories that do not themselves have narrative structure, but which nevertheless feature as part of the narrative. For example, 'images' from the past in the form of what are called 'flashbulb memories', where one has an immediate image of where one was when one saw the second plane hit the Twin Towers on 11 September 2001, will not *on their own* be narrative in form.[16]

---

[16] For seminal work on the idea of flashbulb memory in psychology, see Brown and Kulik (1977). For discussion, see e.g. Rubin (1986).

It is familiar that memory comes in various kinds. Experiential memory, of which flashbulb memory is a kind, is often contrasted with semantic or propositional memory, broadly understood as memory of facts. Experiential memory is memory of an experience more or less (and subject to what follows) as it happened at the time. We characteristically report our experiential memories in non-propositional form: 'I remember seeing Janet for the first time at a fancy-dress party.' In contrast, my remembering *that* 1800 was the date of the Battle of Marengo is an instance of semantic or propositional memory, as is my remembering *that* I first saw Janet at a fancy-dress party. However, it has been persuasively argued that the distinction between semantic and experiential memory is one of degree: memories of episodes of your past experience can come to you with diminishing experiential detail over time, to the point at which one's memory becomes merely semantic (Rowlands 1999). For example, what was once a rich experiential memory of my first seeing Janet can fade to the point where all that remains is the semantic or propositional memory, perhaps with just a residual trace of uncertain experiential detail.

My contention is that diverse kinds of remembering of one's past characteristically get pulled together in autobiographical narrative remembering—semantic memories, all sorts of experiential memories, traces of thought and imagination, fragments of 'flashbulb' memory, almost dream-like sequences that flit through one's mind from time to time, perhaps many of them hardly reaching a level of conscious awareness, and much else besides. And, as we will see with narrative imagining, there will as a result be considerable indeterminacy in any attempt to indentify at any time precisely what kind of remembering is in play.

Empirical support for the idea that autobiographical memories are integrated in this way is found from the work of Martin Conway and colleagues, which shows that autobiographical memories 'contain knowledge at three levels of specificity'.[17] First, there are memories of *lifetime periods*, such as the time I was at university, or my unhappy first marriage. Secondly (and importantly for what follows), there are memories of what Conway calls *general events*. These are memories of a recurring event, such as of my mother helping me to clean my teeth when I was a child. What

---

[17] Conway and Pleydell-Pearce (2000: 262); cf. Barsalou (1988); Conway (1992, 2003); Schachter (1996: 89). For discussion of the developmental and cultural role of autobiographical memory, see Nelson (2003); Nelson and Fivush (2004).

I remember is not any particular episode of teeth-cleaning, but the general event. And, thirdly, there are memories of particular episodes, what Conway calls *event specific knowledge*, such as my memory of dropping a glass of wine when I was at that reception in Buckingham Palace, or my memory of seeing Janet for the first time, dressed in a sheet at that fancy dress party.

Marya Schechtman (1994: 7) has a nice discussion of the importance of autobiographical memories other than memories of particular episodes:

we often summarize information about our pasts, remembering simply *that* we engaged in certain sorts of activities, or had certain sorts of experiences. For instance: I may remember that when I first moved to the city I used to go out to eat often; that for a while I was doing a lot of cooking; that there was a stretch of time when I was always traveling, that when I was depressed I used to go to the movies all the time to cheer myself up, and so on. Furthermore, I can have these sorts of memories without remembering in detail any particular instance of what is remembered, or remembering some instances distinctly, some vaguely, and some not at all.

One might think that the two kinds of memory, experiential and semantic, map neatly onto Conway's 'levels of specificity', with all memories of lifetime periods and of general events being semantic (as perhaps Schechtman's comments might suggest), and all memories of particular episodes being experiential. But this would not be right. First, as we have already seen, an experiential memory of a particular episode might fade into a semantic memory, as I might now merely remember *that* my father fell down drunk at my twenty-first birthday party, where the point at which it becomes merely semantic is indeterminate. Secondly, and more interestingly, memories of lifetime periods and of general events can be experiential. (Thus it would be more accurate to reserve the term 'episodic memory' for experiential memories of particular episodes, allowing the term 'experiential memory' to include more than just memories of particular episodes.)

Here is a nice example of an experiential memory of a general event:

I have a particularly vivid memory from a series of childhood holidays in the south of France. Every year we would visit a campsite in a small village and, for every day that we were there, we would walk down a long, dusty track to reach the rock-beach. The track was flanked on one side by vineyards that stretched away into the distance and on the other by the river. As a child, the walk seemed to take an eternity each time and the heat and dust stay with me to this day. When I consider this memory I know full well that I cannot pick out which particular day it was that I am remembering. Nor do I think it likely that any individual day *was* like this. But, for all that, I do not think it is a false or misleading memory. I suspect it is a blend of various experiences and all the more valuable for it.[18]

General events are very often thought through and remembered in this way in narrative thinking.[19] We remember those holidays in France. Or we remember the days before the clinical depression set in, when we would happily get up in the morning and go for a run whilst it was still dark; then we remember how, after the depression set in, we would for a long time be unable even to summon the energy to pull our socks on in the morning.

The capacity of narratives to capture general events and connect them to lifetime events, and also to particular episodes, is one of the features that give narratives their special explanatory, revelatory, and expressive power, as contrasted with causal accounts. General events do not feature in this way as part of a causal account. (Causal laws and statistical generalizations might be appealed to—'smoking causes cancer'; 'high voltage electric shocks cause death'—but these are appealed to in order to explain particular cancers and particular deaths.) Narratives too are concerned with particulars, of course, but they are not concerned *only* with particulars. They are concerned also with various kinds of general description, including in particular what I am calling general events.

One of the most famous opening sentences of a book is Marcel Proust's in *A La Recherche du Temps Perdu* (1992: 1):

For a long time I would go to bed early.

This captures precisely the sort of thing I have in mind: there is a kind of pattern to young Marcel's activities, in which going to bed early was something that he would regularly do at this time of his life. What is notable here, and in the other examples I just gave, is the 'frequentative'

---

[18] This example is from Andrew Routledge, M.Res. essay, University of Manchester, 2010; thanks to him for discussion here.

[19] See the discussion of the development in children of this kind of memory of general or 'generic' events in Hoerl (2007). Brad Shore (2009: 96–7) provides an interesting account of how these kinds of experiential memories of general events can be shared in a group—paradigmatically a family—through shared narratives. 'Rather than framed in historical time these "routine" memories are framed in what we might call "ritual time". They are often narrated in the format "*we used to*" or "when we were kids *we always*..." '

use of the word 'would'. Ian McEwan (2010: 9) in his novel *Solar* uses the same verb aspect in his discussion of general events in relation to the collapse of the protagonist's marriage:

But even if he ate late with friends, he was usually home before her, and was forced to wait, whether he wanted to or not, until she returned, though nothing would happen when she did. She would go straight to her room, and he would remain in his, not wanting to meet her on the stairs in her state of post-coital somnolence. It was almost better when she stayed over at Tarpin's. Almost, but it would cost him a night's sleep.[20]

Here we do not have a causal account or explanation of a particular event, but rather appeal to a kind of pattern of activity and passivity, one that is all too familiar: the pattern of how a collapsing relationship tends to unfold. We will see in Chapter 3 some examples of how general events are related in narratives of grief.

As Martin Conway and his colleagues show, the three 'levels of specificity' of memories are characteristically integrated. Thus a memory of my early teens might be thus: 'When I was in my early teens I would go to bed early. One night I was sitting on the edge of the bed with a knife in my hand when my father burst in.' We have integrated in this mini-narrative the memory of a lifetime period (being in my early teens), the memory of a general event (going to bed early), and the event-specific memory of my father bursting into the room whilst I had a knife in my hand. To illustrate this integration, Conway and his colleagues cite an example of a subject's memory of the declaration of the beginning of the Second World War in September 1939:

My own memory... occurred when I was aged 6 years and 6 months. I have a clear image of my father standing on the rockery of the front garden of our house waving a bamboo garden stake like a pendulum in time with the clock chimes heard on the radio which heralded the announcement. More hazily, I have an impression that neighbours were also out in the adjoining gardens listening to the radio and, although my father was fooling around, the feeling of the memory is one of deep foreboding and anxiety. I have never discussed this memory with anyone and very rarely thought about it. (Conway and Pleydell-Pearce 2000: 262)

Here we have, again integrated into one narrative memory sequence, a lifetime period (being six and a half years old), a general event (playing in

---

[20] Note also the free indirect style in the penultimate sentence of this citation.

the garden), and event-specific knowledge (his father waving the bamboo stick like a pendulum).

Free Indirect Style and Memory

Now, the idea is this: these diverse ways in which we remember our past, integrated in autobiographical memory, are ineluctably infected by the ironic gap, which, as we have seen, can be triply ironic. And what is fascinating about this is the way in which the autobiographical memories are thought through in the psychological correlate of free indirect style, simultaneously closing the ironic gap and drawing attention to its distance. In this last example, of the man's memories of September 1939, there is the portentous way in which the man remembers his father's actions in the garden that afternoon, infected by the feeling of its significance, and the feeling of foreboding and anxiety that now accompanies those events: all of which, as a child of six and a half years old, he surely would not have appreciated at the time.

We can now go back to an earlier example that I gave, of the story of how last night I went to the office party and stood on the table and sang 'Love is like a butterfly' at the top of my voice. What I gave was an autobiographical narrative, with the triply ironic gap opened up and simultaneously bridged in free indirect style:

> I shamefully made a ridiculous fool of myself last night, getting up on the table and gleefully singing some stupid song.

The idea now is that the ironic gap is expressed not only in the way I narrate it, but also in the way I remember what happened; in memory my external and internal perspectives are integrated in free indirect style. I tell it the way I remember it, and I remember it the way I tell it.

There is an immediate objection that could be raised here. One might accept that the *semantic* or *propositional* memories of last night's episode with my colleagues can be infused with my external perspective on what happened, from the privileged position of the next day ('I remember *that* I shamefully made a ridiculous fool of myself'). But one might nevertheless object that my *episodic* memory of last night will still be 'imprinted in my mind' (an interestingly unscientific notion of a memory trace or 'engram') just as I then experienced it, as if I am 'replaying in my mind' the events as they were then experienced by me. So, according to this objection, my episodic memory *cannot* be infected by what I now know, or by how I now evaluate and respond emotionally to what I did. Instead, the objection continues, there will necessarily be two things: my episodic memory of what happened just as it then took place, just as I then experienced it from the inside; and my external evaluation and emotional response to that memory, expressed in my semantic memory. So the objection is that the psychological correlate of free indirect style cannot, as I am arguing it is, infect the way I episodically remember what happened. Free indirect style is then merely a feature of semantic memory— merely a linguistic gloss on one's retrieval of what happened through episodic memory. Free indirect style cannot bridge the ironic gap between episodic memory and what I now know.

But episodic memories by no means need be like this, and, I suggest, characteristically are not like this, particularly when there is a significant and important ironic gap. (A very important exception is memory after traumatic experience, which I will consider in Chapter 3.) In order to see how this is possible, I need to introduce a distinction between two different ways in which we can have episodic memories. (The same distinction applies to experiential memories of general events, but I will focus just on episodic memories.) This is the distinction between 'field' and 'observer' memories—a distinction that has been discussed in the philosophical literature (although not in these terms: Locke 1971; Moran 2001), and that now has considerable empirical support (Nigro and Neisser 1983; Robinson and Swanson 1993; for discussion, see Eich et al. 2011). In field memory, one remembers 'from the inside', the events as they look place. In observer memory, one remembers 'from the outside', so that one is oneself part of the content of what one remembers. This is a quite familiar phenomenon, as Richard Moran (1994: 91) notes: 'A familiar but remarkable fact about the psychology of memory is that the visual phenomenology of a memory of performing an activity like swimming across a lake will often be presented from a point of view above or behind the figure doing the swimming (that is, *oneself*).' Don Locke (1971: 88–9) has a similar example: 'I might, for example, remember falling down some stairs, but when I remember it, I "see" it, in my image, as if I were a spectator watching myself fall.' Moran mentioned his example in connection with the parallel notion in imagination, where one can perceptually imagine oneself from an external perspective: that is, one perceptually imagines oneself from a perspective, but from the perspective of no person within the imagined scene, so that one appears oneself as part of the content of what one imagines.[21] This kind of memory is genuinely experiential, and is characteristically replete with detail. (I say 'experiential' rather than 'episodic' because it might be a memory of a general event.)

One might think that observer memories are not really memories at all. In his biography of Tolstoy, A. N. Wilson seemed to think this. He objected to Tolstoy's claims to remember much of his childhood, insisting instead that Tolstoy made it all up, that he confabulated. Wilson's evidence for this was this passage from Tolstoy's notes:

I am sitting in a tub and am surrounded by a new and not unpleasant smell of something with which they are scrubbing my tiny body.

Wilson's objection, of course, was that if Tolstoy has genuinely episodically remembered this event, he would not have used the word 'tiny' (Wilson 1988: 19), for a child does not see his own hands as being tiny. When I first read this, before I knew about the phenomenon of observer memory, I thought that Wilson's objection was decisive. But there is no good reason to assume that observer memories are not genuine memories, or that they cannot provide us with some kind of direct epistemic access to our past.[22]

Observer memory is predominant where the memories are of events that took place a long time ago, especially, as Freud suggested, childhood memories.[23] In his *Screen Memories*, Freud (1899/1974: 311) quoted one of

---

[21] For seminal discussion of this sort of imagining, see Wollheim (1984). In Ch. 4, I will consider various structural similarities between experiential memory and experiential imagining.

[22] Dorothea Debus (2007) considers a number of arguments against the claim that observer memories are genuine experiential memories, all of which she finds wanting. She rejects what she calls the Past-Dependency-Claim, that all experiential memory must 'inherit' its spatial characteristics from the past experience of which it is a memory; as she puts it, every recollective or experiential memory 'has its spatial characteristics in virtue of the subject's present awareness of the spatial characteristics of a *past* perceptual experience' (p. 178); she argues instead for what she calls the Present-Dependency-Claim, which, roughly, holds only that the spatial characteristics of the experiential memory must depend on the present perceptual experiences of the subject. She discusses what she calls the Argument from Reconstruction, which I will consider shortly. And she discusses the Argument from Causal Dependency, which holds that all recollective or experiential memories must causally depend on the original perceptual experience, a condition that observer memories cannot fulfil; Debus accepts the condition, but holds that it can be met by observer memories.

[23] See e.g. Nigro and Neisser (1983); and for discussion Eich et al. (2011).

his patient's memories of his childhood: 'I see a rectangular, rather steeply sloping piece of meadow-land [...] Three children are playing in the grass. One of them is myself (between the age of two and three)...' However, age of memory is not the only factor that determines whether field or observer memory predominates. Another factor is the degree of irony between the occasion remembered and the time that the remembering takes place. Of course there will typically be a high degree of irony in childhood memories, but it can also occur in recent memories.[24] And my memory of my performance at last night's party is just such a case. Knowing what I now know—that they were laughing at me and not with me, and so on—I now naturally adopt the observer perspective, 'seeing' myself as others saw me, as if I too were a member of the audience, seeing myself as an object of ridicule.

Furthermore, where there is a high degree of irony, the observer perspective in memory will characteristically involve emotions that one did not experience at the time. Thus, in remembering myself making a fool of myself last night, I experience feelings of shame that I did not have last night. The empirical research literature would seem to show that field memories correlate with more emotionality: for example, Robinson and Swanson (1993: 176) say, 'If subjects oriented to their feelings while recollecting, they were more likely to report a field perspective.' The tendency in the literature is to conclude from this that the emotions experienced from an observer perspective are less emotional: as Eich et al. (2011: 27) put it, 'the observer perspective has less impact on emotion than field perspective'. My suggestion is that the contrast in emotion between field and observer memory should not be between more emotionality and less emotionality, but rather between recall of the emotions that were experienced at the time remembered, and the emotions that were experienced at the time of remembering. Thus if one were trying to 'orient' to one's feelings at the time one would naturally adopt the field perspective, whereas if one were trying to orient to one's feelings now, one would naturally adopt the observer perspective. For example, if I remember doing that thing which I thought at the time was cool and insouciant but now I think is shameful with the observer perspective, the

---

[24] This would seem to have some empirical support; see Libby and Eibach (2002) and Libby, Eibach, and Gilovich (2005). For discussion, see Eich et al. (2011).

experience of shame is likely to be more salient than glee, and vice versa with the field perspective.

I can now give the first part of my response to the objection, that episodic memories cannot be infected with irony though the psychological equivalent of free indirect style. It is as follows: observer memory can be infected with the irony and with the emotions that one now feels in remembering what happened, so that I can quite accurately say, of what I remember from last night:

> I can *see* myself now, shamefully making a ridiculous fool of myself in front of all those people, getting up on the table and gleefully singing some stupid song.

In this way, not only the irony of what I now know, but also the irony of how I now feel about what I now know, infuses the entire memory; in effect, I remember it as I now feel about it. Just the same way of remembering can come into play in my other, earlier example of free indirect style, in which I stupidly bought a forged ticket from a conman, who seemed honest enough to me at the time. Now that I know that he was a conman, it is in fact no easy feat to remember him as he then seemed to me; the shifty way he kept looking over his shoulder is now clear evidence to me of what wasn't known then—how *could* I have missed it at the time?

The second part of my response is that field episodic memories—memories of what happened 'from the inside'—can also be infected with irony, with what one now knows, and how one now feels about what one now knows. One's perspective in the literal, perceptual, sense, is internal, from the inside, but the evaluative perspective, which can be external, can infect the field memory itself. An extreme example of this will be where one now can deploy concepts in thought that one could not deploy then, as might be the case with childhood memories of sexual abuse (Hacking 1995). But infection of episodic field memory can take place without the need for possession of new concepts. To show this, let us go back to the example from Martin Conway and his colleagues, of the man who has a childhood memory of the beginning of the Second World War. Let us assume that he remembers the events, not as an observer from the outside (which is, as we have seen, characteristic of childhood memories), but as a field memory, from the inside. In his autobiographical mini-narrative he said, in what I think is a telling phrase, that 'the feeling of the memory is one of deep foreboding and anxiety'. In this way the feeling that he now has about what he remembers can infuse the episodic memory itself, so that the feeling can be invested both into the content of what is remembered, and into the way of remembering what is remembered, in effect vesting the remembered scene itself with an ominous tone that was not fully appreciated by the child at the time. And just the same can apply to my field memories of that shameful incident last night: however much I might try to focus on remembering the glee that I felt at the time, the shame that I now feel ineluctably infects my memories; and thus, in such cases, one does tend to be drawn to the observer perspective, where the external evaluative perspective coincides with the external observer perspective on one's own follies.

Construction not Retrieval

There is a more general concern that might arise now, once I have responded to the objection that episodic memories cannot integrate internal and external perspectives through the psychological equivalent of free indirect style. This general concern is that we seem to be losing track of the idea that the role of memory, as Paul Ricœur (2004: 21) puts it, is to be 'faithful to the past', for now it seems as if memories are no longer faithful to the past, but also have to be 'faithful' to the present—to how one now feels about the past.

Indeed. We can contrast two views of the way in which the past is recollected. In one view, the past is understood on an archaeological model, where the past is initially hidden, and is waiting to be retrieved through excavation. In the other view, as Nicola King (2000: 12) has put it, 'memory inevitably incorporates the awareness of "what wasn't known then"'. So memory is more of a construction than an excavation and rediscovery. King reminds us of Freud's concept of *Nachträglichkeit* (translated roughly as 'afterwardsness'). In one and the same experience of remembering, and at one and the same time, we inhabit the 'omniscience' of our present perspective and the 'partiality' of our perspective at the time, seeing things as we then saw them and seeing them as we now see them, in a new and different light. We can and do, consciously or unconsciously, intentionally or unintentionally, change the way we remember the past, in the light of the triply ironic gap that is opened up and simultaneously bridged by our memories.

It does not follow, though, that what is 'constructive' in memory is the remembered episode as such, as if the whole episode were 'made up'; as Mark Rowlands (2009: 340) says in his discussion of memory as a constructive process:

> there is little reason for supposing that episodic memories are *systematically* false, inaccurate, or otherwise misleading—although, obviously, they may be so in particular cases. ... Rather, on its most sensible interpretation, the expression 'constructive remembering' designates the way in which memories can re-organize, embellish, and transform the original experienced episodes.[25]

My contention in this chapter is that 'the way in which memories can reorganize, embellish, and transform the original experienced episodes' will characteristically be especially marked where the irony between internal and external perspective is at its greatest, with the irony being expressed through the psychological correlate of free indirect style in autobiographical memory. Our memories are infused with what we now know, and with how we now feel about what happened in the light of what we now know. It is thus that we come to fully understand our past, and thereby to be able to make plans for the future. As Freud (1920/1984: 183) said in another context:

> the curious fact makes itself felt that in general people experience their present naively, as it were, without being able to form an estimate of its contents; they have first to put themselves at a distance from it—the present, that is to say, must have become the past—before it can yield points of vantage from which to judge the future.

Conclusion

Søren Kierkegaard said, near the beginning of his *Stages on Life's Way* (1967: 27, 28), that memory 'is merely a minimal condition'; memory 'presents itself to receive the consecration of recollection'; recollection 'involves effort and responsibility, which the indifferent act of memory does not involve ... Hence it is an art to recollect.' Adopting, and adapting, Kierkegaard's contrast between memory and recollection, and bearing in mind Freud's notion of *Nachträglichkeit*, we can now say: Just being able to have an 'indifferent act of memory' of an incident in one's past life is not

---

[25] See also Debus's (2007) rejection of the Argument from Reconstruction.

sufficient for one to be able to have the right kind of evaluation of, and emotional response to, what happened, from the external perspective on one's past that narrative thinking allows. In other words, it is possible sometimes just to remember that it was you *yourself* that did something, and yet you still lack the 'art of recollection': what you remember fails to receive the 'consecration of recollection'. I will turn to this kind of difficulty in the next chapter, where I will consider narratives of grief and, more generally, of trauma.

3

Grief: A Case Study

Introduction: The Narratable Process of Grief

In grieving, we relate to our past in a special way, realizing that things as they used to be, and as we remember them, can never be the same again. Our position is, in just this sense, agonizingly ironic, and our thinking about and remembering our past, from the perspective that we now have on it, can reflect this irony through the psychological correlate of free indirect style. So, to begin with, grieving, as just a particular way of thinking about the past (and indeed the future), can itself involve narrative thinking. In this respect, grief makes a useful case study of the notion of narrative thinking about one's past that I have been discussing in Chapter 2. But in addition to that, I will be arguing in this chapter that grief is an emotion best understood and explained through a narrative.

Against this, one might object that grief is not the kind of thing for which a narrative is appropriate. According to most recent philosophical accounts of emotion, as a brief survey will show, grief is a particular mental state or event, a non-cognitive feeling perhaps, or some kind of cognitive state. And if this is so, one should no more aspire to a narrative of grief than one should aspire to a narrative of the event of perceiving a red cube in front of you. Instead, I argue that grief is not to be identified with any kind of mental state or event, something that—like the feeling of pain, or the perception of a red cube, or the thought that it's time for tea, or the desire to stretch your legs—can be there one moment and not there the next. Grief is a kind of process; more specifically, it is a complex pattern of activity and passivity, inner and outer, that unfolds over time, and the unfolding pattern over time is explanatorily prior to what is the case at any particular time. I will then show that the pattern of a particular grieving is best understood and explained through a narrative, and not merely a causal, account, for narratives, here as elsewhere, have powerful explanatory, revelatory, and expressive powers that other accounts lack. A narrative account of grief, then, is not some kind of gloss, at best superficial, to be improved on through more careful and profound philosophical or psychological analysis: it is the best that there is.

Grief is Not a Kind of Mental State or Event

This is not the place to give a lengthy review of all the accounts of emotion that are in currency, but a brief survey will be helpful. We can divide them into roughly three groups.

First, there are feeling theories, of the kind put forward by William James and his many followers, which identify emotion with a kind of feeling. As William James famously put it, 'our feelings of the [bodily] changes as they occur *is* the emotion'.[1] Feeling theories can be classified as *non-cognitive theories*, in the rough sense that cognition (whatever that might precisely be) is not a necessary part of the emotion itself, even if cognition, such as belief, typically occurs.

Secondly, there are *judgement-based cognitive theories*. Often finding their roots in Aristotle and the Stoics, these theories hold that emotions are to be identified with judgements. For example, Martha Nussbaum identifies emotion with a 'eudaimonistic' judgement, concerning one's own flourishing: 'emotions are appraisals or value judgments, which ascribe to things and persons outside the person's own control great importance for that person's own flourishing' (2001: 4). She specifically rejects the idea that there are any essential non-cognitive elements to emotion; so far as feelings are concerned, 'the plasticity and variability of people . . . prevents us from plugging the feeling into the definition as an absolutely necessary element' (p. 60). In adiscussion that begins with an account of the death of her mother, Nussbaum applies this theory of emotion to grief in particular. She says, 'In the actual event, my grief was . . . identical to a judgment with something like the following form: "My mother, an enormously valuable person and an important part of my life, is dead"' (p. 76). She accepts that imagining, and ways of seeing, are typically also involved in grief: 'grief is the acceptance of a certain content, *accompanied (usually) by* relevant acts of the imagination' (p. 66, her italics). Nevertheless, she insists

---

[1] James (1884: 190); see also (Damasio 1999).

on identifying her grief with the eudaimonistic judgment: 'my concrete judgments entail that one [the eudaimonistic judgement], and that one is the one in terms of which I would wish to identify and define grief' (p. 77).

Thirdly, there are *perception-based cognitive theories* of emotion. These theories either identify emotions with a particular kind of perception, or claim that emotions are to be understood as analogous to perception. Perceptual theories are best understood as a development out of judgement-based cognitivist theories; they claim to inherit their benefits, including in particular their world-directed intentionality, without inheriting their disadvantages. For example, Robert Roberts has argued that emotion is a concern-based construal of a perceptual kind; and Sabine Döring argues that emotion is an affective perception.[2]

All these theories of emotion have two things in common, in spite of differing over whether the chosen state or event is cognitive or non-cognitive. First, they identify emotion, and grief in particular, with a kind of mental state or event.[3] And, secondly, they in effect give priority to the emotion, that is to the favoured mental state or event, *at a time*, rather than to the dynamics of the emotion—to the way it unfolds *over time*.[4]

In a moment, I will turn to an argument that is meant to show that grief, like other kinds of emotion, is a particular kind of mental state or event. But, first, there is an intuitive idea that might lead one directly to that conclusion: the intuitive idea that there is something that it feels like to grieve. And from this idea one might conclude that grief is a certain kind of feeling: perhaps a non-cognitive feeling of certain kinds of bodily changes, or a more cognitive perception-like feeling directed towards the object of one's grief, such as a feeling of intense sadness at the irrevocable loss of someone (or something) loved; the details do not matter at this point.

---

[2] Roberts (2003); Döring (2007). For other perceptual accounts of emotion, see e.g. Deonna (2006) and Elgin (2008).

[3] I say 'state or event' because most of the philosophers I am concerned with make no clear distinction between these two ontological categories, for example not making it clear whether a judgement is a state or an event.

[4] Jenefer Robinson's theory might be thought to be an exception here, as she emphasizes the process aspect of emotion, but nevertheless in the end she identifies emotion with a short-lived, non-cognitive affective appraisal, occurring 'very fast, automatically, and below the threshold of awareness', so any cognitive elements of the experience are excluded as not part of the emotion itself (2005: 41). Also an exception is Karen Jones's (2008) account of the role of narrative in emotion.

Of course there is something that it feels like to grieve. But this admitted fact does not on its own justify *identifying* grief with a kind of feeling, whether broadly cognitive or broadly non-cognitive. Ludwig Wittgenstein made some remarks that, although characteristically gnomic and open to many different interpretations, do at least lead us to question the idea that grief is a kind of feeling. In his *Philosophical Investigations*, he contrasts two sentences that are, on the face of it, grammatically similar: 'For a second he felt violent pain,' and 'For a second he felt deep grief,' and he asks why the latter sounds odd. 'Grief', he says, 'is not the name of a sensation or feeling. He accepts that the question 'But don't you feel grief *now*?' makes sense, and that the answer might be affirmative when, for example, one feels a sudden pang of grief. So although he quite rightly does not deny that grief has a phenomenology, that there is something that it is like to feel grief, still, he insists, 'that does not make the concept of grief any more like the concept of a sensation'.[5] And in this respect, pain and grief are unalike. This is an important intuition, and I think it points to a larger truth than just that grief is not a sensation or feeling. It points beyond that to the idea that grief is not any kind of mental state or event.

Why would one be tempted, as part of a philosophical theory, to identify an emotion with an individual mental state or event of a particular kind, whether feeling, judgement, or perception? What about, one might ask, all the other diverse things that are involved when one is grieving, in addition to feelings of a certain kind?[6] Are these to be dismissed as merely things that accompany grief but are not part of grief as such? It would be an easy answer to say that philosophers just do have this tendency to simplify the contents of our minds, to tidy up the mess inside, and, whenever the opportunity for ontological parsimony seems to arise, to apply Occam's razor: the maxim not to multiply entities beyond necessity. (Instead, perhaps there should be a reverse maxim, not to eliminate entities beyond necessity, and perhaps we have one that expresses that sentiment very nicely, namely Bishop Butler's wisdom, that everything is what it is and not another thing.) But these are *ad hominem* remarks, and so we should turn to a specific *argument* why we should agree that emotion should be identified with an individual mental state or event. I will now address that

---

[5] Wittgenstein (1958: 174). See also Bedford (1957).
[6] For the so-called five stages of grief, see Bowlby (1998) and Kubler-Ross and Kessler (2005).

argument, from Jesse Prinz, before turning to my positive account of grief as a kind of process.

Prinz puts the argument in the form of two problems faced by all 'component theories' as he calls them (theories that do not identify emotion with any individual state), and in particular by what he calls 'encompassing theories', which 'either claim that every instance of an emotion contains all of the kinds of components I have been discussing, or they claim that each emotion must contain at least some of these' (2004: 18). The two problems are the Problem of Parts and the Problem of Plenty. This is what Prinz says:

> By including everything, one can lose sight of how the different parts hang together. Privileging a single part is a way of drawing attention to the feature that is most fundamental for understanding emotions. An encompassing account that fails to do this suffers from what can be termed the Problem of Plenty.
>
> The Problem of Plenty is the counterpoint to the Problem of Parts. The Problem of Parts asks: What components of an emotion episode are really essential to its being an instance of some particular emotion? The tempting answer is that all parts are essential. The Problem of Plenty then asks: If all parts are essential, how do they hang together into a coherent whole? (p. 18)

Prinz argues that component theories cannot deal with these problems. To drive the point home he considers what he calls a 'parody':

> Suppose one wants to provide a theory of conscious visual states. What, one might ask, is a conscious red experience? . . . [O]ne might say that conscious red experiences have several parts. There is a feeling, a thought, an action tendency, an attention controller, and a memory trigger . . . . When asked to point out which one is the red experience, one might point to the whole set of entities. Red experiences, one might say, have many components.
>
> This complexity would be gratuitous. It would be better to say that a conscious red experience is a unitary mental entity that has several functions, properties and effects. (pp. 241–2)

I agree. It would be better to say that a conscious experience of red, such as the perception of a red cube in front of you, is a 'unitary mental entity'. But there seems to be an assumption that is driving both the Problem of Parts and the Problem of Plenty when we are concerned with emotion— an assumption that what we have in front of us to begin with are the parts, the 'unitary mental entities', and that we are then pressed with the question of how these parts 'hang together'. This might well be true of some mental phenomena, and I agree that a conscious experience of a red cube is one such. But it might not be true of all mental phenomena. Perhaps some mental phenomena are primarily processes, and only secondarily can we properly comprehend the mental states and events they are made up of: the parts do not even come into view *as* parts unless and until they are seen as parts of a particular kind of process. The process is thus ontologically and epistemically prior to the parts. This is, more or less, what I will now argue for. Grief is primarily to be understood as a particular kind of process, and the elements of this process can be seen to 'hang together into a coherent whole', to use Prinz's phrase, through the coherence of a narrative of the process—a narrative of a grieving.[7]

Grief is a Kind of Process

Some things are processes and some are not. Sometimes the distinction is made between those things that persist by *perduring*, of which processes are a kind, and those things that persist by *enduring*. A mental state, such as a conscious experience of a red cube, endures, rather than perdures, if, as Thomas Hofweber and David Velleman (2010: 1) argue, 'its identity is determined at every moment at which it exists'.[8] In contrast, a process persists by perduring, as its identity is not determined at every moment of its existing. One of their helpful examples is the process of writing a cheque:

A process of writing a cheque is a temporally extended process, with temporal parts consisting in the laying down of each successive drop of ink. What there is of this process at a particular moment—the laying down of a particular drop—is not sufficient to determine that a cheque is being written, and so it is not sufficient to determine which particular process is taking place.... Not only, then, is the process not present in its temporal entirety within the confines of the moment: it is not fully determined by the events of the moment to be the process that it is. (p. 14)

This process of cheque-writing perdures because it is an object whose 'persistence depends on spatiotemporal or causal continuity'; 'its temporal

---

[7] I am not sure how important this is to my disagreement with Prinz, but I should make it clear that I am not aiming to provide a scientific account of grief, whatever precisely that might be. My aim is to capture what grief is, as we normally understand it.

[8] In what follows, I am indebted to this paper, in which they argue against the familiar distinction between endurance and perdurance in terms of having temporal parts, which they hold to be ultimately incoherent, in favour of the view put forward here. I hope that nothing significant in my overall argument hinges on the success of this argument.

parts do not belong to one and the same object merely by virtue of their temporally local properties, as they would if these properties fully determined the identity of the object to which each part belonged' (p. 20).

With this briefly characterized notion of a process in place, I can now set out my central claim about grief. Grief is a process, and is experienced as a process. It is a kind of process, which, borrowing again from Wittgenstein (1958: 174), I will call a pattern; he said, '"Grief" describes a pattern which recurs, with different variations, in the weave of our life'. The pattern has certain features. It includes characteristic thoughts, judgements, feelings, memories, imaginings, actions, expressive actions, habitual actions, and much else besides, unfolding over time, but none of which is essential at any particular time. It involves emotional dispositions as well as particular experiences, and there will be characteristic interactions between these. Describable as grief, or as a grieving, the manner of its unfolding is narratable in ways that I will shortly put forward. The pattern is understandable as grief because it follows a characteristic shape, although it will be individual and particular to the person, and will no doubt be significantly shaped by cultural as well as biological influences.[9]

Understanding grief as a process throws light on a number of aspects of this emotion that tend to get adumbrated or even hidden completely when grief is understood as an event or as a state.[10] (I will focus just now on the contrast between processes and events, although the points made apply, with some variation, to states.)

First, whilst some processes, such as the process of water coming out of a tap, are homogenous, many others, such as the process of cheque-writing, are heterogeneous, in the sense that there are distinct stages in the process, so that not everything that happens during the process is happening at any one time (Mourelatos 1993). The opening of the chequebook is a stage in the process of cheque-writing; the adding of the flour is a stage in the process of baking the cake. And the feeling of shock is a stage in the process of grieving. None of these stages continues throughout the process. This is what has been called structural (or 'empirical') heterogeneity of a process,

---

[9] See Ronald de Sousa's (1987) discussion of paradigm scenarios for how we come to recognize certain kinds of situation as being ones where a certain kind of emotion is appropriate. For a discussion of cultural variations in grief, see Wierzbicka (2004).

[10] In what follows, I have been greatly helped by discussions with Helen Steward and by her (2011).

as contrasted with the structural homogeneity that one finds in the process of water coming out of a tap (Gill 1993). This is to be distinguished from a semantic feature of all processes, whether structurally homogenous or heterogeneous, namely that they are homogenous in terms of predication: if Mary was baking a cake, then Mary was baking a cake during each stage in the process, when she was adding the flour and when she was stirring the concoction; if James was grieving over the loss of his wife, then James was grieving during each stage of the process, when he was in shock and when he was in denial. If we were to think of grief as an event, then this combination of structural heterogeneity and predicative homogeneity cannot be adequately captured. Moreover, understanding grief as a structurally heterogeneous process further diffuses Prinz's concerns about how the 'components' of an emotion hang together: they do so in virtue of being stages of a structurally heterogeneous process, just as the stages of adding flour and of stirring the concoction hang together as part of the process of baking the cake.

Secondly, processes, unlike events, can be interrupted. Mary's baking of the cake in the morning might be interrupted by her having to give a music lesson to a pupil; James's grieving might be interrupted by his being hit by a car and rendered unconscious for two weeks. After the music lesson, the baking resumes; after consciousness is restored, the grieving resumes. Events are not interruptible in this way; unlike events, processes have what Steward (2011) has called 'modal robustness in virtue of form'.

Thirdly, as Steward has also argued, 'Questions both of causation and of explanation look rather different when one is thinking about processes from the way they look when one is thinking in terms of events' (p. 15). With an event, we look for the cause as whatever it was that triggered it off: the spark that caused the explosion for example. But with a process we look also for what 'sustains it, what keeps it on course, what prevents it from ceasing or disintegrating' (p. 15). If one thinks of grief as an event (or as a state), the question of cause is limited to the question of what 'set off' the grief, something such as hearing the terrible news. But in thinking of grief as a process we look to what sustains it through its various stages. We might well say that love sustains it—a point to which I will return shortly. And when we turn to the explanation of a process, we look beyond just what sets the process off; we look also for the factors that explain why the process took the turns that it did, at those times and in those ways. With Mary's cake-baking, these factors will centrally involve Mary's agency.

With James's grieving, they will involve that blend of activity and passivity that is so characteristic of human emotion. This kind of explanatory task, I will now argue, is best met with a narrative account.

One might summarize in this way the difference between my position and the other philosophical accounts of emotion that I have mentioned: they privilege a single mental state or event amongst a number of mental states and events as the emotion; whereas I privilege no particular mental state or event but rather the process, which is made up of mental states and events, and of much else besides, and which unfolds in a characteristic pattern. Of course, in thinking about and analysing a particular instance of grief, it is possible to pick out one or more particular state or event for closer attention, as one might focus on the moment when one first heard the terrible news, but this does not affect my point about what grief is, namely a process of a certain kind. Nor does it affect my claim that any such chosen state or event (including its content, whether propositional or not), will not be sufficient to determine that the process of grieving is taking place.

The Narrative of a Grieving: Free Indirect Style and General Events

If grief is a process of the kind that I am suggesting, then its identity, its being this particular process, depends on spatiotemporal or causal continuity. Just as the laying down of a particular drop of ink is not sufficient to determine that a cheque is being written, so a particular mental state or event, such as his coming to realize that she is dead, is not sufficient to determine that he is grieving. It is in just this sense that the Problem of Parts and the Problem of Plenty get things back to front. These Problems simply do not get a grip when we are concerned with processes.

Now this might suggest that what is needed for an account of grief is just a causal account, one that will demonstrate causal continuity between the various states and events involved—the 'events of the moment'. Although I agree that a causal account is possible here, I think that the best available account we can have of grief—of a particular process, remember—is one with a high degree of narrativity: a highly narrative account rather than a bare causal account.

As we saw in Chapter 1, narratives have much in common with causal accounts. Like a causal account, a narrative is idiographic: it is concerned with particular facts, events, and individuals. Like a causal account, a narrative cannot be concerned with just a single simple event or state; it must be about one thing happening after another, and the notion of coherence is concerned with how these things happening one after another hold together in some way. Narratives, like causal accounts, are interest-relative. And causal relations play a central part in the coherence of a narrative. However, in addition, as we also saw, relations other than causal ones can constitute part of a narrative. First, narratives can exploit multiple perspectives in a way that gives them evaluative and emotional import of a kind that causal accounts lack. This import is revealed, or expressed, in the narrative in two kinds of perspective: internal perspectives, which are the perspectives of those individuals who are internal to the narrative; and external, which are the perspectives of the narrator, and also of the author where those two individuals are different. Secondly, narratives are better placed to explain general events, by locating them within part of a larger pattern. In this chapter, as something of a case study, I will develop these two features of narrative in relation to the process of grief.

To begin with, I will focus just on narratives that are simply thought through, without there being any public act of narration. Then at the end I will turn to traumatic experiences and to the significant therapeutic benefits—and the dangers too—of narrating one's grieving, or other kind of traumatic experience, to another person. But note that my account of the powers of narratives does not depend on the therapeutic powers of a public narration, important as they are.

Let us return to irony and to the psychological correlate of free indirect style in autobiographical memory. When you grieve, you often look back on the past, on your time together with the person you loved, knowing now what you did not know then: that the person you loved is now dead, and that you now know the manner and time of the dying. Grief is replete with the irony of memories such as these. For example, you remember the last time you saw the person you loved, not knowing, as you do now, that it was to be the last time. And this irony, through the psychological correlate of free indirect style, will infect the way you remember it.

The psychologist and psychoanalyst Tilmann Habermas has a powerful example from one of his patients, Mrs B, whose husband left for the office and, as she later realized to her horror, committed suicide. Mrs B is relating her memories of the last time she saw him:

I still see the day when he comes home and lay down, and when he got up and said he had to go back again to the office. I said: 'Would you like me to come along?' 'No, I still have to do, what I have not finished before'. This was I think around half past five or ... I will never forget the image. I looked after him and I see him walking around the corner, with hanging shoulders ... (Habermas 2006: 505–6; cf. Habermas and Berger 2011)

As Habermas notes, through the immediacy and drama of the narration, 'the listener is pulled into Mrs B's perspective that she had at the time'. But we are also and at the same time pulled into the memory as Mrs B now remembers it: she now remembers it *as* the last time she saw her husband, walking around the corner with hanging shoulders, so that, because of what she now knows, the memory of that day is itself infused with the portent of the terrible future that the earlier experience did not have. In this way, autobiographical narrative thinking can reveal or express both one's internal and external perspective on one's tragic loss, so that these two perspectives are intertwined through the psychological correlate of free indirect style.

Grief is indeed replete with memories. But grief involves not just memories of particular experiences; it also involves memories of general events, and these can be especially poignant given that the remembered general event can no longer be experienced as it used to be. For example, you remember those holidays in France together, and the trips to the beach with the rest of the family, knowing now that they cannot be repeated as they used to be. Or you remember the general event of his coming home from the office as he usually does, knowing now that he no longer will, for *this* time, this particular remembered time, unlike all the others, is the *last* time.

Now, just this kind of thinking is highly characteristic of narrative thinking about grief, whether one's own grief or that of another person. Grief is a kind of pattern that, as I mentioned earlier, takes a characteristic shape, and accordingly the capacity of narratives to incorporate and make sense of general events is especially important here. In grief, we can appreciate that *this* pattern is unfolding in *this* way both as we undergo it, and as we later remember it: 'During those months, every morning I would be too tired even to take the children to school'. The narrative of a grieving will thus reveal how the pattern of grief unfolded over time in a characteristic way.

Narratives of a grieving are also very well suited to showing—returning to my earlier discussion—what sustains the grief through its stages. One thought here is that grief is a process of a kind that ought to come to an end—to a 'natural' end—and that to continue grief beyond its natural end is psychologically damaging, not only to the person who is grieving but also potentially to those who are still living and who are close to the bereaved person. One needs to, and ought to, get over it. The alternative view, which has been argued for forcefully by Robert Solomon and Kathleen Higgins, is that grief is a continuation of love, and that it is this continuing relation between the bereaved person and the deceased that sustains the grief.[11] I believe that Solomon and Higgins are right about this, and that the social pressures to 'get over it' are misplaced. But whether this view is right or not, it is an important fact that it is only once we have in mind that grief is a process that we can address in a meaningful way this question of what sustains grief.

Two Narrative Accounts of Grief

To illustrate the explanatory, revelatory, and expressive powers of a narrative of grief, I will turn to two literary examples—literary, although they are both based on the authors' own lived experiences. One might complain here that these are, precisely, literary, and that accordingly they do not properly capture our 'ordinary' narratives of grief. But I hope that a close examination of the examples will show that, in fact, these are not different in kind from our ordinary narrative practices; they may be well-written and highly evocative narratives, but this is a difference of degree not of kind. (One might compare here the example of Mrs B from Habermas cited above: thoroughly unliterary, but still highly evocative.) I have picked these two examples of autobiographical narratives of grief because they illustrate especially well the properties of narrative that I have been discussing: the ironic distance between the two perspectives of narrator and of protagonist, often fused through free indirect style; and the capacity of narratives to capture the importance of general events in the unfolding process of a grieving. I will not burden the reader with a commentary: I hope they will speak for themselves.

---

[11] The first view is known as relinquishment theory. The alternative is known as the continuing bonds perspective. I am very grateful to Kathleen Higgins here, and to the discussion in her (2011).

The first example is from Alan Bennett's *A Life Like Other People's*. Bennett is describing his regular visits to his mother, who is dying with advanced Alzheimer's in a hospice. The visits unfold in a characteristic way: each time, unsure if this particular visit will be the last, he would try to gain her attention. Here we have a narrative of general events, and, embedded deeper in the narrative, we have further general events, which Bennett is trying to remember experientially in the knowledge that they cannot be repeated. Moreover, we are able to appreciate the two perspectives, subtly intertwined, of Bennett as 'character' in the related events and of Bennett as narrator, from both perspectives seeing the absurdity of his trying to engage emotionally with his mother, who was already lost to the world:

> To make her see me is not easy. Sometimes it means bringing my head down, my cheek on the coverlet in order to intercept her eye line and obtrude on her gaze. In this absurd position, my head virtually in her lap, I say 'Goodbye, Mam, goodbye,' trying as I say it (my head pressing into the candlewick) to picture her with Dad and print her face on my memory, Mam laughing on the sands at Filey with Gordon and me, Mam walking on the proms at Morecambe with Grandma. If this produces no satisfactory epiphany (a widening of the eyes, say, or a bit of a smile) I do it again, the spectacle of this middle-aged man knelt down with his head flat on the bed of no more interest to the other old women than it is to my mother.   (Bennett 2010: 229–30)

The second example is from C. S. Lewis's *A Grief Observed*. During his process of grieving for the death of his beloved 'H', Lewis found four exercise books around the house, and filled them with his 'jottings' about his experiences. Once they were filled up, he stopped: 'I *will not* start buying books for this purpose' (Lewis 1961: 50). The extract I have chosen is from the beginning of the third book, where he comments on a general event: how he experiences the world as does someone who is grieving but who is not at the time thinking of the person grieved over:

> It's not true that I'm always thinking of H. Work and conversation make that impossible. But the times when I'm not are perhaps my worst. For then, though I have forgotten the reason, there is spread over everything a vague sense of wrongness, of something amiss. Like in those dreams where nothing terrible occurs—nothing that would sound even remarkable if you told it at breakfast-time—but the atmosphere, the taste, of the whole thing is deadly. So with this. I see the rowan berries reddening and don't know for a moment why they, of all things, should be depressing. I hear a clock strike and some quality it always had before has gone out of the sound. What's wrong with the world to make it so flat, shabby, worn-out looking? Then I remember.   (p. 31)

At the beginning of the fourth of his exercise books narrating his experiences, Lewis says:

In so far as this record was a defence against total collapse, a safety-valve, it has done some good. The other end I had in view turns out to have been based on a misunderstanding. I thought I could describe a *state*; make a map of sorrow. Sorrow, however, turns out to be not a state but a process. It needs not a map but a history, and if I don't stop writing that history at some arbitrary point, there's no reason why I should ever stop. There is something new to be chronicled every day. Grief is like a long valley, a winding valley where any bend may reveal a totally new landscape. As I've already noted, not every bend does. Sometimes the surprise is the opposite one; you are presented with exactly the same sort of country you thought you had left behind miles ago. That is when you wonder whether the valley isn't a circular trench. But it isn't. There are partial recurrences, but the sequence doesn't repeat.   (p. 50)

This contrast, between state and process, between map and history, expresses very nicely what I have tried to argue for. The emotion of grief is a kind of process—a complex pattern of activity and passivity, inner and outer, that unfolds over time, and the unfolding pattern over time is explanatorily prior to what is the case at any particular moment, and moreover, explanatorily prior to any particular mental state or event at any particular moment that is part of the process. This process needs a history, and more specifically it needs a narrative account, and not merely a causal-historical account, because narrative accounts have such powerful explanatory, revelatory, and expressive powers—as is illustrated by the small segments of narrative that I have included here. It is because grief is a process of this kind, narratable in this way, that its parts 'hang together into a coherent whole'.

Might this be generalized to other kinds of emotion—even perhaps to the kind of example from William James that is made so much of by philosophers, the fear experienced at the approaching bear in the woods? I would like to think that it could. Grief, of course, is a process that continues (perdures) for a relatively long time, but processes can be short-lived too, and there is much work in psychology that throws light on the complex ways in which, for example, an experience of fear unfolds: recognition and appraisal, bodily feeling, bodily response, facial expression, expressive action, action-readiness, motivation, action, and so on, each of them only fully intelligible as part of a continuing process of the experience of fear.

Traumatic Experience and the Desire for Emotional Closure

I mentioned at the end of Chapter 2, Kierkegaard's contrast between memory and recollection, where memory 'presents itself to receive the consecration of recollection'; recollection 'involves effort and responsibility, which the indifferent act of memory does not involve . . . Hence it is an art to recollect' (1967: 27 and 28). Sometimes, especially where the remembered events are in some way tragic or traumatic, one is unable to recollect: one has memory but not recollection, and the possibility of integration seems unachievable; one is locked into the past. The death of a loved one, being fired from one's job, accidentally maiming a child in a road accident, intentionally doing great harm to someone you love, divorce, the loss of a limb: after such events, one often cannot respond emotionally as one should, with the right evaluative perspective. Looking back on it, one might feel shock, puzzlement, horror, anger, or surprise, but these emotions that one now feels may be little more than a painful 'echo' of the response that one felt at the time. Inadequate in themselves, responses like these reveal that one is failing to have the appropriate emotional response from the external perspective that the 'art of recollection' requires; all one has is 'indifferent memory' (with the qualification that indifference here includes emotions such as surprise, shock, puzzlement, horror, or even just numbness).

Empirical research as well as personal experience suggest that it is characteristic of post-traumatic stress to find oneself anxiously going over and over the events in one's mind in this way: in remembering the traumatic events, one might be able to think through a causal explanation that meets the minimal conditions of a narrative, but the explanation is thought through in a matter-of-fact, non-evaluative way that is far from satisfying to the narrator (Barclay 1995: 113; Eich et al. 2011). One feels locked into one's memories of the past (Conway 2003: 5), struggling to find some way out, some way of *working through* the past and reintegrating it into the present, and into one's narrative sense of self.

What is lacking? What is it that one wants or needs if one is to attain the right perspective on past traumatic events? I think that what one wants is to be able to evaluate and respond emotionally to those past events, perhaps with anger or forgiveness, perhaps with shame or regret, but with emotions that are *appropriate* to what happened from the external perspective that one now has. But this is just what patients with post-traumatic stress disorder cannot do. Both their field memories and their observer memories are unsatisfactory—memories without the art of recollection. With field memories, they find themselves locked into seemingly endless repetition of all the negative feelings that they had at the time. With observer memory, they tend to remember factually, without emotion; as McIsaac and Eich put it, 'people who recalled their trauma from the observer vantage point tended to use a rather journalistic style of reporting their experience: Their tone was unemotional and flat, as if they were just reporting the "facts"' (McIsaac and Eich 2004: 251). And the problem here is, McIsaac and Eich continue, 'the short-term relief from emotional distress that is gained by adopting an observer vantage point may actually impede long-term recovery' (p. 252). So they either re-enact the negative emotions from a field perspective, or they have no emotions from an external, observer perspective.

In short, what is lacking is the *closure* that the art of recollection affords. But we need to distinguish here. One possibility is that what is lacking is *narrative closure*. In narrative closure, we achieve what Frank Kermode (1966) has called 'the sense of an ending', with all the loose ends neatly tied together, as they are at the end of a detective novel. But in real life narratives, as opposed to narratives created for aesthetic purposes, to expect this would be naive, or worse than naive—a point to which I will return in detail in Chapter 7.

The second possibility is *emotional closure*: being able to look back *in the right way* on one's past life from one's present external perspective: not just seeing the causal connections, and making sense of why one then thought, felt, and acted as one then did, but also making an external evaluation and having emotional responses that one feels are the appropriate ones to what happened. It is in this sense that, in remembering something, one sometimes asks oneself how one should think and feel about what happened, realizing perhaps that an answer is not readily available, and will not be forthcoming until one can see the past in what we rightly call 'the proper perspective'. Emotional closure is precisely what is lacking in people with traumatic memories: in narrative thinking they can think through what happened from an external perspective, but they cannot achieve emotional closure; all they can manage is flat, unemotional, matter-of-fact reporting.

Here, of course, the possibility raises its head of a narrative that satisfies the narrator, that gives emotional closure, but that is still far from the truth and deeply self-deceptive; the desire for emotional closure transmutes into a desire for smug self-satisfaction, unwarranted vindication, or worse. We all know only too well of this possibility from our own lives, and our own sometimes rather shabbily desperate efforts (conscious and unconscious) to put our past actions in an unreasonably favourable perspective. There are, of course, many issues here concerning truth in narrative, to which I will return in Chapter 7. However, we should not assume that, just because the quest for emotional closure can lead to self-deception, self-deception or simply deviation from the truth, that these things are an inevitable outcome of that quest.

Telling to Others

It may well be that narrative thinking and autobiographical memory are not enough after tragic or traumatic experience: to achieve the art of recollection might also require that one be able to relate what happened to another person, in order to be able to work through the past in the right way. This I think must have been part of what C. S. Lewis was seeking, when he wrote, of his making a 'record' in his notebooks, that it served as a 'defence against total collapse, a safety valve'. Telling really is important here, as psychoanalysis—the talking cure—reveals: it is sometimes only in the telling that one can come to see the past from the proper perspective—to work things through in one's mind. Before that, what happened may be remembered all too well, and one might even be able to think through a narrative of what happened, but still one is unable to evaluate it, and to respond emotionally, in a way that one feels is appropriate; the desire for emotional closure remains unsatisfied, and one cannot have the peace of mind that this would involve. That is what friends (as well as psychoanalysts) are for: to listen.[12]

---

[12] James Pennebaker, Cindy Chung, and colleagues have written extensively about the importance for psychological health when recovering from trauma of expressing one's feelings to others, in writing or verbally. See e.g. Pennebaker and Chung (forthcoming). For the therapeutic powers of grieving narratives, see (Árnason 2000). Thanks to Kathleen Higgins for the reference to this paper.

Often, in such circumstances, one wants both to tell and not to tell the story. One wants to tell it because of the desire for emotional closure—the desire to have the right sort of evaluative and emotional response to what happened. And yet one also wants *not* to tell the story, partly because of the pain one feels in the telling of it, and partly because one knows that one has not yet achieved this emotional closure in one's own mind; so the uncompleted attempt to tell the story to another, and to work out how one feels in the telling, will be made only too plain, both to oneself and to one's audience.

A desire for emotional closure need not be a conscious one (this is why I sometimes talk of 'need' rather than 'desire'), and sometimes one only comes to see how much one needs to be able to tell one's own story from having heard it told by another. I will end this chapter with a marvellous example of this, discussed by Adriana Cavarero in her *Relating Narratives* (1997). It is from Book VIII of *The Odyssey*. Odysseus, after his many and terrible trials, is the honoured guest of Alkinoos, the king of the Phaiakians. No one in the palace, however, knows who he is. There is a great dinner in his honour, and the blind singer Demodokos is asked to entertain those present. Demodokos sings of the great Odysseus and his deeds in fighting the Trojans. At this point, hearing his story told by another for the first time, Odysseus begins to weep, 'pitiful tears', as he has never been known to weep before. Through the song of the blind singer, Odysseus is able for the first time to see what happened as others see it, from an external perspective, and for the first time he is in a position to respond emotionally to what he was already able to remember. He now has an appropriate external perspective on this terrible part of his life. And hearing his story thus told, and gaining this external perspective, he now recognizes a desire he did not realize he had: for he feels impelled to tell his story to another from this newly gained perspective. So, when Alkinoos asks him to say who he is and why he weeps at these tales, he replies with a narrative of not inconsiderable length, saying at the outset, 'Many are the sorrows the gods of the sky have given me.'

Here, the song of Demodokos awoke in Odysseus the desire for emotional closure, so that mere memory could begin to 'receive the consecration of recollection': Odysseus could begin to evaluate and respond emotionally to his trials as he now sees that he should. Here then we see the art of recollection to be the art of narrative, whether the narrative is told to another or whether it is in the mind of a single thinker.

Showing to Others

We have seen how the therapeutic powers of a narrative can be further enhanced when it is publicly narrated, when we need but cannot find emotional closure, and this is as true of grief as it is of other kinds of traumatic experience.

There is an additional power of a public narration, and that is its revelatory aspect, revealing things about the narrator that might or might not be revealed intentionally. This can be very important in interpreting and understanding another person. For example, it can reveal, through the content or the framework of the narrative, that one cares less about what happened than one thinks, or that one cares less about what happened than one is prepared to say. Or the narrative can reveal aspects of the narrator's character or personality of which the narrator might not be aware, as we find the character of Alan Bennett and C. S. Lewis shining out when we read their grieving narratives.

Beyond that, a yet further power of a public narration emerges when we remember the distinction between narrative understood as product and narrative understood as act of narration. For a narrative can reveal or express one's external perspective on one's grief, not just through the content and framework of the narrative but also through the act of narration, which can itself also be expressive of one's grief. For example, a woman might be narrating the horror of finding her husband dead in bed next to her when she woke up in the morning, and suddenly she cries out to her listener 'I just can't *tell* you how awful it was!' And yet in her act of narration, accompanied as it is by a panoply of expressive gestures, she reveals what the narrative itself cannot reveal.

This points to an interesting feature of emotional experience: one's grief might be ineffable, in the familiar sense that it cannot be expressed in language, but it does not follow from this that it cannot be expressed at all. Nicola King (2000: 1), at the beginning of her book, *Memory, Narrative, Identity*, recounts how she heard a talk given by a survivor of Auschwitz, Leon Greenman. In the talk, she says, 'Greenman describes the moment when, after arriving at Auschwitz, he saw his wife being taken away on a truck—to the gas chamber, although, as he said, he "didn't know that then". This phrase', she continues, 'haunted his narrative, repeated several times: it marked the moments when emotion broke through what was otherwise a rather detached, deadpan delivery'. Greenman might have been unable to put his feelings into words, but ineffability is not the same thing as incommunicability.

Conclusion

I hope that this discussion of narratives of grief and other kinds of trauma will have illustrated the special explanatory, revelatory, and expressive powers of narratives, whether just thought through in narrative thinking, or whether publicly expressed to others, in writing or in speech.

The discussion leaves a lot of unfinished business, including in particular the possibility of achieving truth and objectivity in narrative, given the complex ways in which narratives can reveal and express internal and external perspectives, and the other purposes to which narrative can be put, such as satisfying the need to find emotional closure, where these purposes can be at odds with seeking truth and objectivity in narrative. This is the matter of Chapter 7. Before that, I now want to turn in the next chapter, Chapter 4, to narrative thinking about one's future, and then to how narrative thinking about past and future come together in self-forgiveness—which will be my second case study in Chapter 5.

4

Narrative Thinking about One's Future

Introduction: Imagining and Emotion as Guides in Practical Reason

In Chapter 2, I discussed the role of narrative thinking and emotion in autobiographical memories. In this chapter, I turn to how our thoughts and feelings about our past bear on our thoughts and feelings about the future, and, conversely, how our thoughts and feelings about the future bear on the way we think and feel about our past—not only in memory but also in imagining how things might have been otherwise. At the centre of this, of course, is the self: the person who is doing the thinking and feeling about the past and future, the person who can deliberate about how to act as well as how to think and feel.

In this chapter, I will consider the interplay between imagination and emotion in our narrative thinking and planning. This will reveal the important epistemic role of imagination and emotion as a guide in our practical reason. Then, in Chapter 5, I will illustrate these ideas with a discussion of self-forgiveness—a notion that many treat with what I consider to be a suspicion that is unwarranted once we have in place even a rough idea of the narrative sense of self, a sense of oneself with a past and a future for which one can be responsible. This narrative sense of self will be the subject of further discussion in Chapter 6.

Imagination, Emotion, and Branching Possibilities

Let us begin with an example, and then see how we can make sense of it. You are waiting for someone at an agreed location and time: under the station clock at noon. You have agreed with her to catch the train together which leaves at 12.30, and it is very important that you and she travel together—perhaps it is a romantic occasion, a first weekend away together. The time gets to 12.10, and you begin to feel nervous. As the minutes tick by and there is still no sign of her, you begin to imagine what might have happened to her, thinking through various possibilities, various explanations of why she might be late. She might be stuck on the bus, or have had an accident, or got lost somehow, or perhaps she has fallen seriously ill and can't get out of bed. Or is she somewhere else on the station concourse, wondering where you are? What should you do? You try to call her on her mobile phone, but there's no answer. You could try walking around the concourse, but then of course she might be doing just the same thing so you would miss each other.

As you run through all these possibilities in your mind, you have a range of emotional responses, veering from frustration at the thought of her being stuck on the bus (combined with a little bit of anger at her having chosen not to take a taxi as you suggested), to guilt at the thought of her being ill (and here you are at the station not doing anything about it). And so on through the range of possibilities that go through your mind. As more minutes tick by, and the departure time gets closer, in an effort to cheer yourself up, you adopt the strategy of trying to imagine her turning up and thinking through how enjoyable your journey together will turn out to be. Although this does give you a momentary frisson of pleasant anticipation, you're still terrible nervous and uncertain as to what to do, feeling sweaty, slightly out of control, and somehow exhausted, constantly checking your mobile phone, constantly gazing round, constantly looking at your watch. You're in a mess. Then, just before the train is due to leave and your concerns are at their height, you see her, flustered but grinning, rushing up to you saying, 'Let's run; I'll tell you what happened once we're on the train.' You now feel relief—relieved to see her, and relieved that all your untamed worrying turned out to be baseless, although it takes you some time to 'come down' from your nervous state, both physically and mentally.

This particular series of thoughts and feelings represents something of a hypertrophy of a way of thinking that is a very familiar, and important, part of our psychology. This is thinking in terms of *branching possibilities*. Branching possibilities are simply narrative representations of possible ways in which events might come to pass. The image to have in mind is of the trunk and branches of a tree, with the 'flow' of time, so to speak, pointing upward, and each node representing a point at which possibilities diverge. So, while you were waiting for her at the station, her turning up or not turning up can be represented by a node, and then the branch that represents her not turning up will immediately branch again into the various further possibilities—different possible stories of her not turning up. One of these might be her being ill, a node that branches further into a variety of possible stories of illnesses of varying kinds and varying degrees of seriousness.[1]

What kinds of thoughts and feelings can be involved in such an episode of thinking about branching possibilities, and in particular how can the emotions be implicated? Clearly imagination is involved.

Imagining possibilities can involve either propositional imagining or experiential imagining. Propositional imagining is imagining or supposing that something is the case, or that some event occurs, as one might imagine that one is ten years older. Experiential imagining, as I will use this term, is imagining in which you are somehow involved as a 'character' in what you imagine. There is also what I will call perceptual imagining, where you are not involved in this way, as one might perceptually imagine the Prime Minister standing up in the House of Commons, and you might imagine it from the perspective of someone in the Visitors' Gallery, but you do not imagine yourself as occupying that perspective; or you perceptually imagine her lying seriously ill in bed, feeling very sorry for herself, trying to get up, imagining this from a perspective at the foot of the bed, although you are not yourself a 'character' standing at the foot of the bed.

Experiential imagining can be either central imagining or acentral imagining (Wollheim 1984). Central imagining is where you imagine yourself having certain experiences, making decisions, acting in various ways, and so on, imagining what happens 'from the inside', or 'centrally'. In my example you might try to imagine from the inside how delighted you will feel when (if) she turns up in time to catch the train. Acentral imagining is where you perceptually imagine yourself in some scene, but not from your own perspective in the imagined scene. For example, you might try to imagine how delighted you will be when she turns up by

---

[1] What follows is, I hope, neutral as to the metaphysics of possible worlds. The idea has some connections to the idea of branching narratives in artificial intelligence and virtual reality; see e.g. Miller and Shanahan (1994) and Pinto (1998).

imagining yourself jumping up and down with delight, imagining this from a perspective located at the other end of the station concourse, so in your imagination you 'see' yourself as one of that twosome over there.

There are broad structural similarities between these kinds of imagining and the kinds of memory that I discussed in Chapter 2. (Although, for obvious reasons, perceptual imagining, where you are not a 'character' in what is imagined, does not have a correlate in memory.) Propositional imagining is roughly equivalent to semantic or propositional memory: imagining or supposing that you are in Berlin; remembering that you were in Berlin in August 1983. Central imagining, imagining from the inside, is roughly equivalent to field episodic memory (and Wollheim (1984: 104) in fact calls this 'centred event memory'): you imagine yourself in Berlin, having the experience of standing in the shadows of the Brandenburg Gate looking down Unter den Linden; you remember having had just that experience when you were last in Berlin. Acentral imagining is roughly equivalent to observer memory: in acentrally imagining yourself falling down the stairs, you imagine yourself so that you are part of the content of what you imagine; you remember the episode of falling down the stairs in such a way that you are part of the content of what you experientially remember. (Wollheim's notion of what he calls 'acentred event-memory' (p. 102) is not the same as this, as we will see in Ch. 6.) Finally, roughly equivalent to flashbulb memories, one can have a flashbulb image of something one imagines, as you might suddenly have an image of sitting on that train together once she has arrived.

There is a further structural similarity between memory and imagining in relation to general events. We saw in the last two chapters how one can experientially remember general events: you remember the general event of lying in bed in your school dormitory at night, unable to sleep, and you can remember this general event either from a field perspective or from an observer perspective. Similarly, one can experientially imagine the general event of being with your wife and children having breakfast at home, imagining this either centrally or acentrally.

Then there is a similarity in the ways in which various kinds of memory and imagining can merge: just as we saw in Chapter 2 that the levels of specificity of memory characteristically merge, so too can the levels of specificity of imagination. Thus, just as I might remember one night when I was in my younger teens, and used to go to bed early, how I was sitting on the edge of the bed with a knife in my hand when my father burst in; similarly, I might imagine being old and arthritic, confined to a wheelchair, wheeling myself along the drive, when one morning my son arrives unexpectedly with the latest addition to his family.

Connected with this are the indeterminacies that one finds in both memory and imagination. It might be unclear from introspection precisely whether you are remembering something experientially or propositionally, or as field or observer memory, just as it might not be clear whether you are imagining something in one or other of the ways I have been discussing. Given all these structural similarities and shared indeterminacies, it should come as no surprise how often it can be unclear whether one is remembering something or imagining it.

A further structural similarity is that, in narrative thinking about one's future, as in autobiographical narrative memories of one's past, there is an ironic gap. (Of course the structural symmetry masks the fundamental asymmetry, that in respect of the past, you now know what you did not know then, whereas in respect of the future, you now do not know what you then will know—how things will turn out. Whatever might be the metaphysics of time, surely this is *literally* indubitable.) For example, you don't know whether or not she will arrive at the station in time to catch the train. So narrative thinking here too requires an external narrator, as does all kinds of narrative thinking. The external narrator is you now, thinking about and imagining yourself then, in the future, where you are internal to the narrative, internal to the imagined possibility, just as you now are the external narrator in thinking about and remembering your past. This vital point leads us to a consideration of our emotional responses to what we imagine, and to free indirect style.

In imagining some possible unfolding sequence of events, thinking it through in narrative form, it is possible for you to imagine having an emotion, and to have an actual emotion as a result of what you imagine. Imagined emotion is internal to the narrative. Imagine yourself doing something silly in front of a large audience, such as being at a conference and asking a question that reveals your ignorance. This is surely an easy enough imaginative project. If you imagine this centrally, from the inside, you might imagine experiencing—imagine *feeling*—embarrassment. If you imagined it acentrally, you might imagine yourself from the perspective, say, of another member of the audience: from across the room, covered in blushes and consternation; thus you would imagine yourself being embarrassed without actually imagining feeling embarrassed. Or you could simply imagine that you were embarrassed by asking a stupid question. So in each of these three different ways you can imagine having an emotion.

Secondly, it is possible for you—that is, you now as external narrator—to have an actual emotion in response to what you imagine, so that this emotion is not part of the content of what you imagine. Thus you might come actually to feel embarrassed from imagining doing something silly, just as you can come actually to feel embarrassed from remembering doing something silly.

Just as is the case with the structural equivalent in memory, it has been disputed that experientially imagined emotions are possible; it has also been disputed that we can feel actual emotions as a result of our imaginings. I believe that both are possible. Let me begin by addressing an argument against the possibility of having experientially imagined emotional responses to what one imagines. Some kinds of psychological state have counterparts in imagination with which they share, more or less, the same character (Budd 1989: 100–24). For example, the counterpart of believing is belief-like imagining or supposing, and the counterpart of seeing is visualizing or imagining seeing. Some other kinds of state do not have imaginative counterparts. Being drunk is an example. If you try experientially to imagine being drunk, perhaps the best you can do is to imagine *that* you are drunk, and then engage in a kind of pretence in imagination, imagining behaving as if you are drunk.

Gregory Currie and Ian Ravenscroft (2002: 159) have argued that emotion has no imaginative counterpart, and that, uniquely, imagination is what they call 'transparent' to emotion. This is what they say:

emotions are peculiar states in that they are, so to speak, their own counterparts. In imagination we do not take on another's belief or desire; we take on a belief-like or a desire-like imagining that corresponds to those beliefs and desires. But when I put myself imaginatively in the position of someone being threatened, it is genuine fear I come to experience, not an imagination-based substitute for fear.

In this respect, Currie and Ravenscroft say, this unique transparency of emotion distinguishes it from, for example, pain: if I imagine feeling pain, I do not as a result actually feel pain. They suggest that this capacity, to have real emotions in response to imagined situations, evolved partly because of its role in planning: they say (2002: 197), 'Having a system of emotional responses poised to respond to what I imagine is a capacity we would expect to find in creatures able to choose between alternatives.'

There is a lot I agree with here, as can be seen from what I have said so far. In particular, I agree that the role of real emotion in planning is important. Moreover, I welcome the thought that these emotions are not to be dismissed as what Currie used to call quasi-emotions; rather, they are real emotions that are directed towards what is imagined.

What I disagree with is the claim that, as Currie and Ravenscroft put it, emotion has no imaginative counterpart. For it does seems possible, taking their example, for me to imagine something threatening, and to imagine feeling afraid of the threatening thing that I imagine, where the experientially imagined fear is part of the content of what I imagine, and not an external response to what I imagine.[2] It is just here that I agree with Richard Wollheim. He says the following about sexual arousal, making it clear that he believes that the same remarks apply to the emotions:

> I shall use the familiar phenomenon of the erotic daydream . . . Let us suppose that I centrally imagine myself [that is, that I experientially imagine myself, from the inside] engaged in some sexual activity with a strange figure, or a close friend. As I do so, I centrally imagine myself becoming excited over what occurs between us . . . . And as I centrally imagine myself becoming excited, so I become excited.   (Wollheim 1984: 81–2)

So Wollheim holds both that we can have real feelings of arousal as a result of what we imagine, and that we can have experientially imagined feelings of arousal. And I agree that the same holds for emotion.

Why might one reject the possibility that emotions can have imaginative counterparts? One reason might be grounded in a misconception of what a real life emotional experience is, and thus of what its imaginative counterpart might be like. A real life emotional experience such as grief, as I argued in Chapter 3, is a process, one that involves perceptions, thoughts, and feelings (typically directed towards the object of the emotion), and much else besides. So, if an emotional experience were to have an imaginative counterpart, then we would expect it to involve *imagined* perceptions, thoughts, and feelings, typically directed towards the *imagined* object. And this, I believe, is precisely the correct picture. If you experientially imagine, centrally or from the inside, being woken up in the

---

[2] See Moran (1994). Currie and Ravenscroft (2002: 96) say that the real emotion can 'occur within the scope of an imaginative project'. However, this is a rather misleading way of putting it, for the emotion—the real fear for example—is not part of the *content* of what is imagined.

middle of the night by a gang of burglars breaking down your front door with axes, your imagining this—your imagined perceptions, thoughts, and feelings with the right emotionally laden content—just *is* your imagined fearful experience. Imagining being afraid is not something over and above the imagined fearful experience; rather, imagining being afraid just is imagining having a fearful experience, and imagining having a fearful experience just is undergoing the process of having imagined perceptions, thoughts, and feelings, typically directed towards the imagined fearsome object. Currie and Ravenscroft (2002: 96), whilst rightly admitting these kinds of imaginings, wrongly deny that they constitute the imagined emotional experience, and thus wrongly claim that emotion is unique in not having a counterpart in imagination.

There is a further reason for accepting that emotions have imaginative counterparts, that will also be important in what follows. In thinking through branching possibilities as part of deciding what to do, it is often necessary that an imagined emotional experience features in imagined practical reasoning, and thus in imagined action. In other words, it is necessary for you as protagonist in the imagined story to have an emotion. So, if I were to ask you experientially to imagine what you would decide to do, and what you would do, if you saw and heard those burglars breaking down your front door, you need to imagine being afraid, and then, because of this fear, deciding to call the police rather than go downstairs to investigate. Currie and Ravenscroft rightly emphasize the role of emotional response in planning, but surely in such cases the emotion has to be part of the content of what is imagined, logically and temporally prior to the imagined decision and the imagined action, for it to be able to play this role. What they call the 'generated' real life emotion (p. 96) cannot play this role. One can put the point another way, in terms of the internal coherence and meaningfulness of the narrative, of making sense of your thoughts and actions as protagonist in the narrative. If you imagined a story in which you hear burglars downstairs, and decide not to go and investigate but rather to call the police, the narrative would lack coherence and meaningfulness unless, as part of its content, you had made your decision out of fear.

As with memory, internal and external emotion can come apart. Just as our memories can involve emotions that are internal to the memory and emotions that are external to the memory, so we can have internal and external emotions to what we imagine. For example, just as I can remember shamefully making a fool of myself at the party, although at the time I thought what I was doing was highly amusing, so I can imagine shamefully making a fool of myself, although in my imagination I think that what I am doing is amusing. So here again we have structural similarities between imagination and memory.

There is one more structural similarity remaining for me to consider, and that is the role of free indirect style in narrative thinking about our future. In Chapter 2, we saw that the diverse ways in which we remember our past, integrated in our autobiographical memories, are ineluctably ironic, and that the way in which these memories are thought through in the psychological correlate of free indirect style simultaneously closes the ironic gap and draws attention to its distance. How does this work when we imagine how things might be in the future? An example of Richard Wollheim's (1984: 92) might help: 'A woman who lives in the North writes to me that, when she expects friends to arrive for a visit, she finds herself imagining their crashing in hideous ways on the motorway that passes near where she lives.'

Wollheim's purpose in this example is to show that this woman, by imagining this, does not reveal that she desires that her friends crash, but rather than she dreads it. He continues:

She will imagine the crashes occurring, but now she will imagine them as fearful. She again will represent to herself her friends involved in those hideous pile-ups, again she will do so acentrally, but the internal audience, still the sympathetic audience, will look upon the events with disfavour, and she will tend, as a result of what she has imagined, to end up appalled and terrified.   (p. 93)

The way she 'ends up' is what Wollheim calls the 'residual condition', the real emotion in which one finds oneself after imagining something or other (recall here the earlier example of Wollheim's, of imagining a sexual encounter). But let us focus on the way she imagines the events: she imagines them, Wollheim tells us, 'as fearful'. Now let us change the example slightly to make the imagining autobiographical: let us say that a man imagines himself driving home late at night, after slightly too many drinks. Then he imagines himself blissfully falling asleep at the wheel, as a result of which he crashes into a shop window in the high street. Like the woman, the man imagines what happens as fearful, even though, being blissfully asleep, he does not feel fear as part of the content of what he imagines. Putting it in my terms rather than those of Wollheim, my external perspective on what I imagine is integrated in free indirect style into the way I imagine what happens: I do not simply imagine it as being blissful, and respond to it externally as being fearful. In this respect, then, this example of imagining is structurally similar to my example from Chapter 2, of the child remembering his father's actions in the garden that afternoon when the start of war was being announced on the radio: his memories were infected by the feeling of foreboding and anxiety that now accompanies those events, but that, as a child of six and a half, he did not appreciate at the time.

As Kendall Walton (1997) has argued, we can find out things about ourselves from our imaginings; they 'often reflect actual attitudes, desires, values, prejudices and so forth, and are thus subject to esteem and repudiation'. His example is imagining torturing kittens. Let us assume that I try to imagine doing it with gleeful amusement. But as I try to imagine it in this way, I find myself reacting with horror and shame, and these emotions that I feel, from an external perspective to what I imagine, infect the content of what I imagine, through the psychological equivalent of free indirect style. This is, again, structurally equivalent to my remembering my making a fool of myself at that party, standing up on the table and singing that stupid song; in my sober, reflective moments I am no gleeful kitten-torturer, no boastful stander-up-on-tables.

Regret, and Learning from our Mistakes

With the idea in place of imagined and real emotions in narrative thinking about branching possibilities, let me now turn to the role of emotion in planning, and how we can learn from our mistakes. Some of this discussion might seem unduly complex, but in fact it captures what is really a very commonplace and natural way of thinking about our lives. I will begin with hypothetical imperatives. These are imperatives that tell you what you ought to do in order to achieve some stated goal; as Kant (1964: 39) puts it, they 'declare a possible action to be practically necessary as a means to the attainment of something else that one wills (or that one may will)'. Consider, for example, the hypothetical imperative 'if you want to catch the train that departs at 4 p.m., then you must leave the house by 11 a.m.' This has no relevance to you if you do not want to catch that train, but if you do want to, then the means (leaving the house now) are practically necessary for the 'attainment of what one wills' (the end or goal of catching that train).

One morning, the morning when you plan to catch that train, it is shortly before 11 a.m., which is the time you know you ought to leave the house (you know this because you accept the truth of the hypothetical imperative). But, on the spur of the moment, perhaps out of nervousness, you decide to check your emails. Because of this, you finally leave the house some considerable time after 11 a.m. When you get to the station, the train has left, in spite of some frantic rushing on the way. As a result, you experience unpleasant emotions: the panicky feeling involved in rushing for the train; and the feeling of frustration once you find out that it has left.

These negative emotions do not yet include regret. For regret, it is necessary that you engage in counterfactual thinking, thinking back to the crucial moment when you decided to check your emails, and the regret is the external emotional response to what happened—to that decision which you now conceive as regrettable. 'If *only* I hadn't checked my emails!' you say to yourself; 'How *stupid* of me to decide to do that!' It is the negative emotions that generate the counterfactual narrative thinking, the return in thought to the crucial moment, and thus to the if-only regret. There is evidence that most counterfactual thinking—something like 90 per cent—is generated spontaneously by negative emotions felt towards bad outcomes (Roese 1991); after all, why engage in counterfactual thinking if things turn out all right—if you manage to catch the train in spite of having checked your emails? Thus it is not the regret that generates the counterfactual narrative thinking, but the counterfactual thinking, typically generated by negative emotions, that in turn generates the regret.

Recalling the discussion of Chapter 1, we can see that having checked your emails in those circumstances, which in turn caused the late departure from the house, was an *INUS* condition for missing the train: it was an insufficient but necessary part of an unnecessary but sufficient condition for missing the train—necessary because if you had not checked your emails, then the rest of conditions would not have been sufficient for your missing the train. That's why one naturally says that your having checked your emails caused you to miss the train, and that's why, in narrative thinking about the counterfactual as a branching possibility, the natural point of focus for the regret in the narrative, the node, is the point at which you decided to check your emails, just before the time you should have left the house. You are looking back on what happened, imagining the branching possibility as a counterfactual, where that node, that moment of choice, turned out to be crucial. And this is why, looking back on it, you express your regret through self-criticism: 'How stupid of me!'

This is dramatic irony, where you now, looking back on that moment of choice, know what you did not know then—that deciding to check your emails would cause you to miss your train—and the regret that you now feel is from the perspective of 'external narrator', having emotions external to the narrative that are directed towards yourself and your decisions and actions internal to the narrative, although, with the psychological correlate of free indirect style at work, your decisions and actions will be remembered as stupid and regrettable.

Negative emotions, counterfactual narrative thinking, and regrets can have a feedback effect on one's grasp of the related hypothetical imperatives, helping one to learn from one's mistakes. In order to explain this, it is necessary to give a rough outline of the notion of narrative time as I want to use it here. Narrative time (which is to be contrasted with subjective, phenomenal time, or what is sometimes called time-consciousness) is the time *internal* to the narrative. But in addition to narrative time internal to the narrative, there is also our *external* engagement with the narrative, which itself takes place in time.[3] So a narrative of event C that took place in a narrative prior to event E can be conceived as a narrative of what is past, or of what is future.[4] Assume that C is the falling of the rocks, and E is the blocking of the road caused by the falling of the rocks, then in narrative time C is prior to E. But this narrative time is itself neutral as to whether the narrated episode is past or future. You might be about to drive over the mountain pass and you are concerned that a rock fall might block the road before you get there. Or, alternatively, you are concerned that the rock fall might already have happened. In conceiving the narrative of the episode, you can think of it with concern, and feel concerned about it, either as having already happened or as a future possibility; but in either

---

[3] Shaun Gallagher and Dan Zahavi (2008) point out that narrative time is to be compared with McTaggart's B series, whereas our external engagement with narrative time is to be compared with the A series (McTaggart 1908).

[4] It might also be conceived as fictional or as taking place in the specious present, but I will not consider these alternatives here because they are not relevant to what I want to say.

case, the narrative itself and the narrative time will be the same—the falling of the rocks causing the blockage of the road.

Earlier in this chapter, I discussed various structural similarities between memory and imagination. Here is another: whether a sequence of events is remembered or imagined in narrative thinking, the narrative and the narrative time will be the same. Thus, returning to our earlier example, you can think through a narrative of yourself in which you want to catch the train at 4 p.m.; you aim to leave the house on time at 11 a.m., but you decide to check your emails and then arrive at the station after 4 p.m., only to find that the train has already left, and as a result you experience unpleasant emotions and then regret. This narrative can be conceived as past or as future; in either case the internal narrative time will be the same, but the external perspective on it will differ, depending on whether the narrative is remembered in the past or imagined as a future possibility.

With this in mind, we can grasp how counterfactual narrative thinking can feed back into narrative thinking about hypothetical impera-tives, and, as we will now see, into planning more generally. When you conceive of the episode as past, as we have been discussing, you look back on what happened, and at that crucial moment of deciding to check your emails, with regret. As a result, you formulate in your mind a narrative according to which you leave on time, as you ought to, and successfully catch the train; and this narrative thinking might turn into a plan to do just that, with, in the background, a hypothetical imperative that has been shaped by past experience, and is more vivid as a result of it.

Based on this hypothetical imperative, you might then decide to operate on something like a general policy or maxim of action, to be punctual: 'I shall leave on time for appointments and meetings and theatres and trains and boats and planes, and avoid last-minute displacement activity such as checking my emails. Otherwise I will be late in arriving, which would be annoying, and which I would later regret.'[5] This policy or maxim of punctuality gains its vivacity from remembering narratives in which you did what you ought not to have done—and got into trouble as a result.

---

[5] Sue Campbell (2008) emphasizes the forward-looking role of memory; our capacity to remember is integral to our capacity to think about and plan for the future.

Planning, Policies, and Character

In making plans and adopting policies or maxims, and in forming intentions, we are constrained by a range of contingent factors about ourselves, such as our own character and personality traits, emotional dispositions, and abilities. We are also constrained by our own past experiences and what we have learned from them, and it is partly this that I have been discussing in considering how counterfactual thinking and regrets can feed into hypothetical imperatives, maxims, plans, and policies for the future.[6]

As someone develops their character and personality traits and other dispositions over time, certain plans and policies that might once have been seen as realistic and worth considering come to be excluded from deliberation to the extent that they no longer even feature in one's thinking as 'live options'. Ultimately this kind of 'automatic' exclusion of certain possible courses of action can become part of the pattern of dispositions that comprises an embedded character or personality trait: the considerate person wouldn't *dream* of leaving someone in the lurch just because a better opportunity comes up; it simply wouldn't *occur* to the honest person to accept a bribe; the punctual person just wouldn't *think* of dawdling in a way which would make him miss his train or be late for his rendezvous.

Coming to develop one's personality and character through what can roughly be described as 'training' is a complex matter involving a wide variety of techniques, but what I want to concentrate on here are just two ways in which such dispositions can be trained. The first is backward-looking in time, and is really only an extension of what I have just been discussing. The second is forward-looking. These two ways of training can merge into each other, but for purposes of exposition it is helpful to keep them apart. I will begin with training in a skill.

In backward-looking training, the learner goes back over the narrative of a particular situation where the deployment of the skill was called for. This could be done either by the learner alone in his mind, or by the learner in joint discussion with the teacher. And then, at the crucial moment in the recollected narrative when the skill was called for, the

---

[6] We are also, of course, constrained by external circumstances ('events' as the politicians like to say, are the only things that you cannot plan for), and by other people and their plans, policies, and intentions.

learner 'stops the clock', and considers what he might have done instead of what he actually did. For example, you are a beginner at chess. You have just lost a game, and your teacher then resets the board as it was at that crucial moment several moves earlier. She then turns to ask you to reconsider what you then did and what were the alternatives open to you that you excluded at the time of deliberation, or that you failed to notice as possibilities. She thus shows you both the point in time—the node—at which you went wrong in your deliberation and choice, and also what you could have done to avoid going wrong. A football or tennis coach might do the same sort of thing, getting the learner to think back and analyse where things went wrong at the crucial moment. This can be done with the aid of technology, using a video replay, or just by thinking through or *envisaging* the narrative sequence of events as they unfolded.

This is really just the familiar idea of learning by one's mistakes. But we do not need to make mistakes to learn. The idea of 'stopping the clock' has a second aspect, which does not involve going back over what happened but involves setting up hypothetical forward-looking narratives that have to be thought through. The same procedure applies though, in that the learner is asked to consider the various alternative ways in which he might act, starting at the crucial moment, thinking through the various and varying effects of each alternative course of action. Chess puzzles have this feature, as do flight simulators. The advantage of this method of stopping the clock is that you do not have to lose an actual game of chess, or really crash a plane, in order to learn.[7]

What happens in both such exercises is that the learner is trained first to spot the way things are and to evaluate the facts of the situation at the crucial moment, and secondly to envisage the range of possible alternative actions that are 'live options', such as defensive moves that the chess player ought to make to avoid defeat. Each option represents a narrative sequence, and together the options take the shape of a 'tree' of possibilities, each one branching out from the crucial moment, with each node representing a point at which the narrative could take a different course.

Now, as training progresses and the skill develops, the learner improves in a number of ways: options come to be envisaged as they should be; each

<hr />

[7] Bratman (1999: 86) makes a related point in his discussion of temptation and regrets: 'anticipation of future regret or nonregret can be relevant to the stability of a prior intention of a planning agent'.

option can be more readily envisaged; each envisaged option can be more quickly evaluated for possible action; and the range of options that are 'live' options for evaluation will be narrowed down (but not more than it should be). Ultimately, the chess player will reach a level of skill such that only one possible course of action is salient—there is only one live option. At this point she will be able (immediately and non-inferentially) to see that her queen is threatened, and to see precisely what is the right move to make. Thus what is for a beginner at chess an agonizing and very fallible process of conscious inference towards deciding what is the right move becomes a faster process involving less and less inferential thought until finally the process becomes for the expert phenomenologically immediate, with no conscious inference.

Learning to See and to Feel

Character—including those traits of character that are virtues—can, in its essentials, be taught and learned like this. But there is a significant and crucial difference. (More differences will emerge shortly.) In respect of virtue the learner is at the same time trained to have appropriate *emotional* responses. In other words, the disposition reliably to respond differentially concerns not just the disposition to perceive or otherwise recognize the evaluative facts and what action is called for. For virtues also involve emotional dispositions—dispositions to have the right emotions over a complex range of situations and actions, both actual and non-actual. For example, the virtue of kindness involves the disposition to feel compassion or sympathy, and this disposition itself involves the ability to perceive what is salient when someone is in distress and needs help.

With that crucial difference in mind, we can now consider how virtue can be learned through narrative thinking. First let us consider learning from one's mistakes through backward-looking counterfactual thinking. You once upset someone needlessly, and you now feel bad about having done what you did. Perhaps in conversation with a friend, or perhaps on your own, you think through the narrative of what happened, and you now recognize that it really was needlessly mean-spirited. You feel guilt or shame, which you did not feel at the time, and you now regret what you did. You then go on to think through the branching alternative possibilities of the other things that you might have done instead, and you have

emotional responses appropriate to each envisaged action and its consequences.

Just as with skill, as learning progresses each option can be more readily
envisaged and evaluated as it should be, and the range of live options will
get smaller. But narratives have a more explicit and prominent role in
learning a virtue than they do in learning a skill. I have in mind fictional
narratives—not only novels but also the kinds of narrative that constitute a
deeply embedded part of a culture, such as fairly tales, myths, fables,
legends, and so on. When we engage with these, starting from a very
early age, we not only grasp the narrative, but we also often envisage
alternative narratives—branching possibilities—of how events might unfold. Moreover, sometimes the narrative itself relates the deliberation of
one or more of the characters as to what to do in the situation that presents
itself to them. Through gaining insight into the mistakes—and the right
actions—of fictional characters, and through responding emotionally as
audience to what happens to the characters in the narrative, we come also
to have the appropriate external emotional responses, seeing branching
possibilities opening up—or closing down—as the narrative moves forward in narrated time. Of course, to learn from how bad people do wrong,
or from how good people get led astray, it is not necessary that, in the
narrative, they get their come-uppance—whatever the Hays Code might
have said.

Two points should be made here about the role of backward- and
forward-looking narrative thinking in planning and decision-making.
First, as the foregoing remarks imply, the emotional response need not
always be to what you envisage yourself doing; it might be an emotional
response to what a fictional character does, or to what you envisage
someone else in real life doing, or to what happens to someone in real
life. For example, you might feel terror at imagining what might happen
to someone you love who is considering driving home from the party after
having had too much to drink. As a result of your emotional response to
what you imagine you might advise her not to take the car, or offer to give
her a lift.

The second point, as we saw earlier, is that the emotional response
could be an *imagined* response rather than, or perhaps in addition to, an
actual emotional response; in other words, the emotional response could
be part of the content of what you imagine. For example, you might
envisage the possibility of looking in someone's private diary while she is

out of the room, and then imagine the shame that you would feel if you were seen; and you might also then come actually to feel shame at what you imagine—shame at imagining being seen.

As one's learning progresses, certain options, perhaps whilst briefly considered, are not fully thought through. Perhaps without even feeling or imagining feeling a negative emotion, one shrinks from an action 'as an impossibility', to use J. S. Mill's nice expression. And then, ultimately, at least in the more clear-cut situations, alternative courses of action are no longer considered; one just *sees* the thing to do. If later you are asked why you did not look in her diary when the opportunity presented itself, you might say 'Because I would have felt so ashamed if I had done that—it would have been terribly prying. It didn't even occur to me.' 'Shame', as Myles Burnyeat (1980) put is, 'is the semi-virtue of the learner.'[8]

Let me now relate this discussion of backward- and forward-looking narrative thinking to Michael Bratman's very thoughtful and influential discussion of planning and agency. Bratman (2000: 35) identifies three 'core features' of human agency: 'our reflectiveness; our planfulness; and our conception of our agency as temporally extended'. He distinguishes between what he calls *weak* reflectiveness, which is the capacity to have higher-order attitudes concerning our lower-order desires, and *strong* reflectiveness, which is the capacity to 'take a stand as an agent— to determine where *I* stand with respect to a given first-order desire' (p. 38). To help explain this core feature of reflectiveness, Bratman turns to the other two: to our capacity to make plans, which he says is, unlike ordinary desires, 'subject to distinctive rational norms of consistency, coherence, and stability' (p. 42); and to our capacity to 'see my action at the same time as the action of the same agent as he who has acted in the past and (it is to be hoped) will act in the future' (p. 43). Our plans and policies, he says, 'have as their function the support of cross-temporal organization and coordination of action' (p. 47). *Higher-order* policies, those directed towards our plans and (lower-order) policies, are what Bratman calls *self-governing* policies; these are 'attitudes whose roles are

---

[8] Note, however, that this appeal to the feeling of shame is not a justification for the belief that the action would have been prying—in spite of the 'because'. Rather, both feeling and belief are justified by further reasons, such as, perhaps, the fact that the action would have been demeaning to both parties.

appropriately connected to the temporally extended structure of our agency' (p. 48).[9]

Relating Bratman's ideas to my ideas of the role in our psychology of character and personality traits, and of more local, focused emotional dispositions, we can detect a certain tension, which is revealed in the remarks that I made a couple of paragraphs ago: the idea that if one has a certain character or personality trait, or a certain emotional disposition, then a mark of having such a disposition is that certain thoughts or certain kinds of action just do not occur to one. To bring the tension out a bit more, let us examine the examples that Bratman (pp. 47–8) gives of self-governing policies:

One might have, say, a policy of developing and supporting a strong concern with honesty in writing, or of trying to be more willing to be playful or less inclined to be impatient with others, or of trying not to be so attracted to chocolates or other temptations, or of never acting on or treating as providing a legitimate consideration in one's deliberation a desire for revenge, or a desire to demean.

Let us assume that these are all self-governing policies that the person is satisfied with through strong reflective endorsement. Now, what is noticeable about all Bratman's examples of self-governing, higher-order policies is that they are connected with character or personality traits, and in particular: honesty; playfulness; patience; temperance; forgivingness; modesty (or something like it). They are all, in effect, higher-order policies to manifest these character or personality traits in thought, feeling, and action, and to avoid temptation to go against them in some way.

What is immediately clear is that, if someone's character or personality trait were fully embedded in his psychology, that person would have no need consciously to deploy these higher-order policies in his thinking. For example, the honest person would have no need of the higher-order policy to be honest in his writing, given that such dishonesty would never even enter his mind, and if it was suggested to him as a course of action by someone else, he would shrink from it as an impossibility. In other words, these are the kinds of policies that one might expect to find in someone who reflectively endorsed a trait that is less than fully embedded in his psychology, and who therefore has need of strength of will to enable

---

[9] Appropriateness in a necessary feature here because Bratman accepts that it is possible to have higher-order policies that one is 'estranged' from, so he appeals to the idea that one can be *satisfied with* a self-governing policy through strong reflective endorsement.

him to, so to speak, *deliver* on his traits at the right time, in the right way, towards the right people, with the right feelings, and so on.[10] For example, I would strongly endorse my trying to be less inclined to be impatient with others if I strongly endorse patience (which, so people tell me, is a virtue), *and* if I also find myself occasionally being, or being tempted to be, impatient with others. Or I would strongly endorse my eschewing a desire for revenge because I endorse forgivingness *and* because I find myself occasionally tempted to the sweet-tasting vengeful thought, feeling, or deed.

Let us bring this discussion back to narrative thinking about our past and our future. Assume that you are generally a patient sort of person, although you have not given it any particular thought on particular occasions, and certainly have not made any higher-order policies in relation to it. Now, on a certain occasion you behave impatiently towards someone, and she is very upset by what you have said and done. This upsets you too, for you are sympathetic to her feelings, and as a result you engage in the kind of if-only counterfactual narrative thinking I have been discussing, thinking back over what you did, and regretting that moment when you became impatient and let it show; you might now even be ashamed of what you did and said. You have, so to speak, caught yourself out deviating from the path of virtue. You go on to think how easy it would have been to have bitten your tongue, and you think through the narrative of this branching possibility. It is, I would suggest, at just such a point that you would naturally come to form a self-governing policy, one of 'trying to be less inclined to be impatient with others', and you would (or at least you ought to) then come to make plans and form hypothetical imperatives and intentions accordingly. This self-governing policy is needed at just this point in your life, you now realize, in order to keep you on the straight and narrow. We might then add to Myles Burnyeat's nice remark that shame is the 'semi-virtue' of the learner: so too is regret, and the determination for strength of will that is expressed in one's self-governing policies.

The tension here is not very deep, for it is perfectly possible for Bratman to allow that the virtuous person is someone who would, *if* he considered it, strongly endorse these policies if it turned out to be necessary for him to adopt them—if, for example, he were to find that he had deviated a little

---

[10] Holton (2009) has a helpful discussion of this kind of strength of will.

from the path of true virtue. And the fact remains that reflectiveness is a 'capacity' that we humans possess, so we could say that in a fully virtuous person the capacity for strong reflective endorsement of higher-order policies exists, but is not (and need not be) exercised.[11] Nevertheless, the tension does bring out two important points about deliberation. The first point is that people can, and often do, lead unreflective lives, being playful, patient, temperate, forgiving, modest, and so on, without giving any reflective thought to their policies. Consider Bratman's (2000: 41) example of a policy that is *lower*-order, the commitment 'to buckling up one's seat belt when one drives': there is no need to reflect on this policy, or to think through the narrative of what might happen if one didn't fasten one's seat belt, for the temptation not to simply does not arise. My idea is that higher-order policies can, in those with a fully embedded character or personality trait, be unreflective in one's psychology in just the same kind of way; one doesn't think about being patient (or not patient) any more than one thinks about fastening one's seat belt (or not fastening it). One just *does* it. So, the first point is that one does not typically form desires or intentions to act other than in line with one's disposition; in other words, deviation from virtuous thought and action does not present itself to one as a live option.[12]

The second point is that one's dispositions—honesty, patience, modesty, and so on—do not feature in one's deliberations either: they merely serve as background, in the light of which one forms desires, intentions, and so on. The direction of gaze in deliberation is typically outwards, towards the world, and not inwards, towards one's psychological dispositions, just as it is not towards one's occurrent thoughts and feelings. Even

---

[11] In Goldie (2000: 158), I introduced the notion of a *self-monitoring disposition* as part of a character trait—a disposition to 'monitor her own responses as being in line with how, according to the trait, she thinks she ought to respond'. And in Goldie (2004: chs. 3 and 4), I discussed the idea of *fragility of character*, and of being *circumspect* in forward planning, in the *OED* sense of a disposition to 'attend to circumstances that may affect an action or decision; caution, care, heedfulness, circumspectness'. Although not expressed in the same terms, and although placing greater emphasis on the dispositional side of self-monitoring, I think these ideas are quite congenial to Bratman's idea of a self-governing policy.

[12] It is important to distinguish the person who is unreflective about his character in a way that Aristotle would associate with a *natural* virtue (which he considered to be less than full virtue), and the person who is unreflective in the way that I intend here; he meets the conditions that Aristotle set down for virtuous action (e.g. he knows what he is doing, and he is doing it for the right reasons), but he is not consciously reflective in the way that Bratman is discussing.

when we are thinking about what is best to do in the circumstances, thinking through the branching possibilities and responding to each of them as we find appropriate (doing such-and-such would be shameful; doing so-and-so would be inconsiderate), still the direction of gaze is outwards. Though we are reflective creatures, it is only seldom that our gaze turns reflectively inwards towards our own psychology.[13]

Conclusion

The structural similarities between our narrative thinking about our past and about our future are really not surprising, although it is not remarked enough how these similarities manifest themselves in the way we remember the past and imagine the future.[14] All this narrative thinking is done, of course, from the present: the external narrator's perspective is always that of me-now, thinking about me-then in the past or me-then in the future. Thinking about oneself in these ways is part of what it is to have a narrative sense of self, and this narrative sense of self will be the central topic of Chapter 6.

But first, in Chapter 5, I will consider the idea of self-forgiveness, as a case study of how our thinking about our past and our future come together. This is one place where the direction of gaze does typically turn inwards, and it is this, in part, that makes the process one of particular psychological turmoil.

---

[13] See e.g. Blackburn (2001); Brewer (2002).
[14] Richard Wollheim (1984) is an exception of course, as we have seen throughout this chapter.

5

Self-forgiveness: A Case Study

Introduction: The Paradoxical Appearance of Self-forgiveness

The idea of self-forgiveness seems to many people to be a deeply paradoxical notion, as if just by a self-addressed fiat—'Ego me absolvo a peccatis meis'—I can cleanse myself of my past wrongdoings. Forgiveness is surely essentially third-personal and second-personal, concerned essentially with forgiveness of others, not of oneself, and not so easily won.

I want to defend the idea of self-forgiveness, at the heart of which is the narrative sense of self, the sense of oneself as having a past and a future for which one can be, in various ways, responsible. When properly understood, self-forgiveness is, I will argue, a perfectly coherent and psychologically sound notion. It is something that we are all likely to need from time to time in leading a life which is less than perfect, during the course of which, for reasons perhaps not fully in our control, we can do serious harm to others. And it is not so easily won.

Any reasonable account of self-forgiveness needs to start from what is no doubt the paradigm of forgiveness, forgiveness of others. Starting from there, I will argue that self-forgiveness does not obviously, at the first hurdle, fall short of the paradigm of forgiveness thus understood. I will then consider why, and in what circumstances, we need self-forgiveness. Sometimes no doubt we need it when forgiveness from others is not possible for one reason or another. But these are not the only kinds of case. Also, I will argue, there can be moral considerations that outweigh the reasons for seeking forgiveness from the offended person or from any other person, and here self-forgiveness becomes especially important, not only in the life of the person directly concerned, but also in the lives of his or her loved ones, amongst whom, quite possibly, are the injured party or parties. I will then be in a position to put forward a substantial set of norms for self-forgiveness, with the narrative sense of self at its heart. Finally, I will consider an example from Mozart's *Così fan tutte* where pardon from others rather than forgiveness is appropriate, and yet self-forgiveness remains both possible and important when one has tried to resist temptation and failed.

Forgiveness of Others

It is controversial just what the necessary conditions are for forgiveness of others, and here I will assume that the account given by Charles Griswold in his excellent book on forgiveness (Griswold 2007) is the correct one. Although this makes my task easier in one respect, in that I will only be considering one account, it will make it more difficult in another, for Griswold's account of forgiveness is, as we will see, not particularly congenial to the idea of self-forgiveness. So here, in brief, are the conditions for what Griswold thinks of as paradigmatic forgiveness.[1]

The offence

First, there has to be an offence against another. We have done something that has morally wronged another person or persons, and we consider ourselves responsible for what we did. That is to say, we chose to do it, we did it, and we did it for a reason. Importantly, this implies that we have an explanation of why we did what we did. This explanation must not be an excusing one, such as 'The goddess Athene caused the mist to come over my eyes'; or 'It wasn't my fault, I was badly brought up'; or 'I am no different from anyone else; anyone would have done the same in my circumstances'. It must be an account in which we accept that it was our action: we must 'own up to it', precisely in the sense of taking ownership of it.

---

[1] Griswold (2007: 113) thinks that self-forgiveness is possible, but that it falls short of forgiveness in its paradigmatic form. Some, of whom Hannah Arendt is one, think that self-forgiveness is incoherent (Arendt 1958: 243, cited by Griswold (2007: 122)). For other accounts of self-forgiveness see e.g. Snow (1993); Mills (1995); Holmgren (1998); Dillon (2001); Hagberg (2011).

Reactive emotions

The offended person must experience a range of negative reactive emotions to the offence, amongst which the emotions of resentment and anger are the most obvious. These reactive emotions have a natural expression in bodily movement; in facial expression; in verbal expression; and in desire and action, in particular the desire for revenge.

Narrative accounting

We, the offender, have a narrative account of what we did, and why, making ourselves intelligible in a way that 'puts the wrong-doing as well as the self that did the wrong in a context' (p. 51).

Contrition

We, the offender, repudiate what we did: we acknowledge its wrongness; we understand the damage we have done to others; we regret it; and we sincerely avow that we will not do it again.

Commitment for change

It is not enough, though, to have a narrative account, to be contrite, to feel regret at the offence we have caused, and to avow not to do it again. We must also follow up on our avowal by committing to change ourselves for the better, and then we must take serious steps to live up to our commitment.

As we will see, these conditions of Griswold's for forgiveness that the offender has to meet fit very well with my discussion in Chapter 4 of how we can come to regret our past actions, learn from our mistakes, and come to form maxims and self-governing policies in order to keep ourselves on the straight and narrow in the future. All this is bound up in our narrative sense of self, thinking of ourselves as having a narratable past and future with which we, as external narrators, can engage.

Once these conditions for forgiveness have been met, we, the offender, can then ask the offended person for forgiveness. The offended person, forswearing revenge and resentment, finally comes to see us, and himself, in a new light, 'recognizing . . . the shared humanity of both parties' (p. 51). The offended person thus puts to one side his reactive emotions which were directed towards those very actions that I regret and repudiate, and he understands that I see myself as a new person.

The Relation between Forgiveness of Others and Self-forgiveness

These, then, are the necessary conditions for at least the central cases of forgiveness of others. Is self-forgiveness a kind of forgiveness, so that it too can satisfy these conditions? (Self-forgiveness might not be the paradigm of forgiveness, but it does not follow from this that it cannot meet the conditions for forgiveness. Penguins really are birds even if they are not paradigmatic birds.)

To begin with, we must ask whether there need be more than one party for forgiveness to be possible. One thought here is that the person offending and the person offended might be one and the same, so that one could forgive oneself for an offence against oneself. This is indeed possible. For example, it might be possible to forgive oneself for having made a massively foolish financial investment, as a result of which you alone were the one to suffer. However, I am interested here in those cases of self-forgiveness where one is aiming at forgiving oneself for a wrong done to another person or persons. So another person is involved in this sense in this kind of self-forgiveness. And yet Griswold and others seem to think that this still falls short of forgiveness proper, as found in the forgiveness of others. Why might this be?

The first concern seems to be that there is no resentment in self-forgiveness, for resentment is an emotion that one cannot feel towards oneself and one's own actions; as Griswold puts it, in self-forgiveness 'the forgiver cannot easily be said to resent the candidate for forgiveness' (p. xvi, cf. 40). And so, if resentment, and then the forswearing of resentment, is necessary for forgiveness, then self-forgiveness is either impossible or is at least substantially distinct from forgiveness of other people.

However, whilst it is true that resentment of oneself does not make sense, resentment is just one of a group of negative reactive attitudes and emotions, and other attitudes and emotions in the same group can be felt towards oneself. One can, for example, blame or reproach oneself for what one has done (just as one can blame and reproach others). One can be angry with oneself for doing what one did. Moreover, one can also experience other self-directed negative reactive emotions to the kind of person that one thinks one is (to the kind of person that one *must be* to have done such a terrible thing). These include emotions such as shame, and even self-hatred and self-loathing, which might well be expressed in various kinds of self-harm.[2] So all these reactive emotions can be felt towards oneself, just as other reactive emotions in the same group can be felt towards others.

The second concern which might lead people to think that self-forgiveness falls at the first hurdle is that self-forgiveness seems to fail to be a moral relation between two people even when it involves a harm done to another person. As Griswold (p. 48) puts it, it lacks the 'dyadic character of the process [which] permeates it from start to finish'. Related to this is the concern that in self-forgiveness there is not the possibility of a narrative accounting from an appropriate distanced perspective. A version of the difficulty is found in the familiar thought that self-forgiveness is much too easily won (p. 122). Sincere contrition, and a sincere commitment for change, both of which are involved in a narrative accounting, can turn simply into the self-addressed incantation of a few words: 'ego me absolvo a peccatis meis'.

This seems to me to be the central difficulty that an account of self-forgiveness has to address if it is to not to fall short of what forgiveness should be. The solution lies in the narrative sense of self, and in the way in which one can think of oneself as another. Before turning to this, however, we first need to consider why and when we need self-forgiveness.

Why, and in What Circumstances, Do We Need Self-forgiveness?

When we realize that we have done someone a terrible wrong, we can punish ourselves with guilt and shame. We can find ourselves locked into our past, constantly going over and over in our minds what we did, feeling that we can never be redeemed from being the kind of person who could do such a thing. We need to be able to 'move on', to put the past behind us in the appropriate way, and this just seems impossible. There seems to be no way out—we have a thousand possible pasts and no possible future. This can continue even if we have been forgiven by the person we wronged. In such circumstances, which are surely not uncommon, it seems to us that it is the *other's* forgiveness that is too easily won, not our own. It is *ourselves* who must do the forgiving, and yet we continue to

---

[2] Dillon (2001: 58) takes self-reproach 'to characterize the central attitude in the negative stance most generally, recognizing that there is in fact a continuum of stances'.

punish ourselves. It is not only the psychic harmony of ourselves as the offender that is at issue here. Sometimes, perhaps often, we ruin also the lives of those we love and who love us (who might indeed include the ones offended against): it is no easy matter to live with someone who incessantly tortures himself with his past wrongdoing.

In this respect, shame is not unlike grief. And there is another respect in which it is like grief. It is an emotion that one ought to feel—in the one case for the loss of a loved one, in the other case for the wrong that one has done and for who one is—but neither grief at a loss, nor guilt and shame at a wrongdoing, should have hegemony over our thoughts for evermore. We have to be able to get on with our lives, and not end up shamefully hiding from the world for all time, like Lord Jim in Conrad's great novel, condemned after his fateful leap from the *Patna* to be forever on the run— from himself.[3] And yet, of course, neither with grief nor with guilt and shame, should this moving on be too easily won: what we need is to go through a psychological process; one, moreover, of the right kind. This will exclude a lot: psychopharmacology; self-deception; irrational appeal to an imagined forgiver such as an internalized parental figure; drink; joining the Foreign Legion; taking it out on the person we love most; taking it out on the person whom we have offended. So we need to allow ourselves the possibility of self-forgiveness, achieved in the right way and at the right time, in order to be able to get on with our lives, and not to damage the lives of others who are close to us.

When do we need self-forgiveness? Charles Griswold (p. 123) discusses three kinds of case. First, we need it when the offended person is unwilling to forgive us when he ought to. Secondly, we need it when the offended person is unable to forgive us when he ought to, perhaps because he has gone mad, or died. In these two kinds of case, Griswold argues, the forgiveness is obtained vicariously, done 'in the victim's voice', even though it is self-forgiving by the offending person (p. 123). And, thirdly, we need self-forgiveness in those cases where the victim or offended person is willing to forgive us if the necessary conditions are met; once all the norms for the other's forgiveness are in place, then self-forgiveness straight-forwardly follows.[4]

---

[3] For discussion, see Dillon (2001: 64–5) and Goldie (2004).

[4] Griswold (2007: 125–8) is particularly concerned with the role of self-forgiveness with respect to injuries done to oneself; but, as I said earlier, this is not my concern here.

I think that all these kinds of case are possible. But, if one thought that these were the only kinds of case, I can see why one might also think that self-forgiveness falls short of the notion of forgiveness proper. For each of them, in one way or another, seems to be parasitic or dependent on the other's forgiveness.[5] However, there are other kinds of case which are important, and where self-forgiveness has a crucial role of its own, not parasitic or dependent on the other's forgiveness. These are cases where it would be morally wrong to seek forgiveness from the other person. In other words, the 'dyadic character of the process' involving another person is precluded for reasons which are moral. Let me consider some examples.

A week ago, let us imagine, I made a cruel joke about a good friend behind his back, stupidly, doing it only to impress the people I was with— to show them that I was a man of the world. Although my friend has never got to hear of it, there is no doubt that I have committed an offence against him. So, quite appropriately, I feel guilt and shame about what I did. Should I tell him what I said, and then seek his forgiveness? I think there are strong moral reasons not to do this. One could say that it is dishonest to keep my act of disloyalty from him. Perhaps. But, on the other hand, one could say that if my friend did get to hear of it, he would consider it to be a betrayal (reasonably enough, because it was), and that could be the end of our friendship, which is of such value to both of us. So, because of what I said, whatever I do is problematic and I have to make a judgement about what is, all things considered, the right thing to do. I believe that, in these circumstances, the right thing to do might well be not to tell my friend of my disloyalty, and thus not to seek his forgiveness.

Similar examples can be drawn from what are sometimes called 'sins of the heart'—cases where one has a bad thought, perhaps a deeply disloyal adulterous thought, and yet one does not put the thought into action, perhaps for contingent reasons rather than because of a lack of intention. Here again there may be good moral reasons not to own up to one's loving partner, not to confess the disloyal adulterous thought to which the thinker alone has direct access. (A Christian would add that God also has direct access to one's thoughts. In his famous interview with *Playboy* in November 1976, Jimmy Carter said: 'Christ said, "I tell you that anyone

---

[5] e.g. Nancy Snow (1993: 79–80) argues that self-forgiveness is a 'second-best alternative' to forgiveness from others. Jon Mills (1995: 406) rejects this, but still insists that self-forgiveness is conditional on forgiveness from others. See also Holmgren (1998).

who looks on a woman with lust has in his heart already committed adultery." I've looked on a lot of women with lust. I've committed adultery in my heart many times.' Whether or not one accepts the truth of the conclusion, the logic is impeccable.)

In cases of this kind, self-forgiveness is very important, for it can provide the psychological wherewithal for the wrongdoer (or wrongthinker) to go through the same necessary process of contrition and commitment to change that would be involved in asking forgiveness from the one that has been wronged, but without the collateral damage that would arise from the wrong—perhaps the wrongful thought—being confessed to the other. And of course it is also important because it precludes the insidious alternative of simply putting the whole incident behind one, forgetting about it, and just hoping that it will not happen again. That is the worst of all possible worlds.

Another kind of case where forgiveness from the people offended against is precluded for moral reasons can be drawn from Wittgenstein's life.[6] Perhaps the example is not fair to Wittgenstein, and so I will simply hypothesize a person, W, who was involved in the following events. W, a young man, was teaching children in a village abroad. On more than one occasion he lost his patience with his pupils and cruelly mistreated them, often doing lasting physical harm. Once he hit a child particularly hard, causing him to collapse, at which point W immediately left the village, planning never to return. But what he had done remained on W's conscience, and many years later, when the children in the class were now adults with children of their own, he reappeared in the village, and, to their astonishment and horror, asked them for forgiveness for what he had done.

I think that this was an act of extreme selfishness by W. Surely the last thing that those people would have wanted was to be reminded of their childhood suffering under such a hard master. Perhaps it is right that most of us, unlike W, would have put that time of our lives behind us and simply papered it over in wilful forgetting. Contrition and commitment for change of the kind that is involved in forgiveness are indeed important. But what W should have done is to have sought self-forgiveness, accepting that there are strong moral reasons against reopening old wounds by asking forgiveness from the offended parties.

---

[6] I am relying here on Monk (1991: 232–3, 370–2).

A third kind of case where self-forgiveness is especially important is where the pardon of others is more appropriate than their forgiveness. My example here will be from Mozart's *Così fan tutte*, and I will deal with it at the end, after considering the norms of self-forgiveness.

The Norms of Self-forgiveness and the Narrative Sense of Self

We are, as has often been remarked, reflective animals, capable of thinking about, and of seeking to change, our own thoughts, feelings, and dispositions of character and personality. A part of that capacity, as I have been discussing in earlier chapters, is the ability to deploy in thought and feeling a narratable conception of oneself: with a narratable past, which one now remembers, interprets, and evaluates in various ways; with a present; and with a narratable future, concerning which one can make plans and resolutions, have hopes and aspirations, and so on. This conception of oneself is the narrative sense of self. We have seen that, in narrative thinking about oneself and one's past and future, one's stance is essentially ironic: one takes an external perspective on oneself at that past or future time, in effect seeing oneself as another. This opens up the epistemic, evaluative, and emotional ironic gaps that are at the heart of the notion of narrative: an epistemic gap because one now knows what one did not know then; an evaluative gap because one can now take an evaluative stance that differs from the stance that one then took; and an emotional gap because one can now have emotions directed towards one's past that one did not have at the time.

Narrative thinking about one's own past, from this ironic external perspective, is, in this sense, dyadic: it involves *you now* thinking about *you then*. Of course, thinking about your past self in this way does not imply that there are literally two people involved; you now are the *very same* person that you were then, and it is precisely because of this that self-forgiveness is possible. To illustrate this, let us return to my example of the hurtful remarks I made about my friend behind his back.

To begin with, I have autobiographical memories of what I did, of the kind I discussed in Chapter 2. As we saw, this involves taking an evaluative stance on what I did from the external perspective of myself now, as external narrator, seeing myself then as a 'character' internal to the narrative. I now remember what I said then as being boastful, vain, disloyal, and contemptible, whereas at the time I thought of it as sophisticated and amusing. (Note here how naturally my description and my memories—'I did it to show that I was a man of the world; how boastful that was'—captures the ironic evaluative and emotional stance through free indirect style.)

As external narrator, thinking through this part of my life, I am thus immediately in a position to have the appropriate negative reactive emotions towards what I said about my friend—emotions of self-assessment such as shame. These negative emotions of self-assessment, from the external perspective that I now have, then naturally lead, in these circumstances, to contrition. Evaluating what I did as being wrong, I now feel regret. Unlike the regret I felt for missing the train because I decided at the last minute to check my emails, this is moral regret, regret for a moral wrongdoing, and not merely prudential. But, as with the earlier example, my regret returns me in thought to the crucial moment, thinking to myself 'If only I hadn't decided to say that—I really didn't need to.' Again and again, I go back over what happened, unable to get it out of my mind, thinking of all the other things I might, and should, have done, conceiving the episode in terms of branching possibilities. And looking back on it now, I might express my regret through evaluative self-criticism: 'How *vain* of me to have done that!'[7] These self-directed negative reactive emotions have great psychological power—greater than resentment, for they go to work directly on the person who committed the offence; and moreover, of course, greater because they can be directed not only to actions but also, as we saw with Jimmie Carter, to unexpressed thoughts and feelings: one can be ashamed of the adulterous thought; of having wished she were dead; of having felt a secret thrill of pleasure at her failing to win that important contract.

So far, then, we now have in place the first four of Griswold's conditions for forgiveness which can equally well be satisfied by self-forgiveness: the offence; negative reactive emotions to the offence and the offender; narrative accounting; and contrition.

---

[7] Another possibility is that I realized at the time that what I was doing was wrong; but, what the hell, I thought, it would be such a good way to impress the others. In such circumstances, I now ought to see my wrongdoing as even more culpable because I knew at the time just what I was doing.

What about commitment for change? In self-forgiveness, this should be no different in principle from the commitment for change that is involved in seeking forgiveness from others. The discussion in Chapter 4 of the role of narrative thinking about one's future is essential here, especially in the way that counterfactual thinking can feed into planning about the future, and in particular into self-governing policies. When I think back on my stupid, vain, disloyal joke at my friend's expense, feeling regret and having counterfactual thoughts about that moment of choice, at the same time I determine not to do that kind of thing in the future, forming self-governing policies of trying not to get carried away by the moment, to think before I speak, and never to forget where my loyalties really lie. Engaging in narrative thinking of myself in the future, imagining myself acting on the self-governing policies that I have now adopted because of my regrets for what I did in the past, I can now conceive of myself in future episodes, acting as I now know I should. And I now feel, external to the narrative, emotions that express my satisfaction, through strong reflective endorsement, with my self-governing policies. In the long run, my aim is that these policies will become embedded in my character and personality traits, so that the policies no longer need to be conscious, explicit parts of my self-governance. By then my commitment for change will have been fully met.

Now all the conditions for self-forgiveness are in place so that one can forgive oneself for what one did. One may continue to have reactive emotions when one thinks back on or remembers one's past thoughts and deeds, but meeting the conditions of self-forgiveness means that one need no longer have continuing reactive attitudes towards one's continuing self, such as shame, self-contempt, and self-loathing.

Before turning to self-forgiveness and pardon, let me first consider a general concern that is sometimes raised about this whole cluster of reactive attitudes and emotions, including self-directed shame and contempt. These reactive emotions are sometimes criticized in a Kantian spirit on the grounds that it is not the appropriate moral stance to take—towards oneself in the case of shame, or towards another in the case of contempt. Kant's criticism, echoed by others since, is that they are in effect attitudes that are taken from a spectator's standpoint, from that of an observer of moral life rather than from that of a participant. Moreover, it is said, these attitudes involve a 'globalizing' tendency, in which the person as a whole is thought to be vicious, and so excluded as a member of the moral community and denied all moral worth.[8]

There is no doubt that this globalizing attitude is possible, and it is, I think, a particular notable tendency in shame: because shame is self-directed, and because the dear old self is seldom if ever out of one's thoughts, shame at a shameful deed (or thought) is harder to put out of one's mind than contempt at another person's contemptible deed. One can be haunted by shame in a special way, as so wonderfully and horrifyingly exemplified by Lord Jim, causing one to seek complete withdrawal from the moral community. Just here, then, self-forgiveness is especially important: Jim's shameful insistence on hiding himself away from the moral community arose precisely because of his refusal to forgive himself, and his insistence on writing himself off as a person, denying himself all moral worth.

This way in which, through shame, one is tied to one's past self is very well expressed by Emmanuel Lévinas:

[Shame] is the representation we form of ourselves as diminished beings with which we are pained to identify. Yet shame's whole intensity . . . consists precisely in our inability not to identify with this being who is already foreign to us and whose motives for acting we can no longer comprehend . . . It is that one seeks to hide from the others, but also from oneself . . . What appears in shame is thus precisely the fact of being riveted to oneself, the radical impossibility of fleeing oneself to hide from oneself, the unalterably binding presence of the I to itself. (Lévinas 1935/2003)[9]

What, then, are we to say about shame and contempt as moral emotions? Are they necessarily insidious in this globalizing way? If so, perhaps self-forgiveness becomes impossible. For self-forgiveness requires contrition and a commitment to change, and globalizing shame would seem to preclude this: one sees oneself, riveted to one's past, as being unchangeably and irredeemably bad. But Kate Abramson has argued persuasively and in detail that these attitudes need have no such globalizing implications.[10]

---

[8] '[T]he censure of vice . . . must never break out into complete contempt and denial of any moral worth to a vicious human being; for on this supposition he could never be improved, and this is not consistent with the idea of a *human being*, who as such (as a moral being) can never lose entirely his predisposition to the good' (Kant 1797/1996: 6: 463–4).

[9] Thanks to Alba Montes for bringing this citation to my attention.

[10] Abramson (2009). She also in the same place argues persuasively that the sentimentalists, and Hume in particular, are not guilty of thinking of shame and contempt in these insidious ways.

And my account of how self-forgiveness is possible shows how this is true in particular of shame and other self-addressed attitudes and emotions. One does indeed see oneself as another, and in that sense it is from an external perspective and 'spectatorial', but nevertheless you think of your past self as unequivocally *you*, and of your past actions as unequivocally *yours*. In contrition and commitment for change, you come to see your earlier self, who you were then, and what you did then, in a new light. The possibility of self-forgiveness and redemption, then, arises just because you can see your earlier self from the perspective of a renewed, changed, self, who is now able to rejoin the moral community. None of this would be possible if shame were, as a matter of psychological necessity, a globalizing attitude. Of course it can be, as Jim's attitude to himself revealed.

'An earlier self'; 'a changed self': how can this talk be reconciled with my insistence that your past self and your future self are unequivocally *you*? As we will see in Chapter 6, some philosophers want to take seriously, non-metaphorically, this idea of becoming a new person, as if one's very identity and survival is threatened. I will argue against this view, holding that it blocks off even the possibility of the sort of radical personal change—of *progress*—that I have been discussing in this chapter: moreover, it blocks off the very possibility of *self*-forgiveness if you are literally no longer the same person.

Pardon and Self-forgiveness

Finally in this chapter, I want to consider the role of self-forgiveness where pardon from others is more appropriate than forgiveness. My example is from Mozart's wonderful opera, *Così fan tutte*, although I will also draw on the famous social psychology experiments on obedience carried out by Stanley Milgram in the 1960s and 1970s.

In its essence, the plot of the opera is as follows. Don Alfonso, an old cynic and misogynist, rejects as naive and false the insistence of two young officers, Ferrando and Guglielmo, that their betrothed lovers, the sisters Dorabella and Fiordiligi, are faithful. 'Woman's faithfulness is like the phoenix,' Don Alfonso insists: fabulous but non-existent. He offers the two men a bet that he can prove that the two sisters are just like other women, on the condition that the men do exactly what he says. They accept willingly. The plan, in pursuit of which Don Alfonso recruits Despina (the sisters' maid) as willing assistant, is to deceive the women that their lovers have been called to war. Only a few hours after their departure, two dashing and amorous 'Albanians' arrive—in reality the lovers in disguise. They proceed to make love to the sisters, reversing roles, with Ferrando assailing Fiordiligi, and Guglielmo Dorabella. As the deception continues, real passions begin to emerge. The women begin by rejecting all their advances, but weaken and finally give way after their suitors have (so it seems) attempted suicide out of passion. Don Alfonso, to seal his victory and the deception, sets up a double wedding (with Despina disguised as the lawyer), and then, as the sisters' signatures are still wet on the marriage contract, a military chorus announces the return of the two officers. The 'Albanians' disappear in a hurry, and the young officers march in, apparently outraged at what they discover. Don Alfonso admits to the sisters that the plot was his idea, and encourages all four lovers to laugh it off. The experiment is over, and we can all learn a lesson from it. The disillusioned friends should take the women 'as they are. Nature couldn't make an exception, do you the favour of creating two women of a different clay, just for you'; it is 'a necessity of the heart' (*necessità del core*), and the important thing is to be 'philosophical'. All the proof one needed was there to be examined, and the case is closed. There is no phoenix, and no one is perfect.[11]

   The structural similarities between *Così* and Stanley Milgram's experiments on obedience in social psychology will already be apparent to those who are familiar with Milgram's work. In a series of experiments, participants were deceived into believing that they were involved in a learning test, giving real electric shocks to people, when in fact they were involved in experiments in obedience, and the shocks were not real. Milgram showed that some 65 per cent of subjects administered the maximum

---

[11] As Ernst Gombrich (1954) has pointed out, the librettist Lorenzo da Ponte's plot device of a deception to test a lover goes back as far as the myth of Cephalus and Procris, in which, according to Ovid, Cephalus tests his suspicions of his wife's fidelity by pretending to go on a journey, and then he reappears disguised as a lover brandishing presents. Procris is tempted, and Cephalus then reveals his identity. This plot reappears in all its essentials in Ariosto's *Orlando Furioso*, which da Ponte certainly drew from directly. The additional element of the wager, which da Ponte uses to such effect, is to be found in one of the tales in Boccaccio's *Decameron*. For further discussion, see Steptoe (1981).

shock level on their supposed victims, and that whether or not they did so bore no relation to their character traits.[12]

So both Don Alfonso and Stanley Milgram used deception with the aim of showing what people in general will do, regardless of their character traits. Don Alfonso, the principal 'experimenter', with Despina as his assistant, showed that 'thus do all women', or if not *all* women, then very nearly so, and at least our two sisters were no exception; as Ernst Gombrich (1954: 373) puts it with understandable overstatement, 'not to yield thus to the seductive passion embodied in Mozart's music would be impossible to any human being'. And, just as in Milgram, what we have, citing Gombrich (1954: 373) once more, is 'an experiment about human nature'.

But there are differences of character, even if they are not revealed in action. Fiordiligi, unlike Dorabella, struggles fiercely against her temptation, falls more desperately, and suffers remorse more agonizingly. The aria 'Come scoglio immoto resta' (as a rock remains unmoved) expresses a real and profound determination to resist. And later, when she feels herself beginning to fall in love with Ferrando, but before she has truly fallen, she reveals, in a recitative and a subsequent aria ('Per pietà'), first, the strength of her new passion, then recognition of her betrayal and weakness of will, then her need for forgiveness, and finally her determination never to reveal and always to withstand the temptation which she so strongly feels. Then at last we come to what is generally agreed to be the central, crucial, point of the work. Fiordiligi, dressed in soldier's uniform, desperately hoping to follow Guglielmo to battle, finally relents on the sudden and entirely unexpected appearance of Ferrando. We have something more like resignation to her fate, a kind of *giving way*, albeit a giving way that is chosen. In this respect, her giving way is very much like that fateful leap of Lord Jim off the side of the *Patna*.

And in the Milgram experiment too, we can see differences in character of the participants beginning to emerge when Milgram reports their comments after the experiment was over. One, Mr Braverman, was amongst those who went to the maximum shock level. He, very much like Fiordiligi, suffered internal conflict and regret. During

---

[12] See especially Milgram (1974). I discuss Milgram's experiments in some detail in Goldie (2000).

the experiment, he showed signs of conflict and emotional stress, laughing uncontrollably, clenching his fist and pushing it on the table. And afterwards, he said 'What appalled me was that I could possess this capacity for obedience...as my wife said, "You can call yourself Eichman"' (Milgram 1974: 71). In the light of these and other remarks, it is hard to believe that this man, like Fiordiligi in this respect too, was not psychologically damaged by his experience. Thank goodness that Milgram's experiment is no longer allowed! Thank goodness that Don Alfonso's experiment was part of a work of fiction!

Charles Griswold contrasts forgiveness and pardoning or excusing. Pardon, unlike forgiveness, involves not holding the agent responsible, on the grounds that what they did was, in Aristotle's special sense of the term, involuntary. In particular, Griswold says, pardon is appropriate for those occasions when, to quote Aristotle, 'someone does a wrong action because of conditions that overstrain human nature, and that no one would endure'.[13] If Don Alfonso is right about his lesson for lovers, that no one could resist, then it seems that it is pardon, not forgiveness, that must be possible. Anyway, for the sake of the discussion, let us assume that it is.

Even if forgiveness from others is not possible, there might still be a place for Fordiligi's self-forgiveness, allowing her to redeem herself from the feelings of shame that her aria, 'Per pietà', points towards. This might seem paradoxical, on the grounds that, as Griswold (2007: 129) puts it in a very sensitive discussion of self-forgiveness after giving way under torture, 'it makes no sense to forgive oneself for something for which one is not responsible'. But I think we need to distinguish here between different ways in which one can be not responsible for an outcome in which one is causally implicated. First, there are those cases where one is not responsible for a bad outcome that was caused by you but that was not brought about by an action of yours. For example, whilst sleepwalking you turned on the gas in the kitchen, and this caused the house to catch fire. Secondly, there are those cases, such as arise in moral luck, where an action of yours has bad consequences which you could not reasonably foresee. Bernard Williams's (1993: 124) famous example is of the lorry driver who, through no fault of

---

[13] *Nicomachean Ethics* 1110^{a}24–6, cited in Griswold (2007: 4).

his own, runs over a child. And, thirdly, there is a case of the kind under consideration here. Indeed, one is not responsible in precisely the sense that Aristotle had in mind, and yet it does not follow that one is not responsible in the other two senses. For example, the man who gives way under torture chose to do what he did, and he foresaw what the consequences were—the giving away of some secret to the enemy perhaps, which would cause much harm to his own side.

At this point I need to explain, in outline, a distinction that Richard Moran (2001) makes between two kinds of stance that one can take towards oneself: the essentially first-personal deliberative or practical stance, and the theoretical or empirical stance. When we are deliberating about what to do, it is the former that is at work, and the question 'What am I going to do?' has 'a practical and not a theoretical application' (p. 56): 'What we're calling a theoretical question about oneself, then, is one that is answered by discovery of the fact of which one was ignorant, whereas a practical or deliberative question is answered by a decision or commitment of some sort, and it is not a response to ignorance of some antecedent fact about oneself' (p. 58). So, in deciding what one ought to do (or think or feel), it is a feature of the deliberative or practical stance that what one will decide is not treated as an empirical fact about oneself; if it is, the deliberative 'ought' becomes merely a theoretical or predictive 'ought'.

This distinction is important because it allows us to see why self-pardon is deeply problematic, whilst self-forgiveness remains possible. Pardon for someone else's having done something for which he is not responsible in the Aristotelian sense really involves seeing the other from a theoretical stance, in the sense that the other person is seen as just one amongst a number of similar cases. We thus abstract from their reasons for action, and from their personal choice, just to look at the bare fact of what they did, and at the bare statistical fact that all (at least near enough all) do the same in the same circumstances, so blame and resentment are not appropriate, but pardon is.

Self-pardon, though, is problematic because it would involve seeing one's action in just this way, from a theoretical stance, as just a part of a larger statistical fact, whilst at the same time seeing one's action from the deliberative or practical stance as chosen, chosen indeed when one could have chosen otherwise, which is the only possible way one can see a choice from this perspective. It really is a form of bad faith—a dangerous mixture of the practical and the theoretical stances—to say 'I chose to do it, but I couldn't have chosen otherwise.'[14]

Even though self-pardon is problematic for these reasons, self-forgiveness remains possible, and it is often very important psychologically in such circumstances. It is possible just because it maintains the deliberative, practical stance throughout: one makes a choice in the face of terrible temptation which one tries and fails to resist, and in this sense one is responsible for what one chose to do. That is just why Fiordiligi and Mr Braveman were so self-critical in their narrative thinking about their past actions: they saw that they could have done otherwise—that there were real branching possibilities open to them, and that this is still so even if they were in conditions of the kind that 'no one could endure'; for after all, what no one could endure might still be endurable.[15] And self-forgiveness is needed just because these people suffer so much for having fought temptation and failed. It follows from this that a condition on self-forgiveness in such circumstances—and also on pardon from others—is that one must have tried—and tried hard—to resist the temptation. Neither self-forgiveness nor pardon is open to the person who readily goes along with what they are being 'pressed' to do, as did Dorabella, and as did many of Milgram's subjects.[16]

Even though Fiordiligi's autobiographical narrative thinking about her past is thoroughgoingly personal in Moran's sense, this perspective can still enable her to accept what Griswold (2007: 14) calls 'our irremediable imperfection', of which she is just one instance, and this should help her in achieving self-forgiveness. If the experiments in *Così fan tutte* and in Milgram show us anything, they certainly show us our imperfections. Here, as much as anywhere, we need self-forgiveness. As T. S. Eliot once said, 'Human kind cannot bear very much reality.'

[14] Especially relevant here is Moran's discussion of the akratic gambler; see his (2001: sect. 3.2).

[15] The dark doctrine of 'ought' implies 'can' raises its head here of course, but the point is essentially one about freedom.

[16] I discuss one such subject of Milgram's, Mr Batta, and contrast him with Mr Braverman, in Goldie (2000: 172).

Conclusion

Consideration of self-forgiveness illustrates many of the features of the narrative sense of self that I will be putting forward in Chapter 6. In particular, as we will see, it reveals its importance in how we think of ourselves, as having a past, a present, and a future. Moreover, it reveals how our memories of our past, our deliberation and plan-making about our future, infuse our understanding of ourselves, and of others, in the present. I will then locate this discussion of the narrative sense of self in the context of the recent debate between narrativists and anti-narrativists about personal identity. My own position will turn out to be in neither camp.

6

The Narrative Sense of Self

Introduction: A Metaphysically 'Light' Sense of Self

In earlier chapters, we have seen how narrative thinking plays a central part in our engagement with our own past and future. Implicit, and sometimes explicit, in this discussion has been the narrative sense of self. In this chapter, I want to address in more detail the question of what the narrative sense of self is, and to consider how it relates to other ideas of selfhood, including three in particular: the idea of personal identity, concerned with the metaphysical question of what it is that makes someone the very same person over time; the idea of survival; and the idea of a stable self, whose defining traits remain relatively stable over time. I will try to show that the relationship between the narrative sense of self and personal identity is not as straightforward as might sometimes be supposed: one's narrative sense of self as I conceive it really has no direct connection with the metaphysical question of one's identity over time. As we will see, the expression 'narrative self' can have quite different, much more substantial, connotations that I wish to avoid; I consider the notion of a narrative self to be otiose. Nor does the narrative sense of self have any direct implications for the question of what constitutes survival. And so far as concerns the stable self, again the relation is highly oblique.

Marya Schechtman, in contrast, has argued that having a stable self over time is a condition of one's identity and survival, as part of her important and influential work on narrative and the self. For my past actions to be part of my narrative, she argues, I must be able to identify with them, or have what she calls empathic access to them, which is a necessary condition for my personal identity and survival. This is at the heart of her notion of narrative self-constitution or narrative self-understanding. I will give reasons to reject this view, one such reason being that the requirement for survival of empathic access to one's past in effect blocks off the possibility of profound personal progress through radical change; on my account, one can have a whole gamut of self-directed reactive attitudes and emotions towards one's past, and many of these attitudes and emotions presuppose a profound sense of one's continuity as a person; self-forgiveness is just one such. I acknowledge the importance of having relatively stable defining traits over time, and agree that radical change in one's defining traits is not something that can happen often. Nevertheless when it does, at times of mental conflict and confusion, personal progress can be made, so that one can emerge as a better person. The role of autobiographical narratives is especially poignant here.

The Narrative Sense of Self

The narrative sense of self is a quite simple notion. It is the sense that one has of oneself in narrative thinking, as having a past, a present, and a future. I emphasize the 'sense' in the expression 'narrative sense of self', for it is, according to me, a way of thinking of oneself, or of others, in narrative thinking. (This is not the only sense we have of ourselves of course; for example, we have a visual sense of self, a way of recognizing ourselves through vision—in the mirror, in photographs, and so on.) To avoid doubt, perhaps I should anticipate here: the narrative sense of self does not imply that there is such a thing as a narrative self; having a narrative sense of self is not the same as having a sense of a narrative self.[1]

The discussion of earlier chapters showed how we think of ourselves as agents persisting over time. You, the thinker, the 'external narrator', can think of yourself *in past episodes*, doing and saying things, and you now do this in a way that enables you to conceive of the episode as having an emotional import that you did not recognize at the time, and thus you are now able to have an emotional response that you did not have at the time. Correlatively, when you engage in narrative thinking of yourself in the future, for example acting on the self-governing policy that you have now adopted because of your regrets for what you did in the past, you now are

---

[1] Kristján Kristjánsson distinguishes the self-concept from the self, but he goes on to argue that the self (*idem*) is distinct from the metaphysical notion of self-sameness (*ipse*), although it presupposes it. The self, he says, is 'the set of a person's core commitments, traits, aspirations and ideals: the characteristics that are most central to him or her' (Kristjansson 2010: 5).

thinking of yourself *in future episodes*, acting as you should, and you now feel, external to the narrative, emotions that express your satisfaction, through strong reflective endorsement, with that self-governing policy. Aspects of our narrative sense of self can thus be expressed through narrative thinking, and they can be expressed to others—in speech or in writing.

Our narrative sense of self is present to us not only when explicitly thinking of our past and future or when explicitly engaged in narrative thinking. It is also intricately involved in the way we engage with and think of our present environment and of ourselves and other people. This kind of awareness, more or less conscious, more or less something in which one is actively engaged, shapes the content of our thoughts and feelings about ourselves, others, and the world. We see other people, and we think of them, as we do of ourselves, as having a past and a future, so we have a narrative sense of others whom we know, as we do of ourselves.

Let us begin towards the passive end of this continuum—the way in which we passively experience things and events in the world as part of what has been called the specious present. Other people, other things, do not seem to be things that have only just now come into existence; our knowledge of them as having a past and a future colours the way we think of them and perceive them. I will borrow some of the expressions used by Peter Strawson to capture this idea: 'It seems . . . not too much to say that the actual occurrent perception of an enduring object as an object of a certain kind, or as a particular object of that kind, is, as it were, *soaked with* or *animated by*, or *infused with* . . . the thought of other past or possible perceptions of the same object. . . . Non-actual perceptions are in a sense represented in, alive in, the present perception' (my emphases).[2] Strawson had in mind enduring objects such as tables and chairs and umbrellas, but the idea can readily be extended to the way in which we perceive particular other people as enduring over time. When you meet your good friend for lunch, your perception of her is soaked with your knowledge of her past: with memories of all the times you have spent together, of her life when you were apart, and with thoughts of the myriad ways in which things might have been different. And your perception of her is equally soaked with the future, and with the branching possible ways in

---

[2] P. F. Strawson (1974: 53). For a helpful discussion of the perception of time, and the relation between temporal and spatial reasoning, see Hoerl (1998).

which things might turn out. When we see complete strangers sitting opposite us on a train, we are aware of their having a narratable past and a future, even though in this case we have no knowledge of the narrative. We might fill the idle moments with speculation: his face looks lived in, as if he has had a rackety past; her eyes look bright with hopes for the future.

Towards the active end of the continuum, there is the more reflective way in which we think about the past and future of ourselves and of others in our environment, choosing to remember what happened in the past, and explicitly thinking through branching possibilities in the future. This is active narrative thinking of the kind that I have been discussing in the last four chapters. But between active and passive, unreflective and reflective, there are plenty of possibilities. It is possible for a whole past episode to come flooding back, perhaps prompted by some external event, as, for example, Proust's tasting of the madeleine spontaneously brought back memories of his childhood: 'immediately the old grey house upon the street, where her room was, rose up like a stage set to attach itself to the little pavilion opening on to the garden which had been built out behind it for my parents' (Proust 1992: 54). Or, to use a rather Sartrean example, I might be waiting for my friend Stewart in a café, noticing that he is late as usual, looking out for him amongst the people wandering in, and finding that my mind is filled with recollection of all those past times when he has been late, with these past times merging into a general event—into the memory of his habitual lateness.

In such ways, our experience of other people in our environment can be bound up with our awareness of ourselves as having a past and a future: a past that we can remember, and about which we can provide an autobiography based in part on those memories; and a future, in relation to which we can form intentions, make plans and resolutions, and so on. For example, not only is my sense of Stewart, my way of thinking of him, infused with my memories of his habitual lateness; also my own sense of myself, my own way of thinking of myself, is infused with these memories. In this way my immediate feelings of frustration and boredom are animated by my own experiences of his past and future latenesses, which I might express by asking myself why on earth I bother to turn up on time when I always just end up waiting.

We can thus have a narrative sense of ourselves and of others. I have a narrative sense of myself and a narrative sense of my friend Stewart, the latter being built up of what I know of Stewart's past, and of him now, and of his plans for the future. Typically, of course, your narrative sense of yourself will be more replete than the narrative sense that others have of you, but this is by no means necessarily so: if someone has very significant amnesia, or has lost all their childhood memories, then others might have a more replete narrative sense of that person that he has himself. In this respect, then, any asymmetry between narrative sense of self and narrative sense of other is contingent on the extent of knowledge of self and of other; in a rather Rylean spirit, one might say that we generally happen to know more of our own past.

Partly recapitulating what we have discussed in earlier chapters, let me now make a number of observations that will help to illustrate the relationships—asymmetries and well as symmetries—between one's narrative sense of oneself and one's narrative sense of another.

First, there is, of course, the important difference between the narrative sense that we have of ourselves, and the narrative sense that we have of other people that is captured in the obvious fact that, in expressing my narrative sense of self, only I can do so using the first-person pronoun 'I'. However, this does not mean that my narrative sense of self cannot be expressed by others. When I use the first-person pronoun to express something about my past, for example 'I had a lonely childhood,' as part of my narrative sense of self, what is expressed can be expressed by another person using the second or third person, 'You had a lonely childhood,' or 'He had a lonely childhood.' Borrowing from Mark Sainsbury (2010) here, we can put it like this: although my narrative sense of self is only expressible by me in this first-personal way, as the rule is that English speakers should just use 'I' to refer to themselves as themselves, what I thereby express is by no means private or inexpressible by others. So in principle the content of my narrative sense of myself can be isomorphic with the content of your narrative sense of me. The narrative sense of self, as an aspect of self-knowledge, is 'not some distinctive thing known, but a distinctive way of knowing something which others can know in a different way'; 'the same content can be accessed from different perspectives' (p. 255).

Secondly, the use of 'I' when engaging in narrative thinking about one's past need not involve experiential memory, and in this respect it is no different from the narrative sense that we have of other people. As we saw in Chapter 2, I might remember seeing my father drunk at my twenty-first birthday party, remembering this from the inside or from an external perspective; or I might just remember that my father was drunk on that occasion; or I might merely believe that my father was drunk, perhaps believing it on the grounds of the testimony of my mother. The narrative sense of self is capable of being 'compiled' from multiple sources, and we might surmise that it typically will be, given what we know from recent work on memory of the kind we considered in Chapter 2. So memories are by no means all that goes to make up my narrative sense of self; events, or even whole episodes, that I have forgotten are still in principle narratable and can thus constitute part of my narrative sense of self. For example, there might have been a lost weekend at some point in my life, so that I have no memories at all of what happened and of what I did, but still I might be able to narrate what happened (the police report might help here—'I became very abusive when they turned me out of the restaurant'), and the events of that weekend (and their repercussions, which I might remember rather better) can thus all form part of the sense that I have of my past—a past that is in principle publicly narratable by me or by others.

Thirdly, having a narrative sense of oneself is part of the capacity that we self-reflective human beings have, and in this respect, one's narrative sense of oneself has an importance to each of us that it does not have to another. I care in a special way about my own capacity to think about my own past, present, and future. However, the use of 'I' in autobiographical thinking of my own past does not require that I *identify* with it in any substantial way, even though I think of it as *my* past. For example, there may be something that I did in my druggy youth from which I now feel totally alienated, but still I can use the first-personal pronoun to refer to what I did. We can 'own up to' our past actions without identifying with those actions. I will return to this point in more detail later.

Fourthly, my narrative sense of myself is the sense that I *now* have of myself with a past and a future, infusing how I now think of myself. Sometimes, as we discussed in earlier chapters and as we just saw, I can think of myself as another, from an external perspective. I see myself in my youth making a fool of myself at that party, or I see myself in my dotage, sitting in a wheelchair with a rug over my knees. In both of these examples, I see myself as another and in doing so in this way, I can come to feel alienated from myself at those other times. But still, of course, I—I now, as external narrator in the act of narrative thinking—am thinking about *myself*—about me then, as a 'character' in the narrative who is, precisely, me. So although I am alienated from myself, I am still able to use the first-person pronoun—I am that callow youth; I am that pathetic figure in the wheelchair. This way of thinking of oneself, in one way thinking of oneself as another, in another way thinking of that other absolutely as riveted to oneself, is by no means a confusion: it is at the heart of how we think back ironically on our past, and how we make plans and resolutions for our future in the light of our past. We can also think of ourselves now as another, perhaps thinking back to our youth, and wondering what that youth, me then, would think of me now. I might see my young self as callow, but might he see me now as boringly middle-aged, bereft of any worthwhile aspirations?[3]

Fifthly, the narrative sense of self does not require any deep narrative coherence in the content of one's autobiographical narrative. A brick from the building site falls on your head as you make your way to the church to get married, rendering you unconscious for three years, and when you return to consciousness your fiancé is no longer your fiancé. Why did this happen to you? How can the narrative of this element of your past have any real narrative coherence? Of course, these things can in principle be explained (they are not freaks of nature), and they can, so far as possible, be made sense of, but they lack the kind of coherence that one might expect from a certain kind of fictional narrative: there might be no *reason* why that brick landed on your head at just that time in your life (although no doubt there was a cause). Stuff happens, and not all narratives are narrative *explanations*, which succeed in explaining why stuff happens. This contrast between real life and fictional narratives will feature at more length in Chapter 7.

However, and this is the sixth observation, there is coherence in your autobiographical narrative in the sense that it is a narrative of *your* life. Factual autobiographical narratives presuppose what John Campbell (1997: 107) has called the 'transparent unity of the self in memory'. The grounding for this, he argues, 'is provided only by the conception of the self as spatio-temporally continuous', and this in turn 'requires the conception of time as linear' (pp. 107–8).[4] We can thus be assured of inferential integration of all first-personal autobiographical narratives of one's past:

One of the most basic principles of plot construction is that the remembered I traces a continuous spatio-temporal route through all the narratives of memory,

---

[3] Robin le Poidevin (2011) has a nice discussion of an example such as this.

[4] 'To suppose that time is linear is to suppose that times are ordered by "earlier than" in a way that is irreflexive, anti-symmetric, transitive and connected' (Campbell 1997: 105).

a route continuous with the present and future location of the remembering subject. It may be that there are interruptions in what one remembers, but these can never be taken to imply violations of that principle, and, of course, the mere existence of gaps in memory does not imply violation of the principle. The principle imposes a kind of unity on all the narratives; there has to be a coherent story to be told about my movements which will fit the content of all my various memories.   (p. 110)[5]

This then excludes the possibility of a branching autobiographical past with two or more narrative threads not temporally related to each other. We should reject, as Campbell (p. 107) insists, narrative theories according to which 'there is no more to the facts than is reported in the narratives, just as there is little more to the truth about a set of fictional characters than the text reveals to us'. So whilst the narratives of one's past might be patchy and piecemeal, with significant explanatory gaps here and there, and in *that* sense they can lack coherence, still they cannot violate the principle that requires the continuous 'trail' of the subject through space and time, with all memories temporally related to each other, as earlier than, or later than.[6]

These six observations about the narrative sense of self have implications that I would now like to consider, concerning both the relation between the narrative sense of self and various accounts of personal identity and survival, and the relation between the narrative sense of self and various accounts of what is required for self-understanding over time.

The Narrative Sense of Self, Personal Identity, and Survival

My claims about the relation between the narrative sense of self and personal identity are, in one respect, quite modest, and, in another respect, quite bold. Let me explain.

---

[5] It is, in part, this that distinguishes a real life autobiographical narrative from a fictional one; this is again something to which I will return in Chapter 7.

[6] John Campbell (1997: 112) also argues that psychological continuity theories (what he calls 'functionalist' theories) do not exclude the possibility of a branching past, and that for this reason they should be rejected in favour of 'the conception of the self as a persisting substance'. However, I wish to remain neutral as to whether psychological continuity theories might be supplemented in some way to accommodate our conception of time as linear; it is, one might say, just a condition of my account that any theory of personal identity should accommodate this conception.

My account of the narrative sense of self is not committed to any particular theory of personal identity. If my account of narrative thinking is more or less correct, then no doubt a narrative sense of self is at the heart of how we think of ourselves as having a past and a future, and how we make plans for the future in the light of the past. In this respect, it is no exaggeration to say that having this ability to think about our past and future is part of what it is to be human, for our lives would surely be bereft without it. But this does not commit me to the idea that our personal identity *consists in* having this ability, or in having the kinds of psychological connections, particularly experiential memories, which are argued for in various theories of psychological continuity that follow on from John Locke. These theories hold, very roughly, that what matters for continuity of personhood over time is psychological continuity, rather than, for example, bodily continuity. As Derek Parfit (1984: 206) has put it, '*Psychological continuity* is the holding of overlapping chains of *strong* connectedness . . . For *X* and *Y* to be the same person, there must be over every day *enough* direct psychological connections.'

It might be helpful here to relate my position to that of Michael Bratman. As we saw in Chapter 4, Bratman, in his discussion of planning, places great emphasis on 'seeing ourselves as agents who persist over time', seeing one's action 'at the same time as the action of the same agent as he who has acted in the past and (it is to be hoped) will act in the future' (2000: 43). As we also saw in Chapter 4, I agree with this. However, Bratman's idea might be read as implying that our thinking of ourselves as a temporally persisting agent, as 'one who begins, continues, and completes temporally extended projects' (p. 59), requires adopting a Lockean, psychological continuity view of personal identity, according to which our 'persistence over time consists in relevant psychological connections . . . and continuities' (p. 54). But this does not follow, at least without additional assumptions: what I am calling the narrative sense of self is consistent with a range of possible views of the metaphysics of personal identity over time, of which the psychological continuity view is just one. What is an important ability as part of what it is to be a human being is one thing; the metaphysics of personhood is another.

None of this is to say that I reject the neo-Lockean account, simply that I am not committed to it. I am, modestly, neutral about the metaphysics, and the neo-Lockean account is just one of a number of accounts of personhood with which my account is consistent. For example, my idea is also consistent with the idea put forward by David Wiggins (2001: 194) that persons are human beings, substances endowed 'with a distinctive mode of activity of their own'.[7] Part of this 'mode of activity' no doubt involves the ability of persons to experience themselves as conscious subjects, and in particular to have experiential memories, but on this view, having these abilities is a *mark* of what it is to be a person, without its being *constitutive* of personal identity over time. This is what Wiggins (pp. 198–9) says:

> If experiential memory is a mark of personhood, and persons need to conceive of this faculty as essential to their own way of being, then that secures its full significance to our expectation that, when people do or suffer something, this will impress itself on their mind, extend their information, colour their experience and influence their future responses. In the absence of that expectation, few if any of our finer-grained interpretations of people or the practices these expectations support could ever be sustained.
>
> If so much is correct, then, because of its central role in interpretation, experiential memory plays a special part in the full picture of personhood. But that finding (I insist) does not imply that experiential memory will impinge on the necessary (or sufficient) conditions of the *survival* of persons or play any role in the statement of sufficient conditions of survival. . . . Locke can be right about remembering as central among the marks of personhood without Locke's or the neo-Lockeans' being right about personal identity.

My account is also neutral about what determines survival of the person. Perhaps Marya Schechtman (2005: 10) is right that it is an implication of the neo-Lockean psychological continuity account that total, irreversible amnesia would be 'a form of death',[8] but I need not be committed to any such thing; as we have seen, experiential memory is by no means essential for a narrative sense of self. I might have lost all experiential memories but still be able to think through a narrative of my past, based on the testimony of others, and amnesia on its own does not exclude my being able to think through and make plans for the future.

So far, then, we have seen that, whilst my account of the narrative sense of self is neutral about questions of personal identity and about survival, it can still be readily appreciated why having a narrative sense of self, with plenty of the right kinds of psychological connections to the past and to the future, should matter to us. It matters because it locates us in our

---

[7] I will not discuss it here, but my account is also consistent with the view that personal identity is a response-dependent property, as has been argued by Mark Johnston (2010).

[8] But see also her discussion of Shoemaker (1984) in her (2004).

relations to our memories and plans that we share with others, and this, with our capacity for self-reflectiveness generally, is particularly valuable for us humans. So my view by no means needs to downplay the importance of having the right kind of psychological connections to our past and future; on the contrary.

One attraction of this position, it seems to me, is that philosophical questions about the nature of personal identity and of survival remain completely open and unsettled; the questions are as intractable and contested here as anywhere in philosophy. Everyone seems to accept that finding answers to these questions matters, but the debate continues to rage about what the right answers are. On my account, we can settle on answers to questions about the narrative sense of self, and on why it is something that matters, without leaving this account prone to attack from one or other view of what personal identity and survival actually does consist in. My view is not hostage to fortune in this sense.

This is the modesty of my account. In contrast my account is bold in that it requires that one's narrative sense of self, which can be expressed in first-personal narrative thinking about one's past, must be grounded in the facts, with the narrative sense of self picking out a continuous spatio-temporal route through one's past life. The point here, which we discussed earlier, and which will be developed in Chapter 7, is simply that it is not up to us to make up narratives of our past. Factual narratives, of which autobiographical narrative is a kind, can, unlike fictional narratives, be literally true or false; the thoughts involved in one's narrative thinking about oneself (and about others) are truth assessable. For example, Tommy might be able to relate an autobiographical narrative, which he sincerely believes to be true, in which he asserts 'I was a tank commander in the Battle of the Bulge in the Second World War.' And yet, in fact, he was not there. Tommy has a narrative sense of self—we can accept that much—but it is not grounded in the way things, in fact, were; he, Tommy, was not at the Battle of the Bulge. This, I think, is consistent with Mark Sainsbury's thought, that 'errors of self identification', such as this one, 'are to be understood as the subject successfully referring to himself, but then making a faulty identification, rather than as cases in which the subject, in using the first person, succeeds in referring to someone or something other than himself' (2010: 259).[9]

---

[9] For an interesting discussion, see Velleman (2006).

The Stable Self and Narrative Self-constitution

As was the case with personal identity, my account of the narrative sense of self is both modest and bold when compared with certain other narrative accounts of the self, and in particular with the account that has been developed by Marya Schechtman in her work over recent years. I will spend some time on this, because I think it is important to appreciate just how different our two views are, in spite of being, broadly speaking, 'narrative-friendly'. So let me begin by explaining Schechtman's views as set out in a number of her publications.

Schechtman begins by comparing her narrative self-constitution account with psychological continuity theories, which, as we have seen, have been developed since Locke. First, both views place less emphasis on identity of the self over time, and more on survival; this, she agrees, is 'what matters'. Secondly, both theories take into consideration connections between psychological states other than just memories: they include, for example, the connection between intentions and action—the kinds of connection that we have seen are emphasized by Michael Bratman. Although Schechtman supports both these developments, nevertheless she holds that psychological continuity theories still do not properly capture what matters in survival. Survival, or what she calls 'continuity of life', depends on continuity not only of consciousness but also of personality, on the *stable self*. And, she argues, the relation between these two is complex. Let us see in more detail what is involved here.

In essence, Schechtman's position is that continuity of personality, broadly understood, matters for survival when the personality traits that continue are 'defining traits'—traits 'which define the person in her stability through change' (2004: 90). It is these defining traits, of which we are not immediately conscious, that provide self-understanding, that make us 'intelligible to ourselves' (2005: 18). In this respect, Schechtman sees her theory as in competition with the neo-Lockean account, as giving a better account of what kind of psychological continuity matters for survival. Psychological continuity in terms of memory and other conscious states but without stability of personality is not sufficient for survival, and so the psychological continuity theory 'stands in need of at least some revision' (2004: 92).

In discussing her self-constitution or self-understanding account and the idea of the stable self, Schechtman introduces and endorses Raymond

Martin's notion of a 'perceiver self'. Martin says this about the perceiver-self phenomenon: 'when most adults experience either their own internal states or objects in the world, they simultaneously experience what they (mistakenly) take to be themselves as fixed, continuous points of observation on those internal states or external objects. . . . It is, I think, a profound form of alienation and, hence, of human suffering' (Martin 1998: 130).[10] This phenomenon is manifested in what he calls the 'many-selves experience', such as when one 'watches' oneself getting embarrassed 'without the "part" that is watching commenting on or judging, or trying to control, the embarrassment' (p. 133).

Schechtman (2005: 19) notes that Martin thinks 'that the perceiver self is an illusion', adding 'and of course in some sense it must be; there is no homuncular entity within people who is the observer of their experience'. In spite of this, she uses this idea of the perceiver-self as 'a process that gives rise to the background sense of a stable self of the sort whose existence seems crucial to personal identity' (p. 19); and elsewhere she says, along the same lines, that it 'should just be thought of as a stable observer who views and records the passing flux of experience, and recognises it as part of a single life' (2004: 90).

The best place to start in locating the differences between Schechtman's views and my own is by considering her very interesting reply (2007) to Galen Strawson's arguments against narrativity. Strawson (2004: 429) draws a fundamental distinction between the human being and the 'self':

> The first thing I want to put in place is a distinction between one's experience of oneself when one is considering oneself principally as a human being taken as a whole, and one's experience of oneself when one is considering oneself principally as an inner mental entity or 'self' of some sort—I'll call this one's self-experience.

Strawson uses 'I★', 'me★', and so on, to represent the self or inner subject, and 'I', 'me', and so on, to represent the human being. With this distinction in place, Strawson (p. 434) puts his anti-narrativity position thus:

---

[10] Along very much the same lines, Julian Baggini (2011: 7) identifies what he calls the 'pearl view of the self': 'Do you have an essential "you-ness"? When asked, most people say they do, but I've yet to meet anyone who can explain clearly what this "me-ness" is. People may describe it as a kind of ever-present "feeling," a sense that is always there in the background, or perhaps even as a kind of "flavour" that runs through all their experiences. Although people recognise that they have changed enormously since they were children, most claim that, nonetheless, their sense of "me-ness" has remained constant'.

I'm well aware that my past is mine in so far as I am a human being, and I fully accept that there is a sense in which it has special relevance to me★ now. At the same time I have no sense that I★ was there in the past, and think it is obvious that I★ was not there, as a matter of metaphysical fact.

Schechtman (2007: 168) summarizes thus: 'Strawson acknowledges quite a strong relation among the temporal parts of his human life taken as a whole. He recognizes that he★ has a special relation to other parts of the life of Galen Strawson, that these are of special emotional significance, and that he has certain responsibilities with respect to them. All that he lacks is an identification of those other parts of Strawson's life and him★'.

This then puts Schechtman in a position to outline two different kinds of narrative account: one of persons or human beings; and one of selves, where the self is the inner subject, me★, which is the continuous point of observation on my mental life of the kind discussed by Martin. A *person narrative* is a narrative that requires one to 'recognize oneself as continuing, see past actions and experiences as having implications for one's current rights and responsibilities, and recognize a future that will be impacted by the past and present' (p. 170). A *self narrative*, in addition, requires that, through the narrative, one is able to identify with, or have empathic access to, one's past self or one's future self. This self will be stable, with 'defining traits', 'which define the person in her stability through change' (Schechtman 2004: 90); these include not only character traits, but also other kinds of psychological disposition including one's evaluative dispositions, sentiments, and personality traits.

It is, in effect, person narratives that I have been addressing in my discussion of autobiographical memories in Chapter 2, and planning and so on in Chapter 4, and it is person narratives that express the narrative sense of self in narrative thinking. I am all for them, and so far as concerns person narratives I think that Schechtman and I are in broad agreement, although she is inclined to put more emphasis on the need for narratives that are explanatory than I do; see, for example, her remarks in (p. 172). In contrast, I consider that the breakdown of narrative in providing internal meaningfulness is perfectly possible in ways which I will discuss later.

Four further observations are relevant here about person narratives. First, Schechtman fully acknowledges (as does Strawson) that, through a person narrative, one can take responsibility for one's past actions, as her (p. 170) nice example of a person narrative shows: 'I need not identify with the self who decided to buy the sports car, but if I signed the loan I need to recognize that it is mine to pay, and that my credit will be impacted if I do not.' So 'I bought that sports car' and 'I owe that money' can be part of my person narrative, expressing the thought that I own up to having done such a thing.

Secondly, in narrative thinking, as part of a person narrative, one cares emotionally and in other ways about one's past and one's future, and about what sort of person one was or will become. And moreover, this kind of caring implicitly (or sometimes explicitly) acknowledges that the backward-looking and forward-looking emotions that are involved include emotions directed towards oneself: they are emotions of self-assessment. This is, of course, true of the kinds of regret and self-forgiveness that we considered in Chapters 4 and 5, and of the kinds of shame and embarrassment about one's past actions that we considered in Chapter 2. It is, as we will see in more detail shortly, essential to these emotions that they are *self-directed*, directed towards the *very person* who is having the emotion.

Thirdly, the idea of a narrator in an episode of autobiographical narrative thinking in a person narrative is not that of a homuncular entity (me★), nor is it an entity that is necessarily stable. The narrative sense of self is the sense of self had by the narrator; and this self is, simply, me now as thinker, looking backwards at my narratable past, or forwards to my narratable future. I might be far from having throughout my life a stable set of defining traits with a past to which I have empathic access, but, as we have seen, this in no way prohibits me from having other kinds of affective relations to my past (such as being riveted to myself through shame), nor does it prevent my using the first-personal pronoun to refer to myself in the past or in the future when I have these thoughts and reactions.

My fourth observation will lead us into a detailed discussion of the notion of a stable self, which, I believe, is in the end deeply misleading. Hypostasizing a *set* of 'central' or 'core' commitments, traits, and so on is just what leads to the horrors of *global* self-belief and *global* self-esteem that Kristján Kristjánsson (2010) and others have so effectively criticized. I believe we would do better to drop all talk of the self as a set or collection of core traits, to be replaced with talk of individual traits, each of which can be more or less central or core, each of which can be the proper object of pride or shame, and each of which can be subject to radical change, but none of which constitutes a stable or core self as such.

The Stable Self and Empathic Access

Let us now look in more detail at the uses that Schechtman makes of self narratives and empathic access, for this is where my disagreement with Schechtman's narrative self-understanding view begins. Schechtman (2007: 171) sets out what is required of self narratives as follows:

> Temporally remote actions and experiences that are appropriated into one's *self* narrative must impact the present in a more fundamental sense than just constraining options or having caused one's current situation and outlook [as they do in a *person* narrative]. These events must condition the quality of present experience in the strongest sense, unifying consciousness over time through affective connections and identification. To include these actions and experiences in my narrative [i.e. my self narrative] I will need to have what I have elsewhere called 'empathic access' to them. In *this* sense of narrative [i.e. *self* narrative], actions and experiences from which I am alienated, or in which I have none of the interest that I have in my current life, are not part of the narrative.

Schechtman (2001: 106) says that having empathic access to an episode of one's past consists of two individually necessary and jointly sufficient elements. First, one must be able to remember episodically what happened from the inside, with a suitable richness of phenomenology. And, secondly, one must have 'a fundamental sympathy for the states which are recalled in this way'. So empathic access is more than just having an understanding of one's remembered past, being able to make sense of it; it is *identification* with one's past. A lack of empathic access to one's past reveals that the stability of defining traits required for a self narrative is in doubt, and thus survival, in what Schechtman calls the 'subtle sense', is threatened. It is these stable defining traits, of which we are not immediately conscious, that provide self-understanding, that make us 'intelligible to ourselves' (Schechtman 2005: 18) through empathic access. Thus the ability to have empathic access to one's past is, in effect, an epistemic route to the stability of the self over time, and without it one's survival is threatened.

It would be helpful to see how this might work out by considering some examples, and Schechtman provides us with some. First, there is the Russian nobleman, a story first told by Derek Parfit (1984). This man in his youth embraces socialist ideals. In the knowledge that he is due at some later date to inherit a fortune, he commits himself legally to transfer his land to the peasants, as he fears his values will change when he gets rich. Ulysses-like, he binds himself by insisting that this transfer can only be revoked with the consent of his wife, which consent he tells her not to give, even if he asks for it. He says 'I regard these ideals as essential to me. If I lose these ideals, I want you to think that I cease to exist. I want you to regard your husband, then, not as me, the man who asks you for this promise' (Schechtman 2004: 91). 'Even if his [the Russian's] claim seems hyperbolic', Schechtman says, 'the basic sentiment makes sense' (p. 93), and she sees it as an advantage of her account that it is at least possible that the Russian lacks the stability of defining traits required for personal survival, so that if he does later ask for her consent, then this would be 'survival-threatening quite independent of what happens to memory' (p. 91). Memories alone are thus not enough, Schechtman (2001: 106) insists, and the second element is also necessary for survival: one must have 'a fundamental sympathy for the states which are recalled in this way', and this is what the Russian nobleman lacks when he loses his socialist ideals.

Schechtman (p. 101) further illustrates the importance of empathic access to one's past with a helpful and amusing discussion of a number of different 'matrons' that we are asked to imagine, each of whom now has all the responsibilities of marriage, motherhood, and a career, and each of whom is now looking back on her youth. One such matron, the 'serious' one, can remember her youth, but not from the inside and without any significant phenomenology, and she 'is so alienated from those desires and passions that she cannot quite comprehend how *she* could have made those choices'. Being alienated from her past in this way, she lacks empathic access to her earlier self, and so her personal survival is threatened. The second imagined matron, the 'somewhat-less-serious' one, has phenomenological memory access to her past from the inside, and, in addition, 'the passions that belonged to the party girl are still there', so that she is able to appreciate her daughter's rather similar behaviour, even if she does not approve of it. So, this matron has empathic access, having both the right kind of memories from the inside and sympathy for those past states, and therefore we can say that 'this woman's change seems like ordinary maturation and development rather than a loss of identity' (p. 102). The third matron that we are invited to imagine is the 'mortified matron'. Like the somewhat-less-serious matron, she too has vivid memories from the inside of her party experiences, but now 'these recollections fill her with shame and disgust', so her 'strong repudiation of these past experiences' means that she lacks empathetic access, and this in turn means that she lacks the required stability of traits for survival: 'the relation the mortified matron has to her past is not strong enough for survival' (p. 105). So this mortified matron is like the Russian nobleman in that she lacks empathic access to her past, not because she lacks memories, but because she is alienated from her past states, without any fundamental sympathy for them.

The first thing to note about this model of empathic access is that it is grounded in the idea that there are two distinct psychological states involved in empathic access: being able to remember an element of one's past episodically from the inside; and having a fundamental, identificatory, sympathy for those remembered states. This *two-state model* matches the way we empathize with another person. In the third-person case (and in the second-person too), in which B is empathizing with A, we necessarily have A's 'target' mental state, and B's 'reactive' mental state, of empathy with A's mental state. And this two-state model generalizes to other kinds of third-person attitudes towards A's target mental state; for example, B can feel contempt towards A's mental state, or admiration towards it. So here, in the third-person case, we necessarily have these two states: A's target state, and B's reactive state. Then, in the first-person case, when it is modelled on this view of the third-person case, we also necessarily have two states: B's own target state, namely his past mental state as recalled by B, and B's present reactive attitude to B's past mental state, whether sympathy or shame or contempt or admiration or some other kind of reactive attitude. For example, the mortified matron has, first, vivid memories from the inside of her party experiences just as she then experienced them, and, secondly, she feels shame and disgust at what she remembers. So on this model, target state and reactive attitude are necessarily distinct, just as they are in the third-person case.

The alternative that I was canvassing in Chapter 2 might be called the *one-state model*, in which B's memories and thoughts about his past can be coloured by B's reactive attitude towards his past, through the psychological correlate of free indirect style. The ironic gap can be expressed in the way the mortified matron remembers what happened—she tells it the way she remembers it, and she remembers it the way she tells it: 'I shamefully remember the disgusting desires and passions of my youth.' Once this 'constructive' view of memory is accepted, the very idea of having direct epistemic access to one's past, involving memories unalloyed by what one now knows and how one now feels, becomes fundamentally suspect.

The Stable Self and its Epistemic Difficulties

If the idea of the stable self, with a stable set of defining traits, is to get off the ground, it will be necessary for the individual to be able to individuate what are, at any particular time and over time, his or her defining traits, for only then is the individual in a position to decide which traits are the ones that he or she identifies with as part of her self-conception. This process of individuation, necessarily prior to the process of identification in Schechtman's strong sense, is fraught with epistemic difficulties.

As Schechtman emphasizes in her discussion of the psychological continuity theory, one's defining traits, which go to make up the stable self, are not conscious; our psychological traits are *dispositional* psychological properties: loving your children, for example, or compassion for the homeless, or being generous, or being an intellectual, or embracing socialist ideals as we saw in the earlier example of the Russian nobleman. Some, such as generosity, are virtues, as commonly understood. Others, such as compassion for the homeless, are sentiments. They are an integral part of our psychic economy.

Although traits are not themselves conscious, we can come to understand a pattern of attention, thought, feeling, motivation, and action as being expressive of a certain trait. This is part of what Crispin Wright calls the process of self-interpretation, and he provides a nice example of it from a famous passage in Jane Austen's *Emma*, in which Emma comes to realize, through self-interpretation, that she loves Mr Knightley:

> Emma's eyes were instantly withdrawn; and she sat silently meditating in a fixed attitude, for a few minutes. A few minutes were sufficient to make her acquainted with her own heart. A mind like hers, once open to suspicion, made rapid progress. She touched—she admitted—the whole truth. Why was it so much the worse that Harriet should be in love with Mr Knightley than with Mr Churchill? Why was the evil so dreadfully increased by Harriet's having some hope of return? It darted through her, with the speed of an arrow, that Mr Knightley should marry no-one but herself.[11]

Wright contrasts such *self-interpretative cases* ('I love Mr Knightley') with other kinds of *avowals*. What he calls 'phenomenal avowals', such as 'I feel tired,' have three features: they are *groundless*, in that any demand that the

---

[11] In Wright (1998: 15). The citation from *Emma* is from the Penguin edn. (Austen 1816/1983: 398).

subject give a reason for the avowal must be inappropriate; they are *strongly authoritative*, in that a subject's being sincerely disposed to make the avowal is a guarantee of its truth; and they are *transparent*, in that being ignorant 'of the truth or falsity of an avowal of this kind is not, it seems, an option' (Wright 1998: 15). What Wright calls 'attitudinal avowals', such as 'I believe that this government is in trouble', are both groundless and transparent, and are authoritative, but what Wright calls *weakly authoritative*. But what is important here is that self-interpretative avowals, such as Emma's interpretation of herself that she loves Mr Knightley, lack all three of these features, as Wright makes clear:

> There is no Groundlessness: the subject's view is one for which it is perfectly in order to request an account of the justifying grounds. There is no Strong Authority: mere sincerity and understanding will be no guarantee whatever of truth... Finally, there is no Transparency: within a context of self-interpretation, it is in no way incongruous if the subject professes ignorance of particular aspects of her intentional psychology.   (p. 16).

The conclusion, then, is that the first-personal epistemology of our traits as psychological dispositions is problematic in a special way.[12] Furthermore, the relation between a trait and its pattern of expression is far from simple. First, traits themselves typically involve a complex of sub-dispositions (Rorty 1988; Mumford 1998), and there is no strict, law-like connection between trait and its expression, and the pattern of expression from which the subject infers the trait is highly diverse. Secondly, what unites the diverse manner of expression into a pattern is the trait, the disposition, and yet we can only infer the existence of the trait on the grounds of its diverse manner of expression *being* a pattern. To borrow an expression from Kant, which he used in another context, a trait is the *ratio essendi* of its pattern of expression; and the pattern of expression is the *ratio cognoscendi* of the trait. This makes the epistemic (and ontological) link between the trait itself and its pattern of expression dangerously tight. Thirdly, the risks of mistake and misattribution are made all the more easy by the psychological fact that an incorrect inference from a series of expressions to a trait can readily become self-fulfilling—an all-too-familiar phenomenon. For example, once one makes the mistaken inference that one is in love with someone,

---

[12] The idea that knowledge of our own attitudes is through introspection is disputed; see e.g. Carruthers (2009).

then one's thoughts and feeling can come to revolve around the object of one's sentiment in a way that they would not if the mistaken inference had not been made; and thus the mistake never comes to light. And fourthly, many of the forms of expression of our traits are not readily accessible to us: not all expressions are in the form of what Wright called phenomenal or attitudinal avowals. Some can be evident to others whilst not readily so to oneself. For example, a muscle twitching in the lower part of one's face, or a bodily posture when in repose or even when asleep, can reveal or 'betray' one's traits to others—traits that one is not aware of having.

These epistemic problems with traits concern a person's traits at a particular time. The problems are exacerbated when one considers the individuation of traits over time, which of course is essential for the idea of a stable self as part of one's self-conception. It is here that empathic access is meant to be our guide. Let us recall that empathic access consists of two elements: being able to remember episodically what happened in one's past, from the inside and with a suitable richness of phenomenology; and having a 'fundamental sympathy' for the states recalled in this way. Empathic access is thus meant to give us access to aspects of our past life, in the form of memories of this kind, and these are memories of what were at the time conscious experiences that were, it is supposed, part of the pattern that was expressive of a certain trait. And then the fact that we now feel sympathy for those remembered experiences reveals, it is supposed, that this trait is still in place, and thus stable.

However, these two elements of empathic access are individually and together neither necessary nor sufficient for stability of traits. To begin with, the sympathy element does not seem to be necessary. There could be an aspect of my recent past to which I do not now have empathic access because I do not have fundamental sympathy for the states as I then experienced them, even though I remember them from the inside, but this does not show that my relevant traits were not stable over that time. For example, let us assume that I am a loving father who has been depressed recently, although I am now over it. Whilst I was depressed, I was not feeling or acting as a loving father should—not caring about the children's exams, failing to collect them from school, and so on. My not being able to have empathic access to my states during that time is not sufficient to show that there is no stability of being a loving father over time. The trait of being a loving father might have been in place but temporarily blocked by my depression; we should not assume an overly simple view of psychological dispositions according to which a disposition must always manifest itself in appropriate ways.[13]

The other element of empathic access, being able to remember episodically from the inside, does not seem to be necessary for the stability of one's traits either. Schechtman (2001: 108) says that personal survival depends on 'the right kind of recollection', which 'must be at least in part iconic in nature, and must be a centred memory so that the rememberer actually inhabits, in some version, the emotions, thoughts, and feelings of the person remembered'. But it is not clear why memory from the inside needs to be insisted on as a necessary condition for epistemic access to a defining trait that is stable over time. First, it discounts the possibility of semantic autobiographical memory. Consider the rock star of the 1960s for whom living a life of sex, drugs, and rock'n'roll was then, and is still, fifty years on, as much a part of his identity as it was when he was 20.[14] He remembers *that* he lived the life of a rock star in those days in the 1960s, but, not surprisingly given how stoned he was, there are no memories from the inside of those times, and all phenomenology is gone. So the rock star has a stable defining trait and yet no memories from the inside. And secondly, the requirement of memory from the inside discounts the possibility of autobiographical memory from the observer perspective, from a point of view of no person within the remembered scene, where you yourself feature as part of the content of what you remember. Recall the example from Chapter 2 of my remembering from an observer perspective my making a fool of myself at the party last night. Such memories, albeit not 'centred' in the sense intended by Schechtman, can be replete with phenomenology.

Schechtman relies here on Richard Wollheim's discussion of what he calls 'centred event memory'. (As we saw in Chapter 4, this is structurally similar to experiential central imagining.) Wollheim (1984: 103) contrasts this with what he calls 'acentred event memory', in which I am 'edited out of' the events that I remember; 'when I acentrally remember an event, I can't figure in the memory'. Wollheim claims that acentred event

---

[13] The point is a general one about dispositions: they can be, to use Mark Johnston's (1992) term, *masked*. Schechtman (2001: 109) accepts that there are epistemic difficulties with empathic access, and that it will not always 'be possible to tell in every single case whether access is retained'.

[14] This is the difference between the rock star and the party girl in Schechtman's example: for the rock star, it's *serious*.

memory is unstable and marginal: 'there is very little of it within the domain of event-memory' (p. 102; cf. Schechtman 2001: 18). However, as John Sutton (2010) has argued, Wollheim's notion of acentred event memory is not the same as observer memory, where the subject does figure as part of the content of what he remembers. Wollheim completely neglects observer memory, which neglect is belied by the wealth of empirical research on observer memory, of which we just scratched the surface in Chapter 2, seemingly basing his rejection on the dubious claim that 'not only must the event that I remember be an event that I experienced, but I must remember it as I experienced it'.[15] There is no good argument why we should reject the possibility of observer memories, in addition to field memories from the inside, as a suitable ingredient in enabling one to gain access to one's past defining traits. For example, you vividly remember an occasion in your youth, from an observer perspective, when you bravely stood up at that meeting and spoke out against your boss's bullying behaviour towards a colleague, and this observer memory, plus sympathy for what you so bravely said and did at the time, gives you epistemic access to your courage at that time, which you consider to be a stable defining trait of yours.

Although this is not so important for my purposes, it would also seem that empathic access to one's past is not sufficient for the relevant stability of defining traits. Consider an example of a man who is now highly compassionate, a trait he considers to be defining of who he is. However, he was brought up in the slums of Rio, and during those years he led a brutal life as the leader of a gang of children, neither feeling not showing compassion to any of his fellow slum-dwellers. Now, as an adult who has successfully escaped the slums for the 'normal' life of a teacher, he has very full memories of those years in the slum, from the inside, and he still has a 'fundamental sympathy' for the states that are recalled in memory; this is evidenced by his deep emotional engagement with films of childhood slum life (*Los Olvidados, City of God*, and so on), in which those memories

---

[15] Sutton (2010: 32) speculates that Wollheim 'may have taken it as obvious that such cases [of observer memory] would not be genuine memories, in that the level of construction required to achieve a stable external perspective on myself, represented as from the outside within the remembered scene, would rule out the kind of causal dependence between experience and memory which he elsewhere argued is essential to experiential memory', but Sutton goes on to argue that this is not so. I am very grateful to Sutton's work here, particularly for putting me right about Wollheim's discussion of acentred event memory.

come flooding back, and he sympathizes fully with the brutal protagonists, feeling the thrill of the bad deed done well, just as he did then as leader of his gang. And if, God forbid, he found himself back in the slums, he would do again just as he did then. So he has full empathic access to those years of brutality, with both the right kind of memories and the right kind of sympathy, and yet he in no way considers that brutality to be a defining trait, or to be one that is stable, that connects the compassionate 'self' that he is now to the 'self' that he was then.

On my account, in contrast to that of Schechtman, the narrative sense of self requires neither empathic access nor a stable self (nor as we saw earlier does it require memory, experiential or propositional). As a result, alienation and mortification and so on are perfectly possible in our engagement with our past, when for example one *cringes* at one's past actions as a callow youth (Beck 2008). There are thus plenty of what Schechtman calls 'affective connections', of just the kind that are often appropriate to one's past, which one would not have if one did not see one's actions or one's traits as precisely one's own. However distant they might be from your current psychology, in shame one is still riveted to one's past. And the same affective connections can be involved in narrative thinking about one's future: one sees oneself in the future as a contemptible commuter amongst millions of others, or as a pitiful old man arthritically vegetating in retirement. In other words, according to me, responses of these kinds by *me now*, seeing *me then* as cringeworthy, shameful, contemptible, pitiful, unworthy of self-forgiveness, and so on, are grounded on a profound sense of continuity of personhood. And yet they are, for Schechtman, threatening to one's survival in the subtle sense, just because there is no stable self in the narrative, reflected in the alienation that I now feel towards my past. My contention, in contrast, is that the basic sense of survival in *person narratives* is all we need, and that, on closer examination, the subtle sense of survival in self narratives adds nothing of any importance.

First of all, the use of the first-person pronoun in a person narrative goes with the basic sense of survival, and the appropriateness of this use depends neither on memories of one's past nor on a 'fundamental sympathy' for one's past states, whether remembered or not; I can perfectly well say 'I fell out of my pram when I was 2 although I don't remember it,' or 'I feel a deep shame about the things that I did when I was in my twenties.' The 'I' in these contexts, both the narrating 'I' and the 'I' of the narrated past, refers to the very same human being.

Secondly, life and death go with the basic sense. Whilst we can and should accept that we think of ourselves as having certain defining traits with which we identify, and that this kind of identification can be important, Schechtman would surely agree that it is a mistake to take their continuation through someone's autobiographical narrative as *literally* a matter of life and death, as if the Russian nobleman's loss of his passion for socialist values really amounts to his literal death (Velleman 2006).

Thirdly, not only the use of the first-person pronoun and literal life and death, but also, as we have seen, legal responsibility and moral responsibility track the basic sense of survival in a person narrative. For example, the Russian's contractual obligations remain firmly in place, as do the mature woman's for having signed the loan agreement on the sports car when she was young. And if a person were guilty of betraying someone's trust when he was in his twenties, which betrayal he remembers perfectly well, it would not exculpate him from those actions if he were now utterly alienated from them; they remain entirely *his* actions. Sometimes being unable to remember what one did, or being alienated from it, might play a role in mitigating one's responsibility, although of course this can get one on the hook as well as off it.

Fourthly and finally, we have seen that the whole gamut of backward- and forward-looking emotions of self-assessment goes with the basic sense of survival. Alienation and mortification and so on are perfectly possible in our engagement with our past and our future, and they in no way bring into question our basic survival; on the contrary, they imply it—we remain riveted to our past as, precisely, ours.

To sum up where we have got to in our discussion so far, my conclusion is that we have no need of a narrative self, a self whose identity and survival in the subtle sense can be threatened when a self narrative breaks down through lack of empathic access. All we need is the self of personal identity, the self to which we refer when using the word 'I' in autobiographical person narratives. Once it is allowed that person narratives and survival in the non-subtle sense are sufficient for the continuing use of the first-person pronoun, for literal life and death, for legal and moral responsibility, and for backward- and forward-looking reactive attitudes and emotions of self-assessment, I think we need to hear more of what actually *follows* if the narrative self fails to survive in the subtle sense.

The Mistaken Ideal of the Stable Self

One thing that follows from the ideal—for that is what it seems to be—of a stable self is that it leaves no room for the possibility of radical change in one's defining traits, of coming to see things in a profoundly new light. Let me explain why I think this possibility of radical change is important and should not be closed off by the mistaken ideal of the stable self.

When we are in the process of revising our deeply valued traits, with which we in some sense identify, we are typically in a state of conflict and confusion. I want to argue that conflict and confusion, even if it can be psychologically very painful, can be a good thing as a necessary part of a psychological progress of profound change in one's values, and in particular changes in one's defining traits, traits with which one identifies. Of course, I am not claiming that conflict and confusion is necessarily a good thing because it necessarily leads to progress. Of course, it can lead to change for the worse. The claim is simply that it is a necessary aspect of profound change in one's traits, change that can (but need not) lead to personal progress, rather than, as Schechtman claims, to a threat to the survival of the narrative self. It typically happens when one is falling in love (when one is, in the words of the song, all shook up), or falling out of love. It typically happens when one is in anguish about whether to make a dramatic change in one's career—perhaps from being a philosopher to being an investment banker.

As an example, the best place to start is with the autobiography of J. S. Mill (1960), who gives a poignant and psychologically realistic account of what he called 'a crisis in my mental history'. For many years Mill had been completely wedded to the 'greatest happiness' doctrine of Jeremy Bentham and of his own father James Mill, and working in accordance with this doctrine filled his life. But then came the crisis:

It was in the autumn of 1826. I was in a dull state of nerves, such as everybody is occasionally liable to; unsusceptible to enjoyment or pleasurable excitement; one of those moods when what is pleasure at other times, becomes insipid or indifferent; the state, I should think, in which converts to Methodism usually are, when smitten by their first 'conviction of sin'. In this frame of mind it occurred to me to put the question directly to myself: 'Suppose that all your objects in life were realized; that all the changes in institutions and opinions which you are looking forward to, could be completely effected at this very instant: would this be a great joy and happiness to you?' And an irrepressible self-consciousness distinctly answered, 'No!' At this my heart sank within me: the whole foundation on which my life was constructed fell down. All my happiness was to have been found in the continual pursuit of this end. The end had ceased to charm, and how could there ever again be any interest in the means? I seemed to have nothing left to live for.

At first I hoped that the cloud would pass away of itself; but it did not. A night's sleep, the sovereign remedy for the smaller vexations of life, had no effect on it. I awoke to a renewed consciousness of the woeful fact. I carried it with me into all companies, into all occupations. Hardly anything had power to cause me even a few minutes oblivion of it. For some months the cloud seemed to grow thicker and thicker. The lines in Coleridge's 'Dejection'—I was not then acquainted with them—exactly describe my case:

> A grief without a pang, void, dark and drear,
> A drowsy, stifled, unimpassioned grief,
> Which finds no natural outlet or relief
> In word, or sigh, or tear.

In vain I sought relief from my favourite books; those memorials of past nobleness and greatness from which I had always hitherto drawn strength and animation. I read them now without feeling, or with the accustomed feeling minus all its charm; and I became persuaded, that my love of mankind, and of excellence for its own sake, had worn itself out. I sought no comfort by speaking to others of what I felt. If I had loved any one sufficiently to make confiding my griefs a necessity, I should not have been in the condition I was.

This is what we might these days loosely call a state of anguished depression. It has a highly characteristic phenomenology, which will be familiar to anyone who has experienced it. One is in a state of turmoil, constantly changing one's mind, doing things and undoing them. One is highly anxious, utterly unable to see a way out of one's condition. And one is in a generally heightened emotional state, inclined to be moved emotionally for no good reason—even the advertisements on television can bring on the tears.

Being in this kind of condition is certainly deeply troubling. And also it would seem to involve irrationality, in the sense that subjective rationality requires that one be consistent in one's attitudes (Kolodny 2005). But even if it were possible that we could go through life without ever being in such a state, is it always desirable that we should be free of conflict and confusion? Might it not be, as it was for Mill, a step—perhaps a psychologically necessary one—in the process of profound personal change, perhaps for the better?[16]

---

[16] So I register, in this respect, disagreement with Stuart Hampshire (1972: 248), who says that mental conflict is 'in itself painful and something that everyone will wish to avoid'.

From this deeply troubling crisis in his mental history, Mill was able to reconstitute his life in ways that I need not discuss here. The point for now is simply that this reconstitution that Mill achieved, turning his back on the values of Bentham and his own father with which he had so strongly identified through his strict education, could not be realistically achieved without the kind of turmoil involved in this 'conversion'. Mill did not deliberate, through a rational step-by-step process, from his existing values to a new set of values. Rather, the conversion took place through an initial rejection of the old values, with nothing new to put in their stead, and then a gradual move to discovery of the new values through poetry (Wordsworth and Coleridge) and through music. The old values had gone before new ones came to take their place; and it is precisely this that leaves one so bereft at such times.

For those who are familiar with it, the workings of this process can be related to the debate between Bernard Williams and John McDowell about the possibility of external reasons (Williams 1981; McDowell 1998). Briefly, and very roughly, Williams argues that for something to be a reason for an agent, that reason must either be part of his existing 'motivational set', or it must be a reason that can be accepted by the agent through a sound deliberative route from his existing motivational set. McDowell argues, persuasively to my mind, that the requirement of a sound deliberative route excludes the possibility of conversion, and of coming to see things in a new light. Mill's conversion seems to me to be a case in point.[17]

The ideal of the stable self makes impossible this kind of personal progress, of which Mill's, as related in his *Autobiography*, is just one example. The conversion of St Augustine, according to Schechtman, is equally a survival-threatening rift, rather than a continuing narrative—a person-narrative—of progress toward the good in the life of one particular person, which Augustine gave voice to in his *Confessions*; at one point Schechtman (2001: 105) remarks that religious conversion is 'frequently cited as a case of identity-threatening psychological change', and

---

[17] As one of OUP's anonymous readers has pointed out, it is possible to insist that there must be *some* deliberative route to the agent's psychological state after conversion, even if it cannot be made explicit, either by the agent or by anyone else, for that matter. Whilst no doubt it is correct to insist that there must be a causal explanation, however inaccessible that might be, it seems to me dogmatic to insist that this explanation must be *psychological*.

comments that the convert often 'retains vivid recollection of lusts and passions that he now finds shameful and horrible', thus, according to Schechtman, lacking the sympathy element required for empathic access to his past. Further examples abound outside religious conversion: the person who in his twenties and thirties thought that being rich was at the heart of his self-conception, and who now realizes his mistake; the woman who for many years thought that having power, being in control of the lives of others, was one of her defining properties, and who now sees that this was ethically wrong. And then there are those people whose defining traits depended on their circumstances, and who can no longer express their traits once their circumstances change: the woman who once saw being a loving mother as a defining trait of hers, but whose children died in a tragic accident, and she must now—somehow—find a new life rather than clinging on to the past, as a loving mother but with no children to love, defined by her grief.

We can all accept—as I readily do—that defining traits with which we identify are important to us, and that these traits should, most of the time, be relatively stable over time. The possibility of radical change in one's traits and values is clearly not a process that anyone can go through often, for it arises only when there is a deep re-evaluation of one's whole life, and of what one holds dear, and this simply cannot happen often: deep values cannot be cast off and new ones taken on as if one is changing one's mobile phone for a newer model.[18]

But our accepting this should not lead us to think that the notion of a stable self in a self narrative is an ideal to which we should aspire. Talk of a 'self' here, whose identity and survival can be threatened, is, I think, a kind of exaggeration, as if loss of one trait is enough for the loss of one's self, as if the mortified matron's very selfhood is threatened by her being mortified by her earlier party-going activities. When the Russian nobleman said 'If I lose these ideals, I want you to think that I cease to exist. I want you to regard your husband, then, not as me, the man who asks you for this promise', we should insist that he is indeed speaking hyperbolically. Admittedly we do often say such things—'he is no longer the same person

[18] If one were like this, one would be like the politician in the joke who, at a fundraising barbecue, stood up to make a speech: 'Folks, I want to tell you what my principles are', and then, after talking for twenty minutes, he ends by saying: 'Folks, so those are my principles. I hope you like 'em, but if you don't I'll change 'em.'

after that operation'; 'she is not herself these days'—but this is simply more hyperbole, just as it is when I step out of the shower saying that I feel like a new man. The ideal of a stable self is a mistaken ideal, and the stable self is mistakenly hypostasized. Here at least I agree with Occam: we should not multiply selves beyond necessity.

Making Up our Minds and Breakdowns in Narrativity

What happens to our agency at times of conflict and confusion? When one is in the throes of mental turmoil, the rational ideal of careful deliberation, of weighing up considerations in favour of and against, of deciding, of acting on reasons, seems utterly remote. Gerd Gigerenzer (2007: 3) tells a story (which he insists is true): 'A professor from Columbia University was struggling over whether to accept an offer from a rival university or to stay. His colleague took him aside and said, "Just maximise your expected utility—you always write about doing this." Exasperated, the professor responded, "Come on, this is serious."'

How, then, does one resolve what is the right thing to do in such circumstances? Sometimes, making up your mind when in a state of confusion can be not so much a matter of discovery, of *finding out* what you think is right, but rather a *decision*, a matter of *making up your mind* (Moran 2001: 57–60). A connected idea is argued for by Michael Bratman, who has drawn on Robert Nozick's idea that, instead of 'weighing up' the options before us when we make a decision, as if the options have their weights exhibited on their sleeves, we make 'a self-subsuming decision that bestows weights to reasons on the basis of a then chosen conception of oneself and one's appropriate life' (Bratman 2007: 127, citing Nozick 1981: 300). This kind of decision, the 'bestowal' of weights, being an expression of one's conception of oneself, is radically first-personal. Especially (but not only) in the ethical case, the existence of dilemmas and difficult choices is often, rightly in my view, taken to throw light not only on the radical first-personal nature of choice, but also, as Rai Gaita (1991) and others have argued, on why the notion of a moral 'expert' is incoherent. Accordingly, this notion of agency cannot be captured with the idea that reflection and decision in the face of conflict is something that can be done on the agent's behalf, 'delegated' to some other 'agency', as one might to an expert (ibid.)—'I don't know what to do. You decide for me.'

There is something just right about this idea of deciding what one feels, of bestowing weights. It captures the thought that one's own psychological states are not revealed to one in a pellucid way, especially at a time of mental turmoil: one's reasons do not come with their precise weights already established; one's feelings do not come with a precise attitude and content already in place. However, what can be misleading about 'deciding' and 'bestowing' is that it can be taken to imply a degree of activity and agency that is not necessarily, or even characteristically, the case. Moreover, the idea of bestowing weights 'on the basis of a then chosen conception of oneself and one's appropriate life' seems to be question-begging at a time of conflict and confusion; at such a time *nothing* is settled, least of all one's conception of oneself and one's appropriate life. Often at these times, deciding is not something that one *does* in any obvious conscious sense: one is not even aware of making a decision at all, or, even more passively, of a decision having been made; instead, one finds oneself acting in a way that is not so much expressive of a decision (this is part of the reason why the term can mislead here), but expressive of a change in one's defining traits, a change that the way of acting reveals to you. In these ways, our agency is threatened at these times, as if we are not in control of our destiny; action seems passive, as if the surface of con-sciousness is being moved by some other deeper force, some tectonic plate below the surface.

Even after the 'decision' seems to have been made (but is it really the final one, or will it be undone later?), we cannot expect the mind—the whole mind—to change at the same time as a result. Even after the changes to one's defining traits have settled down, and are expressed in a new way of living, there are still bound to be residues in the mind, archaic leftovers of our prior dispositions, which can find expression in all sorts of ways, often surprising, and which can continue to reveal the residue of conflict and confusion that remains.

At these times, just because one's mind is in a mess, one cannot say precisely what is going on in it; as Hampshire (1972: 243) says, 'it may even be *impossible* at certain times to give an account that is at once simple and complete, just because his mind is one of confusion and conflict. To be sincere, he must convey the confusion in his sentiments and attitudes, and refuse the determinate alternative'. One might say that one can tell what is in one's mind through the pattern of expression. But what the pattern of expression reveals is not a settled state, but one of turmoil; decisions get made and unmade, actions get done and undone—all revelatory of conflict and confusion.

At some point, out of this mess emerges something that is, finally, more or less settled. I think there is a danger here, in autobiographical narratives, of a prejudicial reconstruction of what happened, seeking to explain what happened, to find agency and internal meaningfulness, precisely where it is not to be found, even though what happened was no doubt caused, and caused by you. The demands of narrativity on us as external narrators looking back on our past, seem to drag us towards thinking of our past thoughts, feelings, and deliberations as more determinate than they in fact were, and as reflective of an agency of which at the time we seemed quite bereft. In our reconstructions, we find ourselves saying things like 'I decided that, all things considered, the best thing to do was to leave him'; and 'Although it was terrible at the time, right through the process I just knew that it would turn out all right in the end'; and (to quote St Augustine here) 'My madness with myself was part of the process of recovering health.' It is as though we cannot bear the thought that there is no narrative explanation available of what happened in a way that provides internal meaningfulness. In *Lord Jim*, when we are told of Jim's fateful leap off the *Patna*, Conrad's Marlow is wise enough to 'refuse the determinate alternative'. The leap itself is not described to the reader; all we are told is that 'it happened somehow'. When Jim later says 'it seems' he had jumped, we should not read the 'seems' as a denial of responsibility, but rather as just a reconstruction that makes the leap the focal point of his terrible shame, a shame that might have been diffused if he had accepted Marlow's 'it happened somehow'—caused in some way which is simply too complex to narrate; as H. Porter Abbott (2010: 15) puts it, in a nice discussion of narratives of conversion, and of Jim's leap, 'narrative can fail, not for lack of causality, but for too much of it'.

Conclusion

It can be seen that my idea of the narrative sense of self is quite modest in many respects, with no pretension to offer an account of personal identity, of survival, or of a self that remains stable, to which we can have empathic access over time. In spite of this modesty, I hope to have shown why having a narrative sense of oneself is an important part of what it is to be human. And finally I hope to have shown how a narrative sense of self is consistent with, and even congenial to, the idea of radical change in what one deeply cares about—change that is not survival-threatening but can represent significant personal progress. Nietzsche's (1920–9: 318) remarks are very apposite here: 'A very popular error: having the courage of one's convictions; rather it is a matter of having the courage for an attack on one's convictions!'

7

Narrative, Truth, Life, and Fiction

Introduction: Truth and Objectivity and the Dangers of our Fictionalizing Tendencies

Let me begin by introducing two concerns about the use to which I have been putting narrative in our thinking about our past and our future.

The first concern is that autobiographical narratives cannot realistically aspire to truth in the same way as, for example, causal explanations; autobiographical narratives, and factual narratives in general, should be assimilated to fictional narratives, 'true to life', perhaps, but not true *period*. I shall try to allay this concern: factual narratives can be true *period*, and there is nothing about the nature of narrative that excludes this possibility.

The second concern follows on from the first. Even if autobiographical factual narratives can aspire to truth (to be true *period*), they are second rate when compared with, for example, causal explanations, for they cannot realistically aspire to objectivity, being ineluctably perspectival. We saw this concern crop up in the discussion of grief in Chapter 3. I shall try to allay this concern too. My response will be to distinguish. If being objective is contrasted with being perspectival, then I agree that narratives are not objective, for they are indeed essentially perspectival, involving the narrator's perspective on the related events. But being perspectival does not imply failure to be objective in another sense of that slippery term.

Discussing these concerns will return us to the important truth which we discussed in Chapter 1: thinking through a narrative, and narrating a narrative publicly, are kinds of *action*, done for reasons, and an account of these reasons can explain why someone thought through or related *this* particular narrative at *this* particular time in *this* particular way (perhaps distortingly, perhaps passionately but without distortion). Because of this, there is a double interpretative task of considerable complexity in understanding an autobiographical narrative, as we all know from our own experience: one has to interpret what is narrated; and one has, at the same time, to interpret the narrator's perspective on what happened as expressed in the act of narration. This double interpretative task does not apply only to an audience's interpretation of a publicly narrated autobiography; it applies equally in self-interpretation—in interpreting one's own autobiographical narrative thinking. Divergence of perspective between narrator and audience is of course possible, but divergence of perspective is possible in self-interpretation too—indeed, it is not uncommon.

However, even if truth and objectivity are possible, as I believe they are, another concern comes to haunt the role of narrative and narrative thinking in our lives. We have what I will call *fictionalizing tendencies*: we tend to structure our autobiographical narratives in a way that makes them dangerously close to fictional narratives, and in particular to fictional narratives of the kind one finds in literature. I will discuss four of these fictionalizing tendencies, and how each of them manifests itself as part of our psychology in our narrative thinking and in the narratives we relate to others. And I will also discuss what is, so to speak, the other side of the coin in certain well-known philosophical accounts of the role of narratives in our lives: these too tend, in one way or another, to assimilate real life narratives to literary narratives. Inevitably, my discussion will not draw too sharp a distinction between these two sides of the one coin.

The thrust of my argument will be to acknowledge that these four fictionalizing tendencies are dangerous. However, I will at this point diverge from some other philosophers who point out these dangers, and who then go on to criticize the role of narrative in our lives and the philosophers who are its proponents.[1] I deny that the fictionalizing tendencies vitiate autobiographical narrative thinking, which has, as I have argued throughout this book, a central place in our thinking about our past, our present, and our future, expressed in the narrative sense of self. Nevertheless, acknowledging the dangers of the fictionalizing tendencies, coming to an understanding of what these tendencies are, and understanding the hazards that they involve, will help us to avoid their excesses, and even to put them to our advantage. An analogy might be helpful here

---

[1] We have already encountered some of the critics of narrative, such as Williams (1985/2007); Vice (2003); Lamarque (2004, 2007); Strawson (2004).

to indicate the thrust of my argument. It might be said that we are often self-critical to excess, and that this is a bad thing. However, one can acknowledge these dangers of excess and then go on to insist that to know about the dangers helps us to avoid them, and helps us to be self-critical as we should, in which case self-criticism can be of benefit to us.

Finally, in the last part of this chapter, I will consider whether these four fictionalizing tendencies have a common source in our psychology. Speculatively, and very provisionally, I will suggest that they have a source in our need for meaning in a bleak, impersonal, disenchanted world.

The Possibility of Truth in Narrative

We should begin by distinguishing between those narratives (such as autobiography and history) that aspire to be true, and those narratives (such as novels) that do not aspire to be true in this sense. All narratives share certain properties in their structural dimension; in other words they all have narrative structure in the ways I discussed in Chapter 1. But not all narratives are alike in their referential dimension: some aspire to reference and to truth and some do not.

Against this simple idea, here are some expressions of the view that there is no real difference between fictional and real life narratives: Christopher Nash says: 'the text is so seamlessly interwoven with all utterances—from which what we call reality itself is inseparable—that questions not merely of "fictionality" versus "truth" but of referentiality versus non-referentiality dissolve altogether' (Nash 1990: 210, cited by Lamarque and Olsen 1994: 231). And Stanley Fish says: 'One might object that (my position) has the consequence of making all discourse fictional; but it would be just as accurate to say that it makes all discourse serious, and it would be better still to say that it puts all discourse on a par' (Fish 1980, cited in Walton 1990: 100).[2]

This is wrong. Fictional narratives do not aspire to be true, whereas real life narratives do—or at least they can. A narrative is fictional not in virtue of its content being false, but in virtue of its being narrated, and read or

---

[2] When Tony Blair's autobiography *A Journey* was first released in hardback a number of people who believed that Blair's book was profoundly inaccurate in its portrayal of the Iraq War moved the volumes from the section called 'Autobiography' to the section marked 'Fiction' or 'Crime'. It strikes me that this amusing subterfuge would completely lose its point if Nash and Fish were right that there is not real difference between fictional and real life narratives.

heard, as part of a practice of a special sort: one that invites the audience to imagine or make believe that what is being narrated actually happened, even when it is known that it did not.[3] Thus the question of reference and of truth simply does not arise within the 'fictive stance': it is just irrelevant.[4] Fiction, of course, can aspire to be true to life, to have poetic truth, and much else besides, but none of these aspirations are aspirations to be true *period*—true in the sense in which factual narratives, whether or not publicly narrated, *do* aspire to be true.

So how can a real life narrative meet this aspiration of truth? Here is not the place to discuss the metaphysics of truth, but we need a rough idea to operate with. Roughly, then, the constituent propositions in a narrative can be true in the sense of corresponding to the facts, in the minimalist sense of truth that is pointed towards by the following instance of what is called the disquotational schema:

> 'James had a lonely childhood' is true if and only if James had a lonely childhood.

This might seem trivial, but it is not.[5] On the left-hand side, in quotation marks, we are concerned with language—roughly speaking, with the proposition that is expressed by the quoted words. On the right-hand side, not in quotation marks, we are concerned, roughly speaking, with facts—with the way the world has to be for the proposition to be true. So it is a mistake to think of a narrative—which is, after all, a collection of propositions—as *being* a sequence of events; to think of a narrative in this way is in effect to assimilate the left-hand side and the right-hand side of the schema—to assimilate language and the world. For example, it is sometimes suggested that life, or parts of a life, such as an illness or a process of grieving, *is* a narrative. This is a simple mistake that, I think, often leads to the worry that real life narratives are fundamentally no different from fictional narratives, as we saw in the earlier citations from Nash and Fish. There can be such a thing as a narrative *of* a life or *of* an illness or *of* a grieving, but to say that a life or an illness or a grieving *is* a

---

[3] A story's being false is neither necessary nor sufficient for its being fictional. Cf. Lamarque and Olsen (1994: 31).

[4] Cf. Currie (1990: 30); Walton (1990: 70–3); and Lamarque and Olsen (1994: 77).

[5] For extensive discussion of this account of truth, and of the disquotational schema, see e.g. Donald Davidson's (2001) collection of papers.

narrative is to run together what is represented with the representation. There are two metaphysically distinct things here, and this is part of what the disquotational schema reveals, trivial as it might initially seem. In this sense, then, the metaphysical notions of reference and truth have application in factual autobiographical narrative, just as they do in, for example, scientific, historical, and causal explanations, whereas they have no application in fiction. So, in respect of what I have called their referential dimension, factual narrative and fictional narrative differ.

If it is right, then, that metaphysical notions of reference and truth have no application in fiction, but do have application in historical and everyday explanation, there also arises, but only in this latter area, the epistemological notion of evidence.[6] I think here again there is no difference between a narrative account and a causal account. Narratives can be verified by appeal to the evidence that is evinced in their support, and competing narratives can be tested one against the other. (It will, however, not be epistemically possible in every case to establish whether a particular proposition is true; but unless one is a verificationist, this does not imply that there is no room for truth in these cases.) What might evidence consist of? It could consist of all sorts of thing: what others say now about what happened then; written documents that were produced at the time of what happened; train timetables; aeroplane tickets. That is, roughly, the equivalent of the historian's primary sources.

Now here is an exaggeration, one which is often made by those who assimilate narratives with what narratives are about; indeed, the exaggeration in part motivates the assimilation. It goes as follows. All these documents are just more texts, multiply open to interpretation, and the distinction, much prized by historians, between primary and secondary sources is a distinction without a difference. This is, in fact, doubly an exaggeration. It exaggerates first the degree to which at least some evidence is open to interpretation. If someone's story is that he was in London on some particular day, and the flight manifest and hotel bills show that this person was in Paris, then the story is, simply, false in that respect. Secondly, it exaggerates in quite another direction: the implication is that we did not realize, until it was kindly pointed out to us, that evidence is indeed open to interpretation. But we already know this: we are, in effect,

---

[6] In what follows, I am much indebted to Richard Evans's *In Defence of History* (1997) and to Lamarque and Olsen (1994).

already epistemological holists, examining each piece of evidence with due care, and considering it only in the light of all sorts of other evidential considerations. For example, if there are minutes of the meeting, which were taken at the time, and which are put forward as evidence in support of a story about what happened that day, we know that we should enquire just who produced those minutes, and consider whether there are special reasons to doubt what they relate. Was the minute-taker unobservant, a fool, the sworn enemy of one of the protagonists, or did he have some other special 'agenda' of his own?

So, within the general constraints of interpretation, there is a perfectly good commonsense notion that there can be evidence which can be appealed to in support of those species of narrative that aspire to be true, of which autobiographical narrative is one such.

The Possibility of Objectivity in Narrative

Even if the general concerns about truth and evidence can be dealt with, and even if all the individual propositions in a particular narrative are true and properly supported by evidence, there remain concerns about objectivity. How can a narrative be objective?

To begin with, we can accept that narratives are perspectival, expressing the narrator's external perspective, but insist that being perspectival does not immediately imply lack of objectivity. A narrative can be objective in this sense: it can be *appropriate*, involving an appropriate evaluation of, and emotional response to, what is related. So it is possible for a narrative to be objective, albeit emotionally engaged and perspectival. Narratives, including autobiographical narratives, do not and should not aspire to be like causal or scientific explanations, dispassionate and non-perspectival. For example, C. S. Lewis's narrative of his loss of H in *A Grief Observed* is appropriate in the sense that the narrative, considered as a whole, reveals and expresses his grief, which emotion is, of course, appropriate.

Narrative appropriateness in this sense, then, goes beyond the truth or otherwise of its constituent propositions, but disagreement between narrator and audience is still possible. For example, I might relate a narrative of my roller-blading into the church on the occasion of my sister's wedding in a way that attempts to make amusement an appropriate reaction. But you, the audience, might disagree—you might think that my behaviour was a crude and self-centred attempt to upstage my sister on her big day. You might even insist on this whilst laughing, in spite of yourself, at the way I tell it.[7]

This example shows that the audience has a double interpretative task. First, it needs to interpret and respond to what is narrated. And, secondly, it needs to interpret and respond to the narrator's external perspective, both as revealed in the narrative itself and as revealed to the audience in the act of narration. This distinction is more or less equivalent to the helpful distinction made by Gregory Currie (2010: 86), which we considered in Chapter 2, between a story's content and its 'framework', understood as 'a preferred set of cognitive, evaluative, and emotional responses to the story'. Currie emphasizes that the distinction is one that is often blurred, sometimes intentionally by the narrator, so that it can sometimes not be clear to the audience precisely what it is about the narrative that they are responding to, and perhaps resisting. And we have seen in earlier chapters that one way in which this blurring comes about is through the use of free indirect style, where it is not clear whether the evaluation of what is being related is to be understood as that of the narrator or that of one of the characters internal to the narrative—one and the same person in an autobiographical narrative.

For these reasons, the audience is interested in the answer to this question: 'Why is he relating to me this particular narrative at this particular time, in this particular way?' Even if the narrative is given in response to a request ('Tell me what happened at your sister's wedding'), it is a legitimate question to ask why the narrator is relating this narrative at this time in this particular way. Is there a kind of 'spin' being put on what is narrated of which one needs to be aware?

So we should as audience seek an explanation of why someone relates a narrative just as we should seek an explanation of other kinds of action.[8] In looking for an explanation, we should look more widely than just to the agent's own reasons for doing (or saying) what he or she did: for the 'spin' might not be intentional. We call an action inconsiderate or vain without suggesting that the agent was motivated by inconsiderateness or vanity as

[7] D'Arms and Jacobson (2000) discuss two senses in which emotions can be appropriate: propriety and correctness. You might agree that amusement is 'fitting', in the sense that it is true that my story was funny, but still you insist that it is not appropriate to be amused. 'I know I'm laughing,' you say, 'but it's not funny.'

[8] As Grice (1989: 28) says, about all kinds of communicative act, we should 'see talking as a special case or variety of purposive, indeed rational, behaviour'.

such. For example, I might relate to you the narrative of how I behaved at my sister's wedding with the intention of showing that, on reflection, I might have been rather self-centred, although I did not realize it at the time. But you the audience still feel that, deep down, I still think that what I did was all rather cool and insouciant, so I still reveal my vanity and self-centredness, even if it was no part of my intention to show off in telling you about what I did.

In this context we might consider the possible reasons that Rousseau might have had for saying in his *Confessions* what we cited in Chapter 2: 'I believe no individual of our kind ever possessed less natural vanity than myself.' Even if we were to accept that what Rousseau said was true, and in that sense unobjectionable, we might still ask ourselves why Rousseau chose to say just what he did; what, we might ask, is he trying to prove? And we might ask the same question of a politician's remarks after being forced to perform a major policy U-turn in the face of a fierce public outcry; she praised her own performance as 'a good example of how humility is a valuable quality in a politician', to which one of her opponents added 'Even if I say so myself!'[9]

So an audience is not bound to accept the narrator's evaluation and emotional responses to the narrative, expressed in his or her external perspective. Indeed, a moment's reflection on the public practice of narrative discourse reveals how often the audience's evaluation of what happened diverges from the narrator's evaluation, even if they agree on what happened. We are always free to come to a different evaluation of the narrated events, and we often take advantage of this freedom.

As an example, let us consider the kind of evaluative and emotional divergence that is often found in a clinical setting, such as in psychotherapy and psychoanalysis. I will take my example from a paper by Vieda Skultans (2003). Skultans is exploring the effects of changing social and economic conditions on Latvian thinking about illness and distress. Her research included psychotherapeutic-ethnographic interviews of some thirty-five patients in a polyclinic in north-east Vidzeme. Skultans says this about these patients: 'Of the thirty-five patients who consulted me two thirds began their narrative by complaining that they could not put themselves in order or that they seemed to have lost control of their lives.' One of these patients was Ingrida, and this is what Skultans (pp. 2423–4) tells us:

---

[9] Reported in *The Guardian*, 18 February 2011.

Ingrida is twenty-nine years old, married and with a nine year old daughter. She feels she is lucky to have a husband who does not drink, a job she likes as a shop assistant, a self-contained two roomed flat and enough money to get by. She knows her circumstances are better than those of her neighbours. And yet, although she evaluates her life as one that should bring about satisfaction and happiness she finds that she cannot contain her anger and exude the calmness that she would like. *When pressed to give an illustration of her failure to live up to cultural ideals she describes coming home from work at eleven at night after a fifteen hour shift and losing her temper because the dishes have been left unwashed and the flat is in a mess. The interesting point relates to the fact that Ingrida blames herself and not her long working hours for her anger. Indeed, she pointed out that she did not have to walk home but that her husband collected her in the family car.*

Let us focus especially on the part that I have italicized. Here we are told that Ingrida related to Skultans a narrative—a mini-narrative—in order to illus-trate what she took to be her failure to live up to her cultural ideals of self-control. In the narrative, Ingrida tells Skultans that she lost her temper. It is clear from what Skultans tells us that she, Skultans, understands and em-pathizes with Ingrida's internal perspective in the narrative, and specifically with Ingrida's ostensible reasons for losing her temper: the unwashed dishes, the messy flat. But there is divergence in external perspective. Skultans tells us that Ingrida's evaluation of what happened, from her external perspective as narrator, is that she was blameworthy for failing to control her temper. Skultans's evaluation, from her external perspective as audience, diverges from Ingrida's, in that she thinks it is the social and economic conditions, and specifically the horrendous working hours, where the real fault lies.

Here, then, we have a very nice example of the double interpretative task in action. Skultans understands the content of Ingrida's autobiograph-ical narrative, accepting her account of 'the facts' (that Ingrida came home from work, that she then lost her temper because of the unwashed dishes and the messy flat). And Skultans also understands Ingrida's external perspective (Skultans understands that Ingrida blames herself for losing her temper). But Skultans also has her own external perspective on what happened, which diverges from that of Ingrida: Ingrida blames herself, whereas Skultans feels that Ingrida is not to blame, that her emotions of self-assessment are not appropriate. It is, in part, the clinician's task to help the patient to see that her emotional responses to the past, as revealed in her external perspective, are other than what they should be.[10]

---

[10] One might say that the point of cognitive behavioural therapy lies in getting the patient to see their lives in a more positive light—to see the glass as half full and not half empty.

There is a further complication—one that is very important. You cannot assume that you yourselves, the audience, are free of bias—perhaps it is your perspective that is distorting and not the narrator's. Thus, your own way of seeing things has also to be taken into account in the interpretative process—a point that applies as much to the clinician as it does to the rest of us. For example, you the audience might unknowingly be influenced in your interpretation of my roller-blading story by your somewhat repressed envy of my cool insouciance which you could never emulate. So it is not as though, to quote a remark of Nietzsche's, 'reality stood unveiled before you only, and you yourselves were perhaps the best part of it' (*The Gay Science*, bk. 2 sect. 57).

I have been making these observations in relation to narratives that are related to another person. But just the same divergences can reveal themselves in narrative thinking, where there is no public act of narration. As we saw in Chapter 2, in which I discussed what I called the problem of the audience, the audience can be oneself in another guise. Perhaps to this day when I think back on my behaviour at my sister's wedding all that time ago, I still cannot resist an inward smirk, although my better self knows it to be inappropriate. In effect, we thus have my external perspective as audience *on* my external perspective as narrator, with the two diverging just as they can in a public narration.

There is an important difference, though, between public narration and narrative thinking. A public narration is an action, done for reasons. Narrative thinking to oneself can be like this, as one might intentionally think through a narrative of a typical day in the upcoming walking trip to the Azores, doing so in order to help one make sure that one has all the equipment that is needed. But often thoughts come unbidden, as one might find oneself going over and over in one's mind that *mauvais quart d'heure* which you would really much prefer to forget. Thoughts also often will not come, even when bidden, as one might find oneself incapable of facing up to thinking through properly precisely what you did on that fateful day. Here self-interpretation does not involve trying to work out reasons that purportedly justify one's intentional action, but rather it involves trying to work out reasons in another sense. We often look for reasons in this other sense, and sometimes find them, in the tangled undergrowth of non-conscious (not necessarily unconscious) motivations. Why do I find myself going over and over in my mind that *mauvais quart d'heure* (which after all wasn't that *mauvais*)? Is it because it reminds me of some other occasion that I have put out of my mind? Is it because I'm afraid of something that I won't acknowledge? It is often on such occasions that we need to relate our narratives to others, as we saw in Chapter 3; to repeat E. M. Forster's words, 'How can I tell what I think till I see what I say?'

There is one final point to make about objectivity and appropriateness. We should not think that once an appropriate narrative has been settled on, whether thought through or publicly narrated, then reconsideration of what happened is no longer needed. Rather, in our narratives of our past, and in our narratives of our history more widely, what is past ought to be permanently open to reassessment in the light of how we now see things—in the light of the perspective that we now have—and this perspective can, and often should, change over time. (Recall Beckett's *Krapp's Last Tapes*, with Krapp listening to his earlier ramblings: 'Just been listening to that stupid bastard I took myself for thirty years ago, hard to believe I was ever as bad as that.') Our narratives should not become ossified, repeated and remembered almost by rote as if nothing has changed, reminiscent of Talleyrand's supposed remark about the House of Bourbon at the time of the French Revolution, that they have learned nothing and forgotten nothing (*Ils n'ont rien appris, ni rien oublié*).

Let me sum up what I want to say about objectivity and appropriateness in narrative discourse and narrative thinking. Objectivity in a narrative is not a matter of being dispassionate, of being free of all emotion, for narratives are (at least paradigmatically) concerned with human values and emotions, and one should not aspire to be dispassionate here. Rather, objectivity in a narrative requires having an appropriate external perspective—of having an appropriate evaluation of, and emotional response to, what happened. To echo the words of Aristotle in his *Nicomachean Ethics* (1106^b20), it is a matter of having the right emotions 'at the right times, towards the right people, and in the right way'. The multi-layered multi-level power of narratives to express or reveal perspectives is not a malign power; on the contrary, it is their strength—it is, precisely, what we use them for.

So far, then, let us accept that it is possible to achieve truth and objectivity in narratives of our lives, remembering always the modesty and revisability of interpretation that is appropriate to this kind of narra-tive. However, the bare possibility of truth and objectivity in autobio-graphical narrative is one thing; its being realized in particular cases is another. For the concern remains that, as a matter of human psychology, we have a tendency to fictionalize our lives, to give our lives a kind of narrative structure that is appropriate to traditional fiction but that is simply not appropriate to real life: in short, to *narrativize*. So let us now examine these fictionalizing tendencies.

The First Fictionalizing Tendency: We Plot Out Our Lives

We often think of ourselves, in a way that is perfectly natural, as plotting the course of our lives. Through narrative thinking, we make plots and plans for the future, form hypothetical imperatives, and so on, often based on narrative thinking about our past. For example, I might think back on how I made myself late for the meeting yesterday by dawdling at home checking my emails, and as a result resolve that tomorrow I will not dawdle. Or I might think through in narrative form what it might be like to work in some different part of the world, and as a result look out for job opportunities there, and then take up one of the jobs as I planned to do.

So there is this connection between narrative and life: as the psychologist Jerome Bruner (1987/2004: 692) puts it, life 'is constructed by human beings through active ratiocination, by the same kind of ratiocination through which we construct narratives'. And when we come to 'act out' our plots and plans there is a sense in which it is true to say that what we are 'acting out' is an 'enacted narrative'. Alasdair MacIntyre (1981: 208), making more or less the same point as Bruner, says that narrative is 'the basic and essential genre for the characterization of human action'. But the dangers readily creep in at just this point when, taking MacIntyre again, it is said that we are the *authors* of our lives: 'What I have called a history is an enacted dramatic narrative in which the characters are also the authors' (p. 215).

What precisely is wrong here? First, there is an exaggeration. There is much that happens in our lives that we do not or cannot plan for in an author-like way; we have at least that much in common with mice. For one thing, as MacIntyre himself acknowledges, we are, at best, 'co-authors' with other people who constrain our lives, and it would be an illusion to think otherwise; 'Only in fantasy do we live what story we please' (p. 213). Moreover, many of our actions are constrained, not only by other agents, but by non-agential forces; this is a point to which I will return shortly.

Secondly, as I have already emphasized, life is not a narrative: to elide or to identify the narrative and the life that is narrated is to lose the distinction between representation and what is represented.[11] And in this sense, there is an equivocation of the notion of author when we pass from narrative (what, for example, is written) to life (what is written about) (Ricœur, 1992: 160).[12] We are not literally the authors, or even the co-authors, of our lives.

The Second Fictionalizing Tendency: Finding Agency in the World Where It Is Not

We have a tendency to find too much agency in the world. We have seen this already in the first tendency: to explain too much of what happens by appeal to our *own* agency. Gregory Currie and Jon Jureidini (2004) have a very nice discussion of this second, wider phenomenon, in which they say that it is 'a near universal feature of the cognitively normal population' (p. 410). For example, we often look for a 'meaning' of some natural event or accident, imputing it to an action by some other person or persons, or by some kind of non-human agency, such as gods, ghosts, and monsters (p. 409). We explain what is sheer happenstance as the product of a conspiracy theory. We attribute symbolic 'meaning' to things in nature, such as finding a four-leaf clover or seeing a solitary magpie. And when something goes wrong in our lives, especially when the same misfortune occurs several times, we see ourselves as being, as Freud (1920/1984: 292) put it, 'pursued by a malignant fate'; 'it was never meant to be', we sigh in despair.

Currie and Jureidini ask why this tendency characteristically reveals itself in narrative. Their explanation, which I find persuasive, is that narratives are especially suitable for representation of agency. Moreover, narratives—acts of narration—are expressive of agency and mind. If an

---

[11] In the passage just cited, MacIntyre seems to be identifying history and narrative, to be identifying the events that are the subject-matter of the narrative and the narrative itself. And yet, as he says elsewhere, in real life 'stories are lived before they are told—except in the case of fiction' (1981: 197).

[12] Vice (2003: 99–100) has similar criticisms of MacIntyre.

event is described in a narrative, then we assume that it is there for a reason, that it is of significance. We expect what is related to have a coherence that the real world does not (Currie and Jureidini 2004: 417–19); again, this is a point I will come back to.

Now let me briefly say what is—quite obviously—wrong with this tendency, and then go on to say why it is a *fictionalizing* tendency. What is wrong with it is that it misrepresents the way the world is: it represents non-agential events as being actions, initiated and controlled by agents of some kind. As we have just seen, this manifests itself in part in conspiracy theories and the like, and in part in finding something agential in the mere forces of nature. R. G. Collingwood (1946) puts very well what is wrong with finding agency in mere nature, as part of his essential contrast between a natural process and what he calls a historical process; the former is a 'process of events' and the later a 'process of thoughts'. He then continues:

There is only one hypothesis on which natural processes could be regarded as ultimately historical in character: namely that these processes are in reality processes of action determined by a thought which is their own inner side. This would imply that natural events are expressions of thoughts, whether the thoughts of God, or of angelic or demonic finite intelligences, or of minds somewhat like our own inhabiting the organic and inorganic bodies of nature as our minds inhabit our bodies. Setting aside mere flights of metaphysical fancy, such an hypothesis could claim our serious attention only if it led to a better understanding of the natural world. In fact, however, the scientist can reasonably say of it, 'Je n'ai pas eu besoin de cette hypothèse', and the theologian will recoil from any suggestion that God's action in the natural world resembles the action of a finite human mind under the conditions of historical life. (p. 217)

Why, then, do I call this tendency a *fictionalizing* tendency? The answer is that the tendency to attribute agency in ways that are not appropriate to real life is in fact *appropriate* to much traditional fiction and literature. In other words, what is wrong in interpreting real life is right in interpreting fiction and literature. Children's stories are replete with ghosts, gods, monsters, and magic. Fairy tales and myths involve explanations of natural disasters—floods, plagues, and so on—as the intentional product of some non-human agent, as part of what Collingwood calls a historical process rather than a natural process. Conspiracy theories are the very stuff of spy novels and thrillers. The predictions of the witches in Shakespeare's *Macbeth* and of the gypsy in Verdi's *Un Ballo in Maschera* (*Masked Ball*) have to be understood as being accurate predictions of what will happen. The mud and fog at the start of Dickens's *Bleak House* must be understood as symbolizing the chaos of the world of the novel (Lamarque 2007: 124); as must the fog that pervades Marcel Carné's film *Quai des Brumes*. And Victorian novels are full of coincidences explained by the intervention of an active god. David Goldknopf, the literary scholar, having given several very nice examples of coincidences from Charles Dickens, Charlotte Brontë, and elsewhere, goes on to say this:

In the cases cited, the author has deliberately *emphasised* the element of fortuitousness, and for the same reason: to liberate a crucial incident from the realistic network of causality. Far from evidencing sloppy plotting, the fortuitousness is as legitimate a part of the work's formal design as are the hovering angels in Renaissance religious paintings. In each instance the author has floated his characters away from the order of mundane connections to bring them under the direct control of an *au courant* God. The purpose of the coincidence, in short, is to make God a character in the novel.   (Goldknopf 1969: 44)

The Third Fictionalizing Tendency: Narrative Thread and the Desire for Closure

The third fictionalizing tendency follows on nicely from the second, and in particular from one of the properties of narrative that Currie and Jureidini point towards to explain the phenomenon of over-attributing agency, namely the property of being expressive of agency.

First, there is the tendency to think of one's life as having an unbroken narrative thread that holds it together, so that the narrative sense of self is, as MacIntyre (1981: 205) puts it, 'a concept of a self whose unity resides in the unity of a narrative which links birth to life to death as narrative beginning to middle to end'. This idea is deeply problematic—and remains so even when we have clearly distinguished the narrative of a life from the life that is narrated. To begin with, as we saw in Chapter 6, the narrative sense of self is massively 'gappy': from our childhood onwards, large tracts of our lives will be lost to us for all sorts of reasons, most notably of course through failures of autobiographical memory, perhaps just because of the passage of time, or perhaps because of some traumatic event that caused memory loss. So, under those circumstances, even if there were a unity of some kind, it is not narratable by the agent, or, quite possibly, by anyone else.

Secondly, the difference between the unity of a real life and that of a fictional life is not just a contingent difference. For, as Bernard Williams (2007: 7) has argued, 'fictional characters have a special unity that no real life can have, that the end of them is present at their beginning. . . . their wholeness is already there, and ours is not'. This is true even of Jean-Paul Sartre's Roquentin in *La Nausée*: as a character in a novel, Roquentin's life necessarily cannot represent the sheer contingency that Sartre wants; his wholeness is already there, including the contingencies.[13] And this special unity that fictional characters have could not apply to any real life, even the life of someone whose narrative is planned out from the beginning, as might be the life of a young prince who is the chosen heir to the throne in an ancient dynasty.

And thirdly, the beginning and the end of our lives are a matter of happenstance. One's life can end *just like that*—bricks land on heads, buses come out of nowhere, babies die. In contrast, when we talk of the 'beginning', 'middle', and 'end' of a narrative, these are *already* narrativized notions: there is already something 'fitting' about them in the narrative. As Noël Carroll (2007: 3) points out in a discussion of Aristotle's *Poetics*, these terms are 'technical'. Discussing the end of a tragedy, he says, 'Aristotle is saying that the sort of narrative representation he is anatomizing concludes in the precisely appropriate place just as a piece of music with closure finishes on exactly the right note.'

We can usefully relate this to Carroll's insightful discussion of what he calls erotetic narratives. An erotetic narrative is one that raises questions and provides answers, and which thus sustains narrative closure. In our engagement with erotetic narratives, we have a desire for all substantial questions to be answered, and accordingly, he says, there is something not right, something frustrating, about a narrative that leaves a major question unanswered. The law of Chekhov's gun is familiar here: if the theatre curtain goes up to reveal a gun on the wall of the room, then at some point during the play something must happen that involves the gun; otherwise the question 'What is that gun doing here?' will fail to be answered.

As Carroll (p. 15) rightly argues, the desire for narrative closure is appropriate for those erotetic narratives that are created 'for aesthetic

---

[13] For discussion of Sartre along these lines, see Kermode (1966: 133–52).

consumption'. And Carroll's view is that this link, between erotetic narratives created for aesthetic consumption and the desire for narrative closure, is a normative link. For he finds confirmation of his thesis 'in our ordinary critical responses to certain narratives': we feel a certain frustrating incompleteness because 'answers to certain questions . . . which were implicitly promised were not delivered'.[14]

Carroll (p. 6) draws a contrast here with narratives of real life, saying that narrative closure 'rarely figures in the stories folk tell their mates about their day at work'. It is certainly generally true that our narratives of our days at work do not achieve narrative closure any more than does a narrative of a whole life, and often a narrative of an incident in a day at work will raise more questions than it answers. For example, if I tell you the story of how my boss came into my office to ask to see me tomorrow about my promotion prospects, we will both be in suspense until tomorrow comes. But *sometimes* a narrative of part of one's life, told to a friend, is, and *ought to be*, erotetic. For example, if I begin by saying to you 'Let me tell you about an amazing escape I had at work last week,' the narrative would fail to achieve its promised closure if I ended the story with myself teetering on the brink of disaster. Or we might think that there is a clear narrative thread to the events involved in someone's getting her 'comeuppance': from a hubristic beginning, her nemesis at the end of the narrative was somehow just as it should be, thoroughly deserved. So whilst we must reject the idea of there being a narrative thread to a whole life, we can accept the more restricted idea of there being a narrative thread to a *part* of a life, where that part is, so to speak, selected by the narrator because of its narrative appropriateness.

What, then, is the dangerous fictionalizing tendency here? Before I answer that question, let me first recall the contrast that I drew in Chapter 3 between the desire for narrative closure and the desire for emotional closure. This latter desire is a desire to emplot a narrative with coherence, meaningfulness, and the right emotional import, which thus enables one to have the appropriate emotional response to what happened.

---

[14] Carroll (2007: 6) rightly acknowledges that some narratives, such as *Last Year at Marienbad*, 'may intentionally skirt closure in order to make a point'. The film *The Italian Job* might be another example. And then there are, of course, many narratives where a sequel is promised and never comes; the film *Master and Commander: The Far Side of the World* comes to mind.

Satisfaction of this kind of desire is especially pressing when someone needs to come to terms with a traumatic event in his or her life. Now, to satisfy the desire for emotional closure, it is not necessary to satisfy the desire for narrative closure. For example, the grieving parents who have lost their child to a sudden and mysterious illness might gain emotional closure through coming to terms with the loss and with their grief, coming to be able, as it is said these days, to 'move on'. But there might still be all sorts of unanswered questions: What was the illness? Why did it happen to this particular child—*their* child? Could more have been done to save the child? It is often the case that part of what it is to find emotional closure is to come to terms with the fact that one will never know the answers to these kinds of question.

It is just here, I think, that the dangerous fictionalizing tendency can begin to manifest itself: not satisfied in the quest for emotional closure, one hopes for, aspires for, narrative closure. One manifestation of this is the refusal to accept that narrative closure cannot be found, and thus to become frustrated in psychologically damaging ways. For example, the grieving parents refuse to 'let go', to 'move on', insisting that they will not rest until they know the answers, although there really is no answer to the question of why it happened to *their* child. This is a common phenomenon with people who lose those whom they love in mysterious circumstances: we often read stories in the press of the widow or parents of the soldier who died in active service, who will not let go until the body has been found, or until they know whether the death was the result of friendly fire or of inadequate equipment.

Alternatively, the quest for narrative closure can manifest itself in self-deception: wanting narrative closure, we avoid frustration by turning life into fiction, where the law of Chekhov's gun holds. For example, the grieving parents might come to believe that the death of the child or the young soldier was in some sense 'meant to be': visited on them by God, perhaps, because of something they had done wrong in the past, or in order to draw their marriage closer together.

The simple fact about life is that 'stuff happens'. Life is messy and to seek a narrative that neatly ties all the ends together has the potential of being dangerously blocking to the possibility of emotional closure, or of being dangerously self-deceptive, and deceptive of others.

Hayden White thinks the desire for narrative closure is equally problematic when we turn to historical narratives, and it is instructive to compare them with autobiographical narratives. 'Narrative', he says, 'becomes a *problem* only when we wish to give *real* events the *form* of story.

... It is because real events do not offer themselves as stories that their narrativization is so difficult' (1980: 8). He continues:

What wish is enacted, what desire is gratified, by the fantasy that *real* events are properly represented when they can be shown to display the formal coherency of a story? In the enigma of this wish, this desire, we catch a glimpse of the cultural function of narrativizing discourse in general, an intimation of the psychological impulse behind the apparently universal need not only to narrate but to give events an aspect of narrativity.   (p. 8)

Insofar as historical stories can be completed, can be given narrative closure, can be shown to have had a *plot* all along, they give to reality the odor of the *ideal*. This is why the plot of a historical narrative is always an embarrassment and has to be presented as 'found' in the events rather than put there by narrative techniques.   (p. 24)

We can see how this might work itself out in relation to the narrative of a particular part of the history of a country. White's (1984: 23) example was Marx's narration of the Eighteenth Brumaire of Louis Bonaparte as a farce—'a "farcical" re-enactment of the "tragedy" of 1789'. To take an example from closer to home, English history of the time of Elizabeth I, we might comprehend a narrative of that period as revealing Elizabeth and England standing bravely alone against the might of Spain and its Armada, finally triumphing against the evil forces which were bent on imposing, through any means at their disposal, Catholic dominion throughout Europe. This perspective on the events might be directly represented as part of the content of the narrative, or indirectly expressed through the framing of the narrative. In just the same way, someone might give an account of his dispute with his ill-intentioned employer in terms of resisting and ultimately triumphing against their greater strength, and doing so on a matter of principle: of right against wrong. Whatever precisely the genre of this autobiographical mini-narrative might be, it seems to have much in common with the story of the struggle of Elizabethan England against the Spanish oppressors.

The Fourth Fictionalizing Tendency: Genre and Character

In fiction, there is a close relation between genre and character. In a subtle discussion of what makes a narrative fictional, Anthony Savile (1998: 137) asks whether it is 'just a fortuitous matter that so much of the content of the fiction we know and love is imaginary'. He argues that it is not, and a central element of his reasoning concerns the relations between genre and character in literature. In literature, Savile argues, the genre determines certain facts about the characters in the fiction: 'a choice of genre . . . obliges the characters to have such and such personalities, and that events of such and such a nature be taken to happen *whether the author explicitly tells his reader so or not*'. In literature, he says, 'it is not open for a tragic hero to be a coward, and cowardly deeds are excluded not merely from the recounted action, but also from the hero's presumed past' (p. 142).

This stands in stark contrast to our notion of character in real life. In real life, someone 'cannot know that his brave friends will not flinch in unforeseen circumstances . . . *just because there is no fact of the matter*' (p. 143). The fictionalizing tendency, then, is to impose genre on life in a dangerous way—in a way that leads to a distortion of the notion of character. We find traces of it in Jerome Bruner's account, in his *Acts of Meaning*, of the spontaneous autobiographies of his subjects.

It [the autobiography of his subjects] was constrained by the events of a life, to be sure, but it was also powerfully constrained by the demands of the story the teller was in the process of developing. . . . The larger overall narratives were told in easily recognizable genres—the tale of a victim, a *Bildungsroman*, antihero forms, *Wanderung* stories, and so on. . . . It soon became apparent not only that life imitated art but that it did so by choosing art's genres and its other devices of storytelling as its modes of expression.   (1990: 120, 121)

This tendency to bring about distortion of character in real life manifests itself in a variety of related ways. The first distortion we have already had a glimpse of in Savile's remarks: this is the tendency to *flatten out* the character of a real life person to a description that *requires* that someone think, feel, and act in a certain way: the real life hero is sure never to go against his heroic 'nature'; the ne'er-do-well is sure never to do well; and so on.[15] As a result, we tend to expect too much of our heroes and too little of our villains (give a dog a bad name). And, as we saw in Chapter 5, this in turn leads to globalizing attitudes of contempt and shame, which 'mistakenly equates the person with certain traits or wrongly assumes that characters

---

[15] For the distinction between flat and round characters, see Forster (1962). For the way in which literature 'links character identity to character description', see Lamarque (2007); he calls it the Character Identity Principle.

are monolithic' (Mason 2003: 258). For example, poor Lord Jim in Conrad's novel of that name expected too much of himself and his courage.
When he let himself down, he saw himself as for all time condemned to a
life of hiding from the gaze of the world, utterly beyond redemption.

Finally, we can recall Freud's discussion of the tendency to blame a
recurring event on fate: what he called fate compulsion (*Schicksalzwang*) or
fate neurosis. Here the fate neurosis manifests itself in seeing one's fate as
ineluctably bound up with one's own unchangeable, fixed character: one
comes to think of oneself as a born loser, a victim, someone who, in the
words of Marilyn Monroe's Sugar Kowalczyk in the film *Some Like it Hot*,
'always gets the fuzzy end of the lollipop'.[16] With this in mind, we can see
just what is wrong—and what is right—with what MacIntyre says about
Thomas Becket, and with Bernard Williams's response. It is in the context
of MacIntyre's claim that 'I can only answer the question "What am I to
do?" if I can answer the prior question "Of what story or stories do I find
myself a part?"' (1981: 216). Earlier, MacIntyre has asked us to 'Consider
the question of to what genre the life of Thomas Becket belongs,' and he
determines that the 'true genre' of Becket's life is tragedy (p. 213). To
which Williams (2007: 6) replies that, even if Becket's life is best described
as a tragedy, 'He certainly did not live it by asking, when considering what
to do, how to carry on the tale of one locked in a tragic relation to his
king.' Williams's response shows clearly what is wrong with MacIntyre's
view: we do not need to know what story or stories we are a part of before
we can make decisions about what to do. But what Freud's discussion of
fate neurosis shows is that Williams is really pointing towards a normative
claim: it is possible—but it is not wise—to see one's life as that of a loser, a
victim, or someone who is locked in a tragic relation with another, and
fate compulsion will quite likely determine that this is just how things will
turn out.

There is, however, another side to this coin: thinking through narratives
of oneself and one's character in a certain light can have important dynamic

---

[16] Freud says that compulsion to repeat is found not only in neurotics but also in 'normal
people': 'Thus we have come across people all of whose human relationships have the same
outcome: . . . the man whose friendships all end in betrayal by his friend; . . . the lover each of
whose love affairs with a woman passes through the same phases and reaches the same
conclusion.' In such cases, 'we can discern in him an essential character trait which always
remains the same and which is compelled to find expression in a repetition of the same
experiences' (Freud, 1920/1984: 292–3).

implications for character development, and can be an important moral force for change for the better. For example, ahead of the meeting about my dispute with my employers, I think through a narrative in which I resist and ultimately triumph against their greater strength. In doing this, I seek to cement my steadfastness in the face of such a powerful, but morally wrong, force. In this way, I set myself to be a particular kind of person, with self-governing policies of the kind of which I approve. Sometimes it involves a certain amount of self-deception; in this example, I might not really be feeling all that resilient to pressure, but I keep that out of the narrative that I think through. This is part of what David Velleman has called 'motivation by ideal', and narrative thinking has an important part to play in this kind of motivation. His example is of the smoker who is trying to quit:

> He imagined that he was not addicted—that he didn't like the taste of cigarettes, wasn't in the habit of smoking them, had no craving for them—and he then enacted what he was imagining, pretending to be the non-smoker that he wanted to be. And I suggest that this make-believe succeeded because it excluded the smoker's tastes, habits, and cravings from the story that he was enacting. That story lacked the narrative background that would have made it intelligible for him to buy, light, or smoke the next cigarette.   (Velleman 2002: 100).

Returning to my example, imagine that, in spite of my best resolutions, on this occasion I failed to hold out against the pressure exerted by my employers, and finally let them have their way. I might then tell (or just think through) the story of my irresolute pusillanimousness in a way that expresses my disapproval of how I behaved; I did not do as I know I ought to have done. Moreover, through my external perspective as narrator, I might also express the thought that I have changed: I am a different sort of person now, I think. In thinking this, I am expressing a reaffirmation of my resolution to change, just as the recently reformed smoker might insist that he does not smoke just after having had a cigarette. In these ways, seeing oneself and one's character in a certain light can help one to stick to one's resolutions, and this can be for the good.

A Summary and a Speculation

So we have these four fictionalizing tendencies: we see ourselves as plotting out the course of our lives; we find agency in the world where it is not; we seek narrative closure where it cannot be found; and we transport notions of genre and character from fiction into real life. I accept that these tendencies are dangerous, and I have pointed out where the dangers lie.

However, there is nothing in these dangers, as I have set them out, that vitiates narrative thinking about our lives. Narrative thinking, as we have seen throughout this book, plays a central role in the way we think about our past, our present, and our future. Nor do I think that those philosophical accounts that indulge these tendencies are simply to be written off as benighted; for they often very well reflect the other side of the coin—the psychological tendencies themselves. Knowing about these tendencies and their dangers can mitigate their effect in our narrative thinking.

Finally, I would like to suggest that there is something that unites these hypertrophies of narrativizing, and which helps to explain why we are we subject to them.[17] First, we seek consolation in meaning because we cannot abide what Frank Kermode (1966: 136, 147, 143) calls the 'horror', the 'loathsomeness', the 'monstrous world' of contingency. We cannot accept the thought that sometimes stuff happens, stuff for which there is no rational explanation, and for which no meaning can be given. Why should *this* child die of this sudden illness, why should it be *this* town that gets buried in the mud slide, why was it *me* who was so lucky to be the only survivor on that flight which was fatal to all the other passengers? Unbearable as it is, there are no meaningful answers to these questions. Asking, and not getting answers to, these kinds of question is a permanent feature of our humanity.

But perhaps there is a second, more recent, explanation of our narrativizing hypertrophies, one that is to be found in the advancement of the scientific age. What we are today confronted with is what Max Weber has called the 'disenchantment of the world', brought about through the scientific revolution. In this disenchanted world we are left with the impersonal view of the sciences, bereft of all agency, not just the agency of gods and monsters that we found in numinous explanations of events in the world, not just the agency of Mother Nature in making us the way we are, but also, perhaps most difficult of all to accept, the agency of mankind itself—*our* agency. Perhaps we simply cannot abide this bleakness, not this

---

[17] No doubt there will be evolutionary explanations, but these need not compete with the kind of explanation I am putting forward.

time of contingency, but of an impersonal world-view with, as Tennyson put it so pithily, 'blind matter behind everything'.

Conclusion

Narrative thinking about our lives, and about the lives of others, is bound up with our emotions and our values. To the complaint that narrative thinking is messy and imprecise, blurring all kinds of nice distinctions—between internal and external perspectives, between what is remembered and how one remembers, between a narrative's content and its framework, between the desire for emotional closure and the desire for narrative closure—the right reply is that this is just what it should be, given that life itself is messy. We must resist the temptation to oversimplify life, the mind, the life of the mind.

References

Abbott, P. (2010). 'Conversion in an Age of Darwinian Gradualism'. *Storyworlds* 2.

Abramson, K. (2009). 'A Sentimentalist's Defense of Contempt, Shame, and Disdain'. In P. Goldie (ed.), *The Oxford Handbook of Philosophy of Emotion*. Oxford: Oxford University Press, 189–213.

Anscombe, E. (1957). *Intention*. London: Blackwell.

Arendt, H. (1958). *The Human Condition*. Chicago: Chicago University Press.

Árnason, A. (2000). 'Biography, Bereavement, Story'. *Mortality* 5: 189–204.

Austen, J. (1816/1983). *Emma*. London: Zodiac.

Baggini, J. (2011). *The Ego Trick*. London: Granta.

Bal, M. (1997). *Narratology: Introduction to the Theory of Narrative*. 2nd edn. Toronto: University of Toronto Press.

Banfield, A. (1973). 'Narrative Style and the Grammar of Direct and Indirect Speech'. *Foundations of Language*, 10: 1–39.

Barclay, C. (1995). 'Autobiographical Remembering: Narrative Constraints on Objectifying Selves'. In D. Rubin (ed.), *Remembering Our Past: Studies in Autobiographical Memory*. Cambridge: Cambridge University Press, 94–125.

Barsalou, L. (1988). 'The Content and Organisation of Autobiographical Memories'. In In U. Neisser and E. Winograd (eds.), *Remembering Reconsidered: Ecological and Traditional Approaches to the Study of Memory*. Cambridge: Cambridge University Press, 193–243.

Beck, S. (2008). 'Going Narrative: Schechtman and the Russians'. *South African Journal of Philosophy* 27: 69–79.

Bedford, E. (1957). 'Emotions'. *Proceedings of the Aristotelian Society* 57: 281–304.

Bennett, A. (2010). *A Life Like Other People's*. New York: Farrar Strauss & Giroux.

Blackburn, S. (2001). *Ruling Passions: A Theory of Practical Reasoning*. Oxford: Oxford University Press.

Bowlby, J. (1998). *Attachment and Loss*. London: Pimlico.

Bratman, M. (1999). *Faces of Intention: Selected Essays on Intention and Agency*. Cambridge: Cambridge University Press.

—— (2000). 'Reflection, Planning, and Temporally Extended Agency'. *Philosophical Review* 109: 35–61.

—— (2007). 'Appendix: Nozick, Free Will, and the Problem of Agential Authority'. In M. Bratman (ed.), *Structures of Agency*. Oxford: Oxford University Press, 127–36.

Brewer, T. (2002). 'The Real Problem with Internalism about Reasons'. *Canadian Journal of Philosophy* 32: 443–74.

Brooks, P. (2002). 'Narrative Desire'. In B. Richardson, *Narrative Dynamics: Essays on Time, Plot, Closure, and Frames*. Columbus: Ohio State University Press, 130–7.

Brown, R., and Kulik, J. (1977). 'Flashbulb Memories'. *Cognition* 5: 73–99.

Bruner, J. (1987/2004). 'Life as Narrative'. *Social Research: An International Quarterly* 71: 691–710.

—— (1990) *Acts of Meaning: Four Lectures on Mind and Culture*. Cambridge, Mass.: Harvard University Press.

Budd, M. (1989). *Wittgenstein's Philosophy of Psychology*. London: Routledge.

Burnyeat, M. (1980). 'Aristotle on Learning to be Good'. In A. O. Rorty (ed.), *Essays on Aristotle's Ethics*. Berkeley: University of California Press, 62–92.

Campbell, J. (1997). 'The Structure of Time in Autobiographical Memory'. *European Journal of Philosophy*, 105–18.

Campbell, S. (2008) 'Remembering for the Future: Memory as a Lens on the Indian Residential Schools Truth and Reconciliation Commission'. Discussion Paper prepared for Indian Residential Schools Resolution Canada, Truth and Reconciliation Commission.

Carroll, N. (2001). 'Interpretation, Theatrical Performance, and Ontology'. *Journal of Aesthetics and Art Criticism* 59: 313–16.

—— (2007). 'Narrative Closure'. *Philosophical Studies* 135: 1–15.

Carruthers, P. (2009). 'How We Know Our Own Minds: The Relationship between Mindreading and Metacognition'. *Behavioural and Brain Sciences* 32: 121–38.

Cather, W. (1918/1980). *My Antonia*. London: Virago.

Cavarero, A. (1997). *Relating Narratives: Storytelling and Selfhood*. Trans. P. Kottman. London: Routledge.

Cohn, D. (1978). *Transparent Minds: Narrative Modes for Presenting Consciousness in Fiction*. Princeton: Princeton University Press.

Collingwood, R. G. (1946). *The Idea of History*. Oxford.

Conrad, J. (1900/2002). *Lord Jim*. Oxford World Classics. Oxford: Oxford University Press.

—— (1917/2008). 'The Warrior's Soul'. In J. Conrad (ed.), *The Tale*. London: Hesperus.

Conway, M. (1992). 'The Structure of Autobiographical Memories'. *International Journal of Psychology* 27: 93.

—— (2003). 'Cognitive-Affective Mechanisms and Processes in Autobiographical Memory'. *Memory* 11: 217–24.

—— and Pleydell-Pearce, C. (2000). 'The Construction of Autobiographical Memories in the Self-memory System'. *Psychological Review* 107: 261–88.

Crane, T. (2001). 'Intentional Objects'. *Ratio* 14: 298–317.

Currie, G. (1990). *The Nature of Fiction*. Cambridge: Cambridge University Press.

—— (2006). 'Narrative Representation of Causes'. *Journal of Aesthetics and Art Criticism* 64: 309–16.

—— (2007). 'Both Sides of the Story: Explaining Events in a Narrative'. *Philosophical Studies* 135: 49–63.

—— (2010). *Narratives and Narrators: A Philosophy of Stories*. Oxford: Oxford University Press.

—— and Jureidini, J. (2004). 'Narrative and Coherence'. *Mind and Language* 19: 409–27.

—— and Ravenscroft, I. (2002). *Recreative Minds*. Oxford: Oxford University Press.

D'Arms, J., and Jacobson, D. (2000). 'The Moralistic Fallacy: On the 'Appropriateness' of Emotions'. *Philosophy and Phenomenological Research* 61: 65–90.

Damasio, A. (1999). *The Feeling of What Happens: Body and Emotion in the Making of Consciousness*. San Diego: Harcourt.

Davidson, D. (2001). *Inquiries into Truth and Interpretation*. Oxford: Oxford University Press.

Debus, D. (2007). 'Being Emotional about the Past: On the Nature and Role of Past-Directed Emotions'. *Noûs* 41: 758–79.

Dennett, D. (1992). *Consciousness Explained*. Harmondsworth: Penguin.

Deonna, J. A. (2006). 'Emotion, Perception and Perspective'. *Dialectica* 60/1: 29–46.

De Sousa, R. (1987). *The Rationality of Emotion*. Cambridge, Mass.: MIT.

Dillon, R. (2001). 'Self-forgiveness and Self-respect'. *Ethics* 112: 53–83.

Döring, S. A. (2007). 'Seeing What to Do: Affective Perception and Rational Motivation'. *Dialectica* 61/3: 363–94.

Eich, E., Handy, T., Holmes, E., Lerner, J., and McIsaac, H. (2011). 'Field and Observer Persepctives in Autobiographical Memory'. 14th Sydney Symposium on Social Psychology. University of New South Wales: <http://www.sydneysymposium.unsw.edu.au/2011/chapters/>, accessed January 2012.

Elgin, C. Z. (2008). 'Emotion and Understanding'. In G. Brun, U. Doğluoğlu, and D. Kuenzle (eds.), *Epistemology and Emotions*. Aldershot: Ashgate, 33–50.

Evans, R. (1997). *In Defence of History*. London: Granta.

Fish, S. (1980). 'How to Do Things with Austin and Searle'. *Is There a Text in This Class? The Authority of Interpretive Communities*. Cambridge, Mass.: Harvard University Press, 197–245.

Flanagan, O. (1994). *Consciousness Reconsidered*. Cambridge, Mass.: Bradford.

Forster, E. M. (1927/1962). *Aspects of the Novel*. Harmondsworth: Penguin.

Freud, S. (1899/1974). 'Screen Memories'. In J. Strachey (ed.), *The Standard Edition of the Complete Psychological Works of Sigmund Freud vol. III*. London: Hogarth, 301–22.

—— (1920/1984). 'The Future of an Illusion'. *Civilisation, Society and Religion*. Penguin Freud Library 12. London: Penguin.

Gaita, R. (1991). *Good and Evil: An Absolute Conception*. Basingstoke: Macmillan.

Gallagher, S., and Zahavi, D. (2008). *The Phenomenological Mind: An Introduction to the Philosophy of Mind and Cognitive Science*. London: Routledge.

Gallup, G. (1977). 'Self-recognition in Primates—Comparative Approach to Bidirectional Properties of Consciousness'. *American Psychologist* 32: 329–38.

Geertz, C. (1973). *The Interpretation of Cultures*. New York: Basic Books.

Gendler, T., and Hawthorne, J. (2003). *Conceivability and Possibility*. Oxford: Oxford University Press.

Genette, G. (1980) *Narrative Discourse: An Essay in Method*. Trans. Lewin, J. Ithaca: Cornell University Press.

—— (1988). *Narrative Discourse Revisited*. Trans. J. Lewin. Ithaca: Cornell University Press.

Gigerenzer, G. (2007). *Gut Feelings: The Intelligence of the Unconscious*. London: Penguin.

Gill, K. (1993). 'On the Metaphysical Distinction between Processes and Events'. *Canadian Journal of Philosophy*, 365–84.

Goldie, P. (2000). *The Emotions: A Philosophical Exploration*. Oxford: Oxford University Press.

—— (2004). *On Personality*. London: Routledge.

Goldknopf, D. (1969). 'The Confessional Increment: A New Look at the I-Narrator'. *Journal of Aesthetics and Art Criticism* 28: 13–21.

Gombrich, E. (1954). 'Così Fan Tutte (Procris Included)'. *Journal of the Warburg and Courtauld Institutes* 17: 372–4.

Grice, H. P. (1989). *Studies in the Way of Words*. Cambridge, Mass.: Harvard University Press.

Griswold, C. (2007). *Forgiveness: A Philosophical Exploration*. Cambridge: Cambridge University Press.

Gunn, D. (2004). 'Free Indirect Discourse and Narrative Authority in *Emma*'. *Narrative* 12: 35–54.

Habermas, T. (2006). 'Who Speaks, Who Looks, Who Feels? Point of View in Autobiographical Narratives'. *International Journal of Psychiatry* 87: 497–518.

—— and Berger, N. (2011), 'Retelling Everyday Emotional Events: Condensation, Distancing, and Closure'. *Cognition and Emotion* 25: 206–19.

Hacking, I. (1995). *Rewriting the Soul: Multiple Personality and the Sciences of Memory*. Princeton, NJ: Princeton University Press.

Hagberg, G. (2011). 'The Self Rewritten: The Case of Self-forgiveness'. In Christel Fricke (ed.), *The Ethics of Forgiveness: A Collection of Essays*. London: Routledge.

Hampshire, S. (1972). *Freedom of Mind, and Other Essays*. Oxford: Clarendon.

Harris, P. (1989). *Children and Emotion: The Development of Psychological Understanding*. Oxford: Blackwell.

Higgins, K. (2011). 'Introduction: Robert C. Solomon and the Spiritual Passions'. *Sophia* 50: 239–45.

Hoerl, C. (1998). 'The Perception of Time and the Notion of a Point of View'. *European Journal of Philosophy* 5: 156–71.

—— (2007). 'Episodic Memory, Autobiographical Memory, Narrative: On Three Key Notions in Current Approaches to Memory Development'. *Philosophical Psychology* 20: 621–40.

Hofweber, T., and Velleman, D. (2010). 'How to Endure'. *The Philosophical Quarterly* 1–21.

Holmgren, M. (1998). 'Self-forgiveness and Responsible Moral Agency'. *Journal of Value Inquiry* 32: 75–91.

Holton, R. (2009). *Willing, Wanting, Waiting*. Oxford: Oxford University Press.

Inglis, F. (2000). *Clifford Geerts: Culture, Custom, and Ethics*. Cambridge: Polity.

James, W. (1884). 'What is an Emotion?' *Mind* 9: 188–205.

Johnston, M. (1992). 'How to Speak of the Colours'. *Philosophical Studies* 68: 221–63.

—— (2010). *Surviving Death*. Princeton: Princeton University Press.

Jones, K. (2008). 'How to Change the Past'. In K. Atkins and C. Mackenzie (eds.), *Practical Identity and Narrative Agency*. London: Routledge, 269–88.

Kant, I. (1785/1964). *Groundwork of the Metaphysics of Morals*. London: Harper Torchbooks.

—— (1797/1996). *The Metaphysics of Morals*. Cambridge: Cambridge University Press.

Kermode, F. (1966). *The Sense of an Ending*. New York: Oxford University Press.

Kierkegaard, S. (1845/1967). *Stages on Life's Way*. New York: Schocken.

King, N. (2000). *Memory, Narrative, Identity*. Edinburgh: Edinburgh University Press.

Kolodny, N. (2005). 'Why be Rational?' *Mind* 144. 509–63.

Kristjánsson, K. (2010). *The Self and its Emotions*. Cambridge: Cambridge University Press.

Kubler-Ross, E., and Kessler, D. (2005). *On Grief and Grieving*. New York: Scribner.

Lamarque, P. (2004). 'On Not Expecting Too Much from Narrative'. *Mind and Language* 19: 393–408.

—— (2007). 'On the Distance between Literary Narratives and Real-life Narratives'. *Royal Institute of Philosophy Supplement* 82: 117–32.

—— and Olsen, S. (1994). *Truth, Fiction, and Literature*. Oxford : Clarendon.

Lévinas, E. (1935/2003). *On Escape: De l'evasion*. Trans. J. Rolland and B. Bergo. Stanford, Calif.: Stanford University Press.

Lewis, C. S. (1961). *A Grief Observed*. London: Faber & Faber.

Lewis, D. (1986). 'Causal Explanation'. In D. Lewis (ed.), *Philosophical Papers vol. II*. New York: Oxford University Press, 214–40.

Libby, L., and Eibach, R. (2002). 'Looking Back in Time: Self-concept Change Affects Visual Perspective in Autobiographical Memory'. *Journal of Personality and Social Psychology* 82: 167–79.

———— and Gilovich, T. (2005). 'Here's Looking at Me: The Effect of Memory Perspective on Assessments of Personal Change'. *Journal of Personality and Social Psychology* 88: 50–62.

Locke, D. (1971). *Memory*. New York: Doubleday.

Lodge, D. (2002). *Consciousness and the Novel: Connected Essays*. New York: Secker & Warburg.

McDowell, J. (1998). 'Might There Be External Reasons?' In J. McDowell (ed.), *Mind, Value, and Reality*. Cambridge, Mass.: Harvard University Press, 95–111.

McEwan, I. (2010). *Solar*. London: Jonathan Cape.

MacIntyre, A. (1981). *After Virtue*. London: Duckworth.

McIsaac, H., and Eich, E. (2004). 'Vantage Point in Traumatic Memory'. *Psychological Sciences* 15: 248–53.

Mackie, J. L. (1980). 'The Transitivity of Counterfactuals and Causation'. *Analysis* 40: 53–4.

McTaggart, J. (1908). 'The Unreality of Time'. *Mind* 17: 456–73.

Martin, R. (1998). *Self-concern: An Experiential Approach to What Matters in Survival*. Canbridge: Cambridge University Press.

Mason, M. (2003). 'Contempt as a Moral Attitude'. *Ethics* 113: 234–72.

Milgram, S. (1974). *Obedience to Authority*. London: HarperCollins.

Mill, J. S. (1960). *Autobiography of John Stewart Mill*. New York. Columbia University Press.

Miller, R., and Shanahan, M. (1994). 'Narratives in the Situation Calculus'. *Journal of Logic and Computation* 4: 513–30.

Mills, J. (1995). 'On Self-forgiveness and Moral Self-representation'. *Journal of Value Inquiry* 29: 405–6.

Monk, R. (1991). *Ludwig Wittgenstein: The Duty of Genius*. London: Penguin.

Moran, R. (1994). 'The Expression of Feeling in Imagination'. *Philosphical Review* 103: 75–106.

—— (2001). *Authority and Estrangement*. Princeton: Princeton University Press.

Mourelatos, A. (1993). 'Aristotle's Kinesis/Energeia Distinction: A Marginal Note on Kathleen Gill's Paper'. *Canadian Journal of Philosophy* 23: 385–8.

Mullan, J. (2006). *How Novels Work*. Oxford: Oxford University Press.

Mumford, S. (1998). *Dispositions*. Oxford: Oxford University Press.

Nagel, T. (1974). 'What Is It Like to Be a Bat?' *Philosophical Review* 83: 435–50.

Nash, C. (1990). 'Slanghtering the Subject: Literature's Assault on Narrative'. In C. Nash (ed.), *Narrative in Culture: The Uses of Storytelling in the Sciences, Philosophy, and Literature*. London: Routledge, 203–22.

Nelson, K. (2003). 'Narrative and the Emergence of a Consciousness of Self'. In G. Fireman, T. McVay, and O. Flanagan (eds.), *Narrative and Consciousness*. Oxford: Oxford University Press, 17–36.

——and Fivush, D. (2004). 'The Emergence of Autobiographical Memory: A Social Cultural Development Theory'. *Psychological Review* 111: 486–511.

Nietzsche, F. (1920–9). *Gesammelte Werke*. Munich: Musarion.

Nigro, G., and Neisser, U. (1983). 'Point of View in Personal Memories'. *Cognitive Psychology* 15: 467–82.

Nozick, R. (1981). *Philosophical Explanations*. Cambridge Mass.: Harvard University Press.

Nussbaum, M. (2001). *Upheavals of Thought: The Intelligence of Emotions*. Cambridge: Cambridge University Press.

Parfit, D. (1984). *Reasons and Persons*. Oxford: Clarendon.

Pennebaker, J., and Chung, C. (2011). 'Expressive Writing: Connections to Physical Health'. In H. S. Friedman (ed.), *Oxford Handbook of Health Psychology*. New York: Oxford University Press, 417–37.

Pinto, J. A. (1998). 'Occurrences and Narratives as Constraints in the Branching Structure of the Situation Calculus', *Journal of Logic and Computation* 8/6: 777–808.

le Poidevin, R. (2011). 'The Temporal Prison'. *Analysis* 71: 456–65.

Prinz, J. (2004). *Gut Reactions: A Perceptual Theory of Emotion*. Oxford: Oxford University Press.

Proust, M. (1992). *In Search of Lost Time*, i. *Swann's Way*. Trans. C. Scott Moncrieff and T. Kilmartin. London: Vintage.

Ricœur, P. (1984). *Time and Narrative*. Trans. K. M. Pellehuer. Chicago: Chicago University Press, i.

——(1992). *Oneself as Another*. Trans. K. Blamey. Chicago: University of Chicago Press.

——(2004). *Memory, History, Forgetting*. Trans. K. Blamey and D. Pellauer. Chicago: University of Chicago Press.

Rimmon-Kenan, S. (2002). 'The Story of "I": Illness and Narrative Identity'. *Narrative* 10: 9–27.

Roberts, R. C. (2003). *Emotion: An Essay in Aid of Moral Psychology*. Cambridge: Cambridge University Press.

Robinson, J. (2005). *Deeper than Reason: Emotion and its Role in Literature, Music and Art*. Oxford: Oxford University Press.

——(1985). 'Style and Personality in the Literary Work'. *Philosophical Review* 94: 227–47.

——and Swanson, K. (1993). 'Field and Observer Modes of Remembering'. *Memory* 1: 169–84.

Roese, N. (1991). 'Counterfactual Thinking'. *Psychological Bulletin* 121: 133–48.

Rorty, A. O. (1988). 'Virtues and their Vicissitudes'. *Midwest Studies in Philosophy* 13: 136–48.

Rousseau, J.-J. (1861). *The Confessions*. London: Reeves & Turner.

Rowlands, M. (1999). *The Body in Mind: Understanding Cognitive Processes*. Cambridge: Cambridge University Press.

—— (2009). 'Memory'. In J. Symons and P. Calvo (eds.), *The Routledge Companion to Philosophy of Psychology*. London: Routledge, 336–45.

Rubin, J. (1986). 'Allegory versus Narrative in Quatremere de Quincy'. *Journal of Aesthetics and Art Criticism* 44: 383–92.

Rudder Baker, L. (1998). 'The First-Person Perspective: A Test for Naturalism'. *American Philosophical Quarterly* 35: 327–48.

Sainsbury, M. (2010). 'English Speakers Should Use "I" to Refer to Themselves'. In A. Hatzimoysis (ed.), *Self-knowledge*. New York: Oxford University Press, 246–60.

Savile, A. (1998). 'Imagination and the Content of Fiction'. *British Journal of Aesthetics* 38: 136–49.

Schachter, D. L. (1996). *Searching for Memory: The Brain, the Mind and the Past*. New York: Basic Books.

Schechtman, M. (1994). 'The Truth about Memory'. *Philosophical Psychology* 7/1: 3–18.

—— (2001). 'Empathic Access: The Missing Ingredient in Personal Identity'. *Philosophical Explorations* 2: 95–111.

—— (2004). 'Personality and Persistence: The Many Faces of Personal Survival'. *American Philosophical Quarterly* 41: 87–105.

—— (2005). 'Personal Identity and the Past'. *Philosophy, Psychiatry and Psychology* 12: 9–22.

—— (2007). 'Stories, Lives, and Basic Survival: A Refinement and Defense of the Narrative View'. In D. Hutto (ed.), *Narrative and Understanding Persons*. Cambridge: Cambridge University Press, 155–78.

Scholes, R., Phelan, J., and Kellogg, R. (1966). *The Nature of Narrative*. New York: Oxford University Press.

Shoemaker, S. (1984). *Personal Identity*. Oxford: Blackwell.

Shore, B. (2009). 'Making Time for Family: Schemas for Long-Term Family Memory'. *Social Indicators Research* 93: 95–103.

Skultans, V. (2003). 'From Damaged Nerves to Masked Depression: Inevitability and Hope in Latvian Psychiatric Narratives'. *Social Science and Medicine* 56: 2421–31.

Snow, N. (1993). 'Self-forgiveness'. *Journal of Value Inquiry* 27: 75–80.

Steptoe, A. (1981). 'The Sources of "Cosi Fan Tutte": A Reappraisal'. *Music and Letters* 62l: 281–94.

Steward, H. (2011). 'Are Processes Continuants?' Unpublished manuscript.

Strawson, G. (2004). 'Against Narrativity'. *Ratio* 17: 428–54.

Strawson, P. F. (1974). *Freedom and Resentment and Other Essays*. London: Routledge.

Sutton, J. (2010). 'Observer Perspective and Acentred Memory: Some Puzzles about Point of View in Personal Memory'. *Philosophical Studies* 148: 27–37.

Velleman, D. (2002). 'Motivation by Ideal'. *Philosphical Explorations* 5: 89–103.

—— (2003). 'Narrative Explanation'. *Philosophical Review* 212: 1–25.

—— (2006). 'Identification and Identity'. *Self to Self: Selected Essays*. Cambridge: Cambridge University Press, 330–60.

Vice, S. (2003). 'Literature and the Narrative Self'. *Philosophy* 78: 93–108.

Walton, K. (1990). *Mimesis as Make-Believe: On the Foundation of the Representational Arts*. Cambridge, Mass.: Harvard University Press.

—— (1997). 'Spelunking, Simulation, and Slime'. In M. Hjort and S. Laver (eds.), *Emotion and the Arts*. Oxford: Oxford University Press, 44–65.

White, H. (1980). 'The Value of Narrativity in the Representation of Reality'. *Critical Enquiry* 7: 5–27.

—— (1984). 'The Question of Narrative in Contemporary Historical Theory'. *History and Theory* 23: 1–33.

Wierzbicka, A. (2004). *Emotions across Languages and Cultures: Diversity and Universals*. Cambridge: Cambridge University Press.

Wiggins, D. (2001). *Sameness and Substance Renewed*. Cambridge: Cambridge University Press.

Williams, B. (1965/1973). 'Ethical Consistency'. *Problems of the Self*. Cambridge: Cambridge University Press, 166–86.

—— (1980/1981). 'Internal and External Reasons'. *Moral Luck*. Cambridge: Cambridge University Press, 101–13.

—— (1976/1981). 'Moral Luck'. *Moral Luck*. Cambridge: Cambridge University Press, 20–39.

—— (2002). *Truth and Truthfulness: An Essay in Genealogy*. Princeton: Princeton University Press.

—— (1985/2007). *Ethics and the Limits of Philosophy*. London: Fontana.

Wilson, A. N. (1988). *Tolstoy*. London: Hamish Hamilton.

Wilson, G. M. (2003) 'Narrative'. In J. Levinson (ed.). *Oxford Handbook of Aesthetics* (Oxford: Oxford University Press), 392–407.

Wimmer, H., and Perner, J. (1983). 'Beliefs about Beliefs: Representation and Constraining Function of Wrong Beliefs in Young Children's Understanding of Deception'. *Cognition* 13: 103–28.

Wittgenstein, L. (1958). *Philosophical Investigations*. Oxford: Blackwell.

Wollheim, R. (1984). *The Thread of Life*. Cambridge, Mass.: Harvard University Press.

Wood, J. (2008). *How Fiction Works*. London: Jonathan Cape.

Woolf, V. (1925/2003). *Mrs Dalloway*. London: CRW.

Wright, C. (1998). 'Self-knowledge: The Wittgensteinian Legacy'. In C. Wright, B. Smith, and C. Macdonald (eds.), *Knowing Our Own Minds*. Oxford: Clarendon. 13–45.

Index